DATE DUE

DEMCO 38-296

The specialized vocabularies of lawyers, ethicists and political scientists obscure the roots of many real disagreements. In this book, the distinguished American international lawyer Alfred P. Rubin provides a penetrating account of where these roots lie, and argues powerfully that disagreements which have existed for 3,000 years are unlikely to be resolved soon. Current attempts to make "war crimes" or "terrorism" criminal under international law seem doomed to fail for the same reasons that attempts failed in the early nineteenth century to make piracy and the international traffic in slaves criminal under the law of nations. And for the same reasons, Professor Rubin argues, it is unlikely that an international criminal court can be instituted today to enforce ethicists' and "natural law" advocates' versions of "international law."

Ethics and authority in
international law

CAMBRIDGE STUDIES IN INTERNATIONAL AND COMPARATIVE LAW

This series (established in 1946 by Professors Gutteridge, Hersch Lauterpacht and McNair) is a forum for studies of high quality in the fields of public and private international law and comparative law. Although these are distinct legal sub-disciplines, developments since 1946 confirm their interrelationship. Comparative law is increasingly used as a tool in the making of law at national, regional and international levels. Private international law is increasingly affected by international conventions, and the issues faced by classical conflicts rules are increasingly dealt with by substantive harmonisation of law under international auspices. Mixed international arbitrations, especially those involving state economic activity, raise mixed questions of public and private international law. In many fields (such as the protection of human rights and democratic standards, investment guarantees and international criminal law) international and national systems interact. National constitutional arrangements relating to "foreign affairs," and to the implementation of international norms, are a focus of attention.

Professor Sir Robert Jennings edited the series from 1981. Following his retirement as General Editor, an editorial board has been created and Cambridge University Press has recommitted itself to the series, affirming its broad scope.

The Board welcomes works of a theoretical or interdisciplinary character, and those focusing on new approaches to international or comparative law or conflicts of law. Studies of particular institutions or problems are equally welcome, as are translations of the best work published in other languages.

General Editors	James Crawford *Whewell Professor of International Law, University of Cambridge* David Johnston *Regius Professor of Civil Law, University of Cambridge*

Editorial Board	Professor Hilary Charlesworth *University of Adelaide*
	Mr John Collier *Trinity Hall, Cambridge*
	Professor Lori Damrosch *Columbia University Law School*
	Professor John Dugard *Director, Research Centre for*
	   International Law, University of Cambridge
	Professor Mary-Ann Glendon *Harvard Law School*
	Professor Christopher Greenwood *London School of*
	   Economics
	Professor Hein Kötz *Max-Planck-Institut, Hamburg*
	Dr Vaughan Lowe *Corpus Christi College, Cambridge*
	Professor D. M. McRae *University of Ottawa*
	Professor Onuma Yasuaki *University of Tokyo*

Advisory Committee	Professor D. W. Bowett QC Judge Rosalyn Higgins QC Professor Sir Robert Jennings QC Professor J. A. Jolowicz QC Professor Eli Lauterpacht QC Professor Kurt Lipstein Judge Stephen Schwebel

A list of books in the series can be found at the end of this volume

Ethics and authority in
international law

Alfred P. Rubin

The Fletcher School of Law and Diplomacy
Tufts University

CAMBRIDGE
UNIVERSITY PRESS

OF THE UNIVERSITY OF CAMBRIDGE

et, Cambridge CB2 1RP, United Kingdom

CB2 2RU, United Kingdom
40 West 20th Street, New York, NY 10011-4211, USA
10 Stamford Road, Oakleigh, Melbourne 3166, Australia

First published 1997

Printed in the United Kingdom at the University Press, Cambridge

A catalogue record for this book is available from the British Library

Library of Congress Cataloguing in Publication data

Rubin, Alfred P.
Ethics and authority in international law / Alfred P. Rubin.
     p.   cm. – (Cambridge studies in international and comparative law)
Includes bibliographical references and index.
ISBN 0 521 58202 4 (hardback)
1. International offenses – Philosophy.
2. International offenses – Moral and ethical aspects.
3. Criminal jurisdiction – Philosophy.
4. Criminal jurisdiction – Moral and ethical aspects.
5. International law – Philosophy.
6. International law – Moral and ethical aspects.
I. Title.   II. Series.
JX5415.R83   1997
341.4′88 – dc21   96–45060   CIP

ISBN 0 521 58202 4 hardback

To my students in Law 203 at The Fletcher School of Law and Diplomacy, who have helped my understanding of much of this, and to my wife, who has helped my understanding of everything else

Contents

ix

Preface

This monograph had two inspirations. Between 1963 and late 1965 I was the junior attorney in the United States Department of Defense General Counsel's office principally responsible for legal questions involved in the Far Eastern entanglements of the United States military. We were not consulted often regarding our Viet Nam involvement. But at the annual meeting of the American Society of International Law in April 1973, some seven years after I had left that office, I was asked to serve on a panel to discuss some aspects of the laws of war as applied (or not) in Viet Nam. One of the other panelists asked some pointed questions about the United States not arresting and trying before its own courts various officials of the Government of South Viet Nam who had been photographed committing what seemed obvious violations of the "positive" laws of war (i.e., those laws adopted through an exercise of human discretion; in this case at least in part by treaty). When I replied that neither general international law nor the pertinent treaties gave the United States the jurisdiction to apply those rules to foreigners acting in their own country, he asserted that the codifying treaties gave all countries the authority to try anybody for war crimes committed anywhere; that "universal offenses" implied "universal jurisdiction" to adjudicate and enforce; thus that violators of the acknowledged laws of war could be legally punished by any country's tribunal anywhere. My response was to question his assertion of law, but, more tellingly in light of what I regarded as an attack on the integrity of myself and my country, to ask why, if his view were correct, his own country had not requested South Vietnam to extradite (or "hand over" in the terms of the pertinent treaties, to avoid the complications of the technical laws of each country relating to "extradition") the accused war criminals and then prosecute them. He clearly had not expected the question and his answer related to his country making quiet diplomatic expressions of concern rather than arrests and trials. Of course, that is exactly what we had done.

When I received my copy of the formal record of the panel for correction prior to its being published in the *Annual Proceedings* of the Society I discovered that he had deleted his acerbic questions, leaving my response to appear an ill-tempered and unprovoked assault which he appeared to have calmly (if rather evasively) answered. Unwilling myself to tamper with a record of fact, I approved the transcript in so far as it recorded my own remarks regardless of the changed context.

In the years following, I mulled the question of the international legal order and the frequent assertions that it contains provisions dealing with "universal crimes" such as "war crimes" and "piracy," and the assumption that with the category "universal crime" there is inevitably a corollary "universal jurisdiction."

In 1981–2, while serving as Charles H. Stockton Professor of International Law at the US Naval War College, I investigated the "piracy" precedents at some length and discovered that the notion of universal crime/universal jurisdiction had in fact been common in the eighteenth and early nineteenth centuries, but had been far more popular with academics than with statesmen; had been given lip service by judges, but rarely applied in cases in which the issues were squarely presented. The result of that investigation was a book, *The Law of Piracy*, published in 1988 by the Naval War College Press as volume LXIII in its "Blue Book" series of International Law Studies. After reviewing all the oft-cited "piracy" cases in the English and American literature, and the history of the concept as reflected also in accounts, literature and diplomatic correspondence contemporary with the events from antiquity to the present, it seemed to me that there were some serious confusions in current "conventional wisdom." The reasons appeared to me to rest on fundamental jurisprudential assumptions. The "ontology," intellectual "models" of the world order, in the minds of those addressing the questions seemed to reflect aspects of culture and definitions of "law" that seemed unrelated to the realities of "authority," its real distribution in the world, and predictable and demonstrable state practice. I found this distance between assertions of "law" by jurists, and the practices accepted as lawful by statesmen, to be demeaning to the law, subversive of its vital influence on civilized behavior, and generally polemical.

In the light of renewed interest in an international criminal court arising from "terrorism" and the public exposure of atrocities in former Yugoslavia and Rwanda, the issues of "universal crimes" and "universal jurisdiction" are again posed. Further analysis of the underlying jurisprudential issues seems urgently needed. Indeed, in the absence of such an analysis, an inappropriate model of the international legal order seems to have been adopted by the UN Security Council in setting up a tribunal to try persons accused of atrocities in connection with events in former Yugoslavia. The inconsistency of that model with the actual distribution of authority in the current international legal order makes it almost certain that the tribunal will fail to achieve its stated purposes. That this is not a negligible error in perception by some of our most effective and well-motivated leaders is a tragedy.

The weaknesses of the intellectual model underlying the new and proposed tribunals are illustrated by an obvious elision: none of the tribunals is given jurisdiction to apply the supposed universal law to the officials of those countries most enthusiastically supporting the idea. To explain this anomaly, advocates of universal law and universal jurisdiction usually cite the "Nuremberg" precedent: the trial of defeated Nazi leaders by the victorious allies of 1945. The pretension is that the allies represented civilized humanity, and only the defeated Nazis had conspired to wage aggressive war, had committed crimes against humanity or had committed war crimes. The pretension is patently false. But the precedent is in fact illuminating. When it was imitated only a short time later in Tokyo, it provoked a dissent by Judge Radhabinod Pal (India) and a partial dissent by Judge Bert V. A. Röling (The Netherlands). And other anomalies were noted in the process. The outstanding "precedential" value of Nuremberg might well be the fact that for fifty years it has *not* been followed. But during this period there has been no shortage of wars, atrocities and moral revulsion.

It seems to me that the reason the Nuremberg "precedent" has failed in the real world has been because the precedent relies on "victory," completely open records and a level of hypocrisy rarely achieved in even this imperfect world. For example, the charge against the Nazi Foreign Minister, Joachim von Ribbentrop, of conspiring to commit aggressive war, managed to avoid mention of the no-longer-secret provision of the Molotov–Ribbentrop Pact under which the invasion of Poland was agreed between Hitler's Germany and the USSR. Yet officials of the USSR were in the prosecution and on the bench at Nuremberg. None was a defendant.

Of course, the inconsistencies of the Nuremberg process in no way excuse the villains who were caught in it. "*Tu quoque* [you, too]" is not a persuasive defense for people who commit atrocities and was specifically rejected at Nuremberg. Assuming that international law in fact forbids atrocities authorized by a national legal order, the vice is not merely in the application of the "international" law directly to individuals; it is in the selective application of the law by pre-arrangement. Lest I be misunderstood, perhaps I should mention that in my view the Nuremberg process was morally important both to the victors and to Germany and politically probably the best alternative available to them both in the aftermath of the cataclysm of the Second World War. I have problems with its legal basis. As pointed out in *Judgment on Nuremburg*, a study by William J. Bosch, published by the University of North Carolina Press in 1970, so do many lawyers.

But enough ink has been poured out over Nuremberg, and this work is not intended to be yet another legal critique of that morally one-sided and legally dubious but in other ways useful and perhaps politically significant event. There is no need now, fifty years later, for further comment on the hypocrisies of trying defeated enemies before tribunals composed in part of representatives of victorious allies some of whose leaders had in fact committed acts possibly as atrocious as some of the acts for which some of the accused paid with their lives.

"Universal crimes/universal jurisdiction" seems to have become part of the false "conventional wisdom" of the most influential international lawyers today. But as I view the philosophical and historical evidence, the model on which at least the "universal jurisdiction" part of the phrase is currently based has shallow roots nurtured by emotional reactions to United States activities in Viet Nam more than twenty years ago; it does not reflect the practice of states or the distribution of authority that has characterized the international legal order for some 350 years (indeed, for some 3,000 years, as shall be seen).

The other tributary to this stream of thought is more superficial. In 1986 I was invited by the Carnegie Council on Ethics and International Affairs to give a talk at Notre Dame University on the function of international law in determining the shape of humanitarianism. I expected that the responsible people at the Carnegie Council and the jurists at Notre Dame would want a paper confirming the common notion that the substantive rules of international law are rules of conscience transferred to the legal arena by the intuitions of statesmen, judges and scholars strongly influenced by social pressures and the writings of theologians and moralists. Eventual publication as a chapter in a book of similar papers was envisaged. I made it clear that I could not support the notion that rules of "law," or at least the substantive rules of public international law, are a sort of crystallized and universally binding set of moral imperatives. I was nonetheless invited. I accepted with pleasure.

The paper that I first drafted set out the conclusions of a fundamentally "positivist" model that I believe reflects the realities of current international society far better than the moral "naturalist" model that has characterized a major part of the scholarly literature of law since the days of Cicero, and of international law in recent years, particularly some writings dealing in principle with so-called "human rights." To support this draft before an audience that I knew would disagree with its jurisprudential assumptions, I found that considerably more explanation was needed; simply setting out a controversial model without more support than a mere assertion that it seemed consistent with my own observations and prejudices was not likely to be useful or persuasive to anybody else. Before I knew it, I was grappling with basic questions of jurisprudence and the legal tradition, and my thirty-page draft had turned into the concluding section of a 150-page monograph.

At the end of an enjoyable visit to Notre Dame in March 1987, it was clear that my concluding section would not suit the editors of the planned book. On a whim, I submitted the entire monograph to the 1987 Lon L. Fuller Jurisprudence competition run by the Institute of Humane Studies in Fairfax, Virginia. It won Honorable Mention and a cash award about equivalent to what would have been paid had the chapter been accepted for the book planned by the sponsors of the Notre Dame session.

Until now, I have found that monograph to be unpublishable either as a long article or short book. The rejections were in only one case accompanied by substantive comments. In that one case, the negative comments did not go to the substance of the piece (which seemed to escape much of any comment), but to some details and to its organization. I now think the reviewers were right about that last. Publication was recommended by both reviewers, but without much enthusiasm. The prospective publisher decided against it.

No doubt the original introduction was more confusing than helpful to those who had not read the conclusion first; an absurdity for which I was solely responsible. I have rewritten both the introduction and the conclusion and much else, seeking the unattainable clarity that alone can overcome entrenched orthodoxy. In taking a long-range historical approach to the evolution of doctrine and its relation to reality I do not know if I have seen farther than others of my own generation. But it has been in all ways rewarding to try. Whether I have succeeded at least in part is for others to decide.

Acknowledgments

Thanks are due to my fellow panelists at the 1973 meeting of the American Society of International Law and to the Carnegie Council on Ethics and International Affairs for the pushes that started this work; to Notre Dame University and the Kellogg Foundation for a stimulating session that spurred it on; and to the Institute of Humane Studies for an award that convinced me that the work was worthwhile despite its being dismissed elsewhere.

I owe thanks also to too many colleagues to mention, even, perhaps especially, to those who in private conversations have disagreed with my reading of the historical texts and the jurisprudential lessons I have drawn from the analysis. Particularly stimulating sessions were organized by Professor Jost Delbrück at the Kiel Institute of International Law in 1992 and 1994. The second was precisely to the issue; its proceedings were published as Volume 117 in the *Veröffentlichungen des Instituts für Internationales Recht an der Universität Kiel* in 1995 under the title *Allocation of Law Enforcement Authority in the International System*.

As with most works with elaborate footnotes, much time was spent in library research. Without the resources and cheerful help of the staffs of the libraries of The Fletcher School of Law and Diplomacy, Tufts University, and Harvard University, the research would have been impossible. I thank them all.

The Fletcher School of Law and Diplomacy gave me a sabbatical semester in Spring 1995 to work on this book, and Tufts University invited me to be Scholar in Residence at their European Center in Talloires, France, in June. A great deal of useful work was done then and I am very grateful for the time and inspiration.

Finally, I owe a debt to those anonymous scholars who reviewed the semi-final typescript for Cambridge University Press. Their suggestions for improving the text were perceptive and I have made several changes and additions as a result.

Of course, I alone am responsible for this work's errors.

Abbreviations

ABAJ	*American Bar Association Journal*
AILC	*American International Law Cases*, Francis Deàk, ed.
AJIL	*American Journal of International Law*
AN	*The American Neptune*
ATTGO	*Attorney Generals' Opinions*
BFSP	*British and Foreign State Papers*
BJIL	*Brooklyn Journal of International Law*
CLR	*Chicago Law Review*
CWILJ	*California Western International Law Journal*
CLR	*Connecticut Law Review*
CTS	*Consolidated Treaty Series*
DJILP	*Denver Journal of International Law and Policy*
D&S	*Diplomacy & Statecraft*
FFWA	*The Fletcher Forum of World Affairs*
FRUS	*Foreign Relations of the United States*
HAN	T. C. Hansard, *The Parliamentary History of England from the Earliest Period to the Year 1803*
HILJ	*Harvard International Law Journal*
HLR	*Harvard Law Review*
HRD	US House of Representatives, Committee on Foreign Affairs, *Human Rights Documents* (September 1983)
ICLQ	*International and Comparative Law Quarterly*
IL	*The International Lawyer*
ILM	*International Legal Materials*

IYBHR	*Israel Year Book on Human Rights*
MJIL	*Michigan Journal of International Law*
NI	*The National Interest*
NILR	*Netherlands International Law Review*
OLR	*Oregon Law Review*
PILR	*Pace International Law Review*
PP	*Parliamentary Papers*
PROC	*Proceedings of the American Society of International Law*
RdC	*Recueil des Cours, Académie de droit international de la Haye*
TER	*Terrorism: An International Journal*
TILJ	*Texas International Law Journal*
TSA	*Thesaurus Acroasium*
UCLALR	*University of California at Los Angeles Law Review*
YLJ	*Yale Law Journal*
UNRIAA	*United Nations Reports of International Arbitration Awards*
UNTS	*United Nations Treaty Series*

Table of cases

International tribunals

United States tribunals

British tribunals

Table of statutes

Table of treaties

1 Introduction

Crime and punishment: jurisdiction to prescribe, to adjudicate and to enforce

The relationship between universal crimes and universal jurisdiction has been disputed by statesmen and lawyers for at least 3,000 years. An incident appears in a papyrus of about 1000 BC:[1]

> I [Wen-Amon, a priest of the Egyptian god Amon-Re from the temple of Karnak] reached Dor [on the coast of what is now Israel], and . . . a man of my ship ran away and stole one (*vessel*) of gold . . . four jars . . . and a sack of . . . silver. I got up in the morning, and went to the place where the Prince was, and I said to him: "I have been robbed in your harbor. Now you are the prince of this land, and you are its investigator who should look for my silver. Now about this silver – it belongs to Amon-Re, King of the Gods, the lord of the lands; it belongs to . . . my lord, and the other great men of Egypt! It belongs to you; it belongs to . . . the Prince of Byblos [apparently scheduled to be a recipient of the money in return for a cargo[2]]."

Apparently, the priest took a rather imperious line, because the Prince of Dor began his response by denying the impact in Dor of the priest's assertions of eminence. The priest records the argument in what seem honest and clear terms:

> And he said to me: "Whether you are important or whether you are eminent – look here, I do not recognize this accusation which you have made to me! Suppose it had been a thief who belonged to my land who went on your boat and stole your silver, I should have repaid it to you from my treasury, until they

---

[1] James K. Pritchard, *The Ancient Near East* (5th edn., Princeton University Press, 1971) 16*ff.*, translating an Egyptian papyrus of the eleventh century BC. This tale appears to be part of the background that inspired the Finnish author Mika Waltari to write his international bestseller, *The Egyptian* (1949).

[2] Pritchard, *Ancient Near East* note 3.

had found this thief of yours – whoever he may be. Now about the thief who robbed you – he belongs to you! He belongs to your ship! Spend a few days here visiting me, so that I may look for him."

Apparently, the priest regarded the theft of religious property to be what today would be called a "universal" crime. In his view, the Prince of Dor had a legal obligation to find the thief and punish him, and to reimburse the priest for his losses. But the local ruler, the Prince of Dor, refused at first to apply to a person of the priest's ship the law that would be enforced had the accused been within Dor's legal authority based on residence ("nationality"?) or territorial jurisdiction to prescribe. Apparently, the Prince argued that the violation of Egyptian law in an Egyptian vessel is not a violation of the law of Dor, where he was the dominant or sole law-making authority. The argument is not wholly clear, but then the priestly author writes with indignation and cannot be taken as an objective reporter of law or fact and it is certainly no mark of disrespect to suggest that the modern translator was apparently not trained in ancient Egyptian and modern international law. In a compromise seeking to preserve the pretensions of both parties, the Prince of Dor offers to seek out the thief and hand him over to the traveling priest to administer whatever law the priest thought best, Egyptian imperial law or divine law.[3]

A later episode in the same papyrus clarifies the jurisprudential assumptions:

[Zakar-Baal, the prince of the port] said to me: "On what business have you come?" So I told him: "I have come after the woodwork for the great and august barque of Amon-Re, King of the Gods. Your father did (it)[4] your grandfather did (it), and you will do it too!" . . . But he said to me: "To be sure, they did it! And if you give me (something) for doing it, I will do it! Why, when my people carried out this commission, Pharaoh . . . sent six ships loaded with Egyptian goods . . . [W]hat is it that you're bringing me[?] . . . If the ruler of Egypt were the lord of mine, and I were his servant also, he would not have to send silver and gold . . . As for me . . . I am not your servant! I am not the servant of him who sent you either! . . . [W]hen Amon founded all lands, in founding them he founded first the land of Egypt, from which you come . . . and learning came out of it, to reach the place where I am. What are these silly trips which they have had you make?"

And I said to him: "(That's) not true! What I am on are no 'silly trips' at all!

---

[3] Ibid. The priest's narration of the particular episode stops there; the final disposition of the affair is not known.

[4] Apparently referring to supplying Lebanese cedar-wood to the religious institution in Egypt. See Pritchard's introduction, *Ancient Near East*, 16.

There is no ship upon the River which does not belong to Amon! The sea is his, and the Lebanon is his, of which you say: 'It is mine!' . . . You are stationed (here) to carry on the commerce of the Lebanon with Amon, its lord. As for your saying that the former kings sent silver and gold . . . they had such things sent to your fathers in place of life and health! . . . If you say to Amon: 'Yes, I will do (it)!' and you carry out his commission, you will live, you will be prosperous, you will be healthy, and you will be good to your entire land and your people!"

But the priest apparently recognized that his divine law argument was not carrying the weight he thought it should have. He yields:

Have your secretary brought to me, so that I may send him to . . . the *officers* whom Amon put in the north of his land, and they will have all kinds of things sent. I shall send him to them to say: "Let it be brought until I shall go (back again) to the south, and I shall (then) have every bit of the debt still (due to you) brought to you." So I spoke to him [italics *sic*].[5]

The priest's model of the world order rests on "divine law," a notion of Egyptian imperial law and an identification of property rights with universal morality and universal "law." The "Prince of Dor" and Zakar-Baal accept the divinity of Amon, but in Dor the authority of the priest to dictate local police action on the basis of that divinity is denied; the Prince accepts Egyptian imperial pretensions but denies the authority of the priest to represent the Pharaoh directly; accepts the notion of universal property rights but denies that the concept is significant to an event happening solely within an Egyptian vessel; and seems to take a territorial view of his own authority to make and enforce law, allowing an equivalent authority in the priest, but drawing territorial lines between the enforcement authority of the two. The resulting compromise adopts the prince's model by proposing a cooperation of the two law-enforcers, each acting within his own sphere of authority. Similarly, Zakar-Baal denies the authority of the priest even while admitting the authority of Amon; denies that past behavior of his princely ancestors is binding on him as customary law; apparently rejects the priest's gloss that made the true exchange one of cedar for Amon's favor instead of for property of equivalent value. Ultimately, the priest gets his cargo by promising both Amon's favor and property in exchange. Both sides maintain their models of legal relationships.

With many variations, the same argument and the same capacity to maintain inconsistent models while getting on with real life has been going on in one form or another for 3,000 years. Theorists of the law,

---

[5] Ibid., 19–21. This fascinating tale goes on; the disputes over authority go on, but this is
    enough for present purposes. The interested reader is advised to read the original.

priests and lawyers, have been seeking to expand their own authority to determine substantive law and require the holders of territorially based authority to enforce it for them; "princes" have been seeking to maintain their authority to determine the law as well as to enforce it free of the moral, religious, or political dictates of those whom they regard as competitors for that authority.

Words and reality

It seems "natural" for every person to construct in his or her own mind an abstract model of reality. We all do it. Without an abstract model (a "paradigm," in the academic jargon of my youth; "ontology" in current philosophical jargon) to give order to our perceptions, every perception would be unique and we would see no order in the world. Of course, it is possible that there is no order in the world and that we deceive ourselves in supposing our models to be useful. But our brains, the intellectual hardware with which we are born, seem to be "wired" to think in terms of generalities and relationships, and we each accept for our own purposes the abstractions and connections that we find enable us best to understand and interact with the world we perceive around us. We label everything, concrete or abstract, things or relationships, with "words." By usage, we find that our conceptions of what the words stand for in the perceived world seem to come sufficiently close to what we take to be the perceptions of others that communication between people seems possible.

The arguments are endless about the meanings of words, their interrelationships, the structure of communication in particular languages and in general, and the connections, if any, between the words we use to represent reality and reality itself, assuming there is any reality behind our individual perceptions.[6]

---

[6] Every worker in this field seems to believe that his or her personal insights are universally valid. Since at least the days of Aristotle, philosophers seem to have preferred to focus more on the patterns of logic than the relationship of words to reality. The beginning of currently fashionable analyses of logic is probably George Boole, *An Investigation of the Laws of Thought* . . . (1854, Dover edn., 1958). The interested reader might prefer to start with a more recent introductory text like Hans Reichenbach, *Elements of Symbolic Logic* (1947, Free Press Paperback, 1966), or W. V. Quine, *Methods of Logic* (Harvard University Press, 1950, 4th edn., 1982), and proceed through Ludwig Wittgenstein, *Tractatus Logico-Philosophicus* (London and New York: Routledge & Kegan Paul, 1922, corrected bilingual edition, 1933) and his superseding work, *Philosophical Investigations* (G. E. M. Anscombe, translator) (New York: Macmillan Publishing Co., Inc., 1953, revised 3rd edn., 1968). On the connections between logic and

Assuming that word-based abstract models of reality are necessary for social thought, and words are the best tools we have for people to communicate their abstract thoughts to each other, some basic agreement as to the processes of logical thinking is also necessary.

Most "logic" seems intuitive and in legal argumentation much more is owed to the influence of models posed by Plato,[7] Aristotle,[8] Cicero[9] and the scholastic philosophers of the high middle ages than to mathematical models or semiotic theories of reality. It was not until the middle of the fourteenth century that a rule was proposed that seems to express the fundamental assumption relating logical thought to reality. *Essentia non sunt multiplicanda praeter necessitatem*: Nothing should be posited unless necessary. This intuitive, unprovable, self-referring rule is "Occam's Razor," the non-logical basis of all logical analyses of reality. It demands that superfluous assumptions be cut out of a proposition; that a model purporting to reflect reality must be the simplest consistent with the

---

"reality," see W. V. Quine, *Philosophy of Logic* (Harvard University Press, 1970, 2nd edn., 1986). The connections between logical thought and perceptions of reality are too many and too complex to be ignored in any serious work involving jurisprudence. Since at least the days of Plato, philosophers have posed models representing the connections they saw between perceptions and reality. The most famous is probably Plato's myth of the cave: *Republic*, Book VII. Plato suggests the existence on a metaphysical level of ideal conceptions perceived only with distortions by fallible human senses. Plato's ideal "reality" does not necessarily exist on a physical level. The impact of his model and various interpretations of it on Western (and some non-Western) philosophy has been incalculable. A relatively new field of study, "semiotics," has been popularized by the novel, *The Name of the Rose* (1980, English translation, 1983), by an Italian academic, Umberto Eco. Eco's more serious works, *Semiotics and the Philosophy of Language* (1984), or his short essay, "Language, Power, Force", in Eco, *Travels in Hyperreality* (1986) at 239, are readily available for those to whom this subject seems interesting. It is only peripheral to this study. Those wanting a provocative foreshadowing might find it amusing to re-read Charles L. Dodgson (Lewis Carroll), *Through the Looking Glass and What Alice Found There* (1861). In the seventh square, the White Knight distinguishes between the name of a song, what the name is called, what the song is called, and reality: the song itself. See *The Annotated Alice* (Martin Gardner, ed., New York, 1960) 306, note 8.

[7] Platonic works addressing the art of rhetoric directly include *Cratylus*, where Plato's protagonist, Socrates, suggests that only a "legislator" has the authority to give "names" to things; and *Phaedrus*, in which rhetorical argument is dissected. There are other Platonic (not necessarily Socratic: Socrates does not appear in *Laws*) dialogues pertinent to a full study, but the subject is only peripheral to this essay.

[8] Aristotle's six treatises on logic are grouped together as the *Organon*. But *Rhetoric*, which deals with forensic argument and appeals to emotion, persuasion, is indispensable to those who would understand the processes of legislation. See below.

[9] Particularly Marcus Tullius Cicero, *De Legibus* [*On Laws*], which contains a much-quoted description of "*vera lex* [true law]," identifying "law" with moral conviction. This will be discussed below.

perceived facts and contain the fewest possible exceptions.[10] It is a fundamental assumption of lawyers and jurists. It is frequently forgotten in the enthusiasm of some to create a model of reality that leads to desired results; by jurists whose approach is normative rather than descriptive, but who prefer to reach their conclusions by making them appear implicit in the system rather than the product of their discretion in accepting unstated assumptions.[11]

"Naturalism" and "positivism"[12]

As illustrated in the tale of Wen-Amon, two major schools, usually denominated "naturalism" and "positivism," have dominated juristic thinking from earliest days. They are different models elaborated, sometimes brilliantly, by scholars and urged by groups of scholars for general adoption as operating models for judges and statesmen of all societies.

"Naturalism"

"Naturalism" in jurisprudential jargon is the system that assumes that rules of human behavior derive ultimately from sources outside the will of mankind. The "nature" that creates those rules has been argued in

---

[10] William of Occam (or Ockam, occasionally Ockham), c.1300–1349, is reputed to have first uttered this famous phrase. I have translated it in a modern sense, using "basic assumptions" as equivalent to the neo-Platonic and scholastic notion of "essences." A concise summary of Occam's achievement is the article by T. M. Lindsay in 19 *Encyclopaedia Britannica* (11th edn., 1911), 965.

[11] An example of the use of Occam's Razor to analyze competing legal formulae, showing the philosophical unacceptability of a purported rule of international law by which merchant ships were considered inherently exempted from being the object of self-defense actions in time of "legal" peace, accepted by many notable publicists as "conventional wisdom" in the 1920s and the 1930s, is Alfred P. Rubin, "Evolution and Self-Defense at Sea," in 7 TSA 101 (1977). The formula preferred by those who wished to establish as a dominant legal principle the immunity from military action of merchant vessels on the high seas in time of peace is shown to require many exceptions, a notional violation of law without legal consequences, and derogations from the law of "self-defense" which many publicists and nearly all statesmen must reject in practice.

[12] There is much confusion in this common branch of jurisprudential analysis which I have tried to disentangle in a short article focusing on how the perceived source of the rule, natural law in one or another of its guises, positive law, or some other normative system, affects the enforcement of the rule. I tried to show that attempts to use the tools of the positive legal order to enforce rules derived from some type of "natural" order either fail or involve making "judges" of particular cases into legislators for society in general. Alfred P. Rubin, "Enforcing the Rules of International Law", 34(1) HILJ 149 (1993) (hereinafter cited as Rubin, "Enforcing").

classical writings to derive actually from at least three very different sources: physical nature; value-based "morality" or "ethics" (which word depends on whether the Latin or Greek conception is being implied); and "divine law." A possible fourth source is social pressures and amoral custom. A fifth is a mixture of the others developed by various scholars with varying weights given to each of the asserted sources of "law."

Aristotle grounded his "naturalist" model of the legal order in physical facts (the Greek word for "nature" is "*physis*"); in the animal nature of mankind, the inherent need to have children, protect them and the family, provide a more efficient economic basis for survival than subsistence farming and pattern a social organization to fit the innate capacities of its members.

Because it is the completion of associations existing by nature, every *polis* exists by nature, having itself the same quality as the earlier associations from which it grew . . . From these considerations it is evident that the *polis* belongs to the class of things that exist by nature, and that man is by nature an animal intended to live in a *polis*.[13]

But Aristotle did not carry this categorization wholly over to the field of law because he did not believe that the sociological and community relationships established by nature always coincided with the relationships demanded by a sense of "justice."

One part of political justice is natural: another is legal. The natural part is that which has everywhere the same force . . . The legal part is that which originally is a matter of indifference, but which ceases to be indifferent as soon as it is fixed by enactment . . . Some hold that the whole of justice is of this [natural] character. What exists by nature (they feel) is immutable, and has everywhere the same force: fire burns both in Greece and in Persia; but conceptions of justice shift and change. It is not strictly true that all justice is legal, though it may be true in a sense . . . True, all our human justice is mutable; but that does not prevent some of it from having a natural origin.[14]

---

[13] Aristotle, *Politics* 1252b and 1253a, taken from Ernest Barker (ed. and translator), *The Politics of Aristotle* (Oxford, 1946, paperback edn., 1975) (hereinafter cited as Barker, *Aristotle*) 5.

[14] Aristotle, *Nichomachean Ethics*, 1134b18, in Barker, *Aristotle*, Appendix II at 365. The translation by H. Rackham for the Loeb Classical Library, Aristotle, *The Nichomachean Ethics* (Harvard University Press, 1939) uses the word "conventional" instead of "legal" in the first sentence. In the original Greek, it says: "*Ton de politikon dikaion to men physikon esti to de nomikon*": Ibid., 294 (Greek)/295 (English). Aristotle carefully distinguishes between "*dikaion*" (justice?) and "*nominos*" (law?). But a full analysis of Aristotle's conceptions of "law" and "justice" and the relationships between them would fill libraries (indeed, they already have filled libraries). In general, it is wise to beware of translations, but a study such as this could not be made without using them.

Obviously, Aristotle considered "law" to include conceptions in the positive order; a product of human discretion. Otherwise his remark about the legal part being morally ("ethically"; in what follows I shall use the two words interchangeably) "indifferent" until fixed by "enactment" would make no sense. He also used the Greek word "*nomikon*," normally translated "laws," to refer to the physical "laws" of nature. Not only do conceptions of "justice" shift and change, thus differentiating the moral laws binding society from the physical laws of non-human nature, like the law of gravity or the law that requires fire to burn the same way in both Greece and Persia, but some of the "natural" relations that seemed obvious to Aristotle as a sociologist seem quaint (indeed painful) today, and many of the laws that Aristotle supposed derived from the "nature" of political societies now seem far less the product of physical nature than the product of human discretion falsely attributed to nature. For example, Aristotle derived the conformity with nature of the Greek patriarchy from the supposed nature of women and the inborn characteristics of those best fitted by nature to be slaves (apparently including all members of societies defeated in war and the possibly brilliant and independent-minded children of "nature's" slaves).[15]

Nonetheless, the identification of physical nature and its phenomena with "law" and this "law" with "justice" popularized (among scholars) a confusion of terminology with implications for legal argument today despite Aristotle's own perception of the differences of the two sorts of "law" and the dangers of attributing identity to concepts that only partially overlap. Aristotle certainly saw human, positive laws improving natural social institutions, like the *polis*. But he did not suggest that natural sanctions, like starvation or physical misery, were superseded by human law. And neither the natural law nor the human law need have anything to do with "justice," which is not "law" in the same sense, but a moral or (using the Greek root) "ethical" notion.

A second category of "natural law" system rests on identifying moral insight with "law" and finding the "moral law" to be superior to human prescriptions in a model in which both "moral" and "human" law are presumed to be part of an undifferentiated whole "law." The great formulator of this view was Cicero. He described the "*vera lex*," the "true law," as:

[R]ight reason in harmony with nature; it is of universal application, unchanging and everlasting; it summons to duty by its commands, and averts

---

[15] Aristotle, *Politics* 1253b*ff*., 1259b, in Barker, *Aristotle*, 5, 8*ff*., 32–33.

from wrongdoing by its prohibitions . . . We cannot be freed from its obligations by senate or people, and we need not look outside ourselves for an expounder or interpreter of it.[16]

The first part of this eloquent statement of personal honor and responsibility has been frequently applied to assert the existence of eternal, universal and constant rules of "law" that bind others who, under the last phrase, must nonetheless serve as their own expounders and interpreters. The notion that all who reason "rightly" must come to the same conclusion on a matter of moral values has had an immense impact on the intensity of both moral and legal argumentation.

Obviously, the Ciceronian assumption of universal, constant and eternal rules of "true law" is inconsistent with Aristotle's assertion of shift and change in conceptions of "justice" unless "true law" and "justice" are differentiated. There seems to be no surviving school of jurisprudence built on such a differentiation. The surviving influence of Cicero's statement seems to rest on its use by naturalist jurists to attribute universality to the rules they discover in their own consciences. Introspection is not regarded as an exercise in discretion, but in the discovery of rules with which all reasonable people must agree; rules which exist independently of human discretion but rest on the nature of mankind and our God-given capacity to reason "objectively." There is much disagreement among scholars as to whether those rules, including such moral imperatives as charity, good faith and honesty, can ever be particularized to cover real situations; and, if they can, whether all reasonable people would apply them in the same way; and, if they would, whether those rules can properly be called rules of "natural law" without confusing them with rules of discretionary, human (positive) law; and, if they can, whether the moral "natural law" should be conceived to nullify the human law in the legal orders erected by human societies.[17]

---

[16] Marcus Tullius Cicero, *De Re Publica*, III, xxii, 3: "recta ratio naturae congruens, diffusa in omnes, constans, sempiterna, quae vocet ad officium iubendo, vetando a fraude deterrat . . . nec vero aut per senatum aut per populum solvi hac lege possumus, neque est quaerendus explanator aut interpres eius . . ." in Cicero, *De Re Publica* and *De Legibus* (C. W. Keyes, translator) (Loeb Classical Library, 1928, 1977) at 210 (Latin)/211 (English). The view that virtue is the result of education, that evil is a product of ignorance, and that all knowledge is inborn, the function of education being merely to help the individual organize his thoughts in a reasonable way, traces back at least as far as Plato's *Protagoras* and *Crito*.

[17] For an argument that the two (indeed, many more) "legal" orders must be conceived to exist side by side and that vindication in one does not mean vindication in another any more than violation of one means violation of others, see Yasuaki Onuma, *Conclusion: Law Dancing to the Accompaniment of Love and Calculation* in Yasuaki Onuma

There is another major problem with Cicero's famous formula. It is that "reason" in his phrase "right reason [*recta ratio*]" has little relationship to deductive, inductive, analogistic, or even rhetorical reasoning. Instead, it seems to involve isolating factors affected by proposed rules, weighing the values implicit in each, and affirming the dominance of the value(s) whose enhancement seems worth the degradation of other values. Decisions are made by intuition usually based on an analysis of predicted social consequences. Ultimately an intuitive judgment is made as to what social consequences are more desirable (to the analyst) than others; how far to accept the diminishing of some values in action by enhancing others, and which should be enhanced at the expense of others to be ignored or diminished. The conception has little or nothing to do with modern analyses of logic and seems to be used often to mean the opposite of what it says if "reason" is taken to imply logical thought processes. It seems to call "right reason" that which is grasped intuitively with little or no "reasoning" involved, but instead a weighing of moral values about which "reasonable" people frequently disagree.

A third confusion must be noted. "Moral reasoning" is itself a concept about which eminent moralists differ. One pattern of moral reasoning consists of a search for a "golden mean."[18] At times, this reaches almost ludicrous proportions as moralists search for extremes between which some apparently *a priori* desired mean can be located.[19]

Some moralists reject the "golden mean" and elevate a single religious, social or personal value to the level of a litmus test against which action can be measured, attributing governing authority to that particular value, making it the sole measure of virtue or "law."[20]

(ed.), *A Normative Approach to War* (Oxford: Clarendon Press, 1993) 333 at 340 and fig. 11.1 at 342–43 setting out in graphic form Onuma's analysis of Grotius's conception of overlapping orders pertinent to an understanding of the overall international legal order in the middle of the seventeenth century. Onuma finds this differentiation among "orders" at the heart of Grotius's analysis of the international legal order. For some independently derived elaboration on this theme as applied in the late twentieth century, see Rubin, "Enforcing".

[18] Aristotle, *The Nichomachean Ethics*, 1106a25*ff.* (Book II, chapter 6*ff.*).

[19] E.g., ibid., 1108a19 (Book II, chapter 7) finding a "truthful sort of person" to be the mean between boastful exaggeration and mock modesty.

[20] This is particularly common in discussions of so-called "human rights," where some particular "right" is held the touchstone of "law" without analysis of other values that might be affected by the rules derived from this approach. See Alfred P. Rubin, "Are Human Rights Legal?", 20 IYBHR 1990 45 (1991). A memorable short story by Mark Twain exposes the contradictions into which single-value moralists fall when elevating a single value, in the story: "truth," to the pinnacle of argumentation. See Mark

Still another pattern of moral reasoning, today the most used in legal argumentation, involves identifying the social or personal values that might be affected by a proposed course of action, and weighing the enhancement of some values against the detriment to others to arrive at a calculus of advantage, such as "greatest good to the greatest number and least harm to any,"[21] supporting the conclusion as "moral" and perhaps even as therefore "legal." Every student of "common law" judicial techniques must be familiar with the "balancing test" by which various legal and moral factors are set forth by a court as pertinent to its finding of implicit "law."[22]

A fourth pattern of moral reasoning, still found occasionally, is to assert definitions, usually involving distinctions between the Latin *"mores,"* the Greek *"ethike"* and the English "morality" or "ethics," to be based on universal conceptions, then to adopt the usages and definitions preferred by the particular author as if universally understood and universally valid. This practice has led to very influential and insightful works that are extremely difficult to read except within their own narrow focus.[23]

Recognizing that Cicero's synthesis, however emotionally and rhetorically compelling its language, rests on subjective conclusions then generalized by assuming them to reflect universal experience by calling the

Twain, "Was It Heaven? Or Hell?" (1902), in *The Complete Short Stories of Mark Twain* (Charles Neider, ed., Bantam, 1958) 474–491.

[21] This particular formula is a common paraphrase of what appears to be a remark in Jeremy Bentham's *The Commonplace Book* (10 Works 142): "The greatest happiness of the greatest number is the foundation of morals and legislation," *The Oxford Dictionary of Quotations* (2nd edn., Oxford 1955) 42:11. The Oxford Dictionary traces it back to a treatise by Francis Hutcheson published in 1725. This technique of "moral reasoning" is common today. For an example, see Sisela Bok, *Lying: Moral Choice in Public and Private Life* (Pantheon Books, 1978).

[22] E.g., *Mannington Mills Inc.* v. *Congoleum Corp.* (Ct. App. 3rd Cir. 1979) 595 F. 2d 1287.

[23] For early examples, see Thomas Hill Green, *Prolegomena to Ethics* (A. C. Bradley, ed., 1883, reprinted by Thomas Y. Crowell, 1969); George Edward Moore, *Principia Ethica* (Cambridge University Press 1903, reprinted 1968). A modern work along the same line as applied to international affairs is *Traditions of International Ethics* (Terry Nardin and David R. Mapel, eds., Cambridge University Press, 1992), especially Murray Forsyth, "The Tradition of International Law" at 23–41. Forsyth's essay attempts to identify the dominant "ethical" underpinnings to basic "legal" conceptions over the centuries, but his notion of what underpinnings were "ethical" depends on largely unstated definitions of "ethics" with which not all readers would agree. Nor can I agree with his characterizations of the underlying conceptions of some of the influential writers he mentions. For a detailed critique of another modern attempt to find "ethical" bases for rules of law in international affairs, see Alfred P. Rubin, "Review Article of Beitz, Political Theory and International Relations", 47(2) CLR 403 (1980).

process "right reason," there have been many attempts to find an objective basis for moral conclusions. Whatever the value of moral logic for each person acting on his or her own responsibility, moral logic cannot form the basis for "law" applicable to others unless it can be generalized. The most influential approach to "objectifying" the analysis of supposedly universal natural law reflects the view that Aristotle impliedly rejected: that if a principle were applied in many different legal orders it can be presumed to rest on universal human perceptions of proper behavior, perhaps on the universal capacity of mankind to reason about it, perhaps on some inborn, intuitive sense of propriety or command of a father-like God to all human creatures. The notion found its way into legal codes at least by the time of the Roman jurist Gaius. In his *Institutes* (AD 165) Gaius distinguishes between the *ius civile* (national, local law, usually called "municipal law" in jurisprudential writings) and the *ius gentium* (the law of nations) defining the latter as "the law observed by all mankind" and therefore to be applied by Roman administrators and judges even to those not subject to Roman law as such:

Every people that is governed by statutes and customs observes partly its own peculiar law and partly the common law of all mankind. That law which a people establishes for itself is peculiar to it, and is called *ius ciuile* (civil law) as being the special law of that *ciuitas* (state), while the law that natural reason establishes among all mankind is followed by all peoples alike, and is called *ius gentium* (law of nations, or law of the world) as being the law observed by all mankind. Thus the Roman people observes partly its own peculiar law and partly the common law of mankind.[24]

---

[24] F. de Zulueta, *The Institutes of Gaius*, Part I (Oxford 1946, 1985), para. 1, 2 (Latin)/3 (English): "Mones populi, qui legibus et moribus reguntur, partim suo proprio, partim communi omnium hominum iure utuntur: nam quod quis/que populus ipse sibi ius constituit, id ipsius proprium est uocaturque ius civile, quasi ius proprium ciuitatis; quod uero naturalis ratio inter omnes homines constituit, id apud omnes populos peraeque custoditur uocaturque ius gentium, quasi quo iure omnes gentes utuntur. populus itaque Romanus partim suo proprio, partim communi omnium hominum iure utitur."
The application of the *ius* (or "*jus*": the "*i*" and "*j*" in Latin are interchangeable, as are the "*u*" and "*v*") *gentium* to foreigners and as a "common law" applicable to Romans in the absence of a *ius civile* superseding rule, are evident in some other parts of Gaius. See, e.g., his provisions relating to the formation of a binding contract in Roman and non-Roman law, in ibid., III, ciii, "Sed haec quidem uerborum obligatio, DARI SPONDES? SPONDEO, propria ciuium Romanorum est; ceterae uero iuris gentium sunt, itaque inter omnes homines, siue ciues Romanos siue peregrinos, ualent [Now the verbal obligation in the form 'Do you promise? I promise' is peculiar to Roman citizens; but the other forms belong to the *ius gentium* and are consequently valid between all men, whether Roman citizens or transients]": Ibid., 180 (Latin), 181 (English). I have replaced Zulueta's unusual English word "peregrines" with the word "transients" because some

The idea was included in Justinian's *Institutes*, compiled in Constantinople by AD 533.[25]

A third category of "natural law" system rests on religious conviction. So-called divine law systems, those that rest on revelation or religious doctrine purporting to come directly from God or gods, are, for present purposes, "natural law" systems because in divine law systems human discretion is purportedly subordinated to other, non-human, non-discretionary sources of law. To those analyzing divine law systems, it is not relevant that the priestly caste or class through whom this law is revealed or interpreted consists of humans because in theory the human agents serve as mere pipelines to transmit orders originating elsewhere.

A fourth category of "natural law" rests on the perception that "custom" is binding as "law." But custom, habits or practices of social behavior, even if called "*mores*" in Latin or "*ethos*" in Greek, might be moral (ethical) but might also be immoral by some standards. It is far simpler to regard custom as a different category; virtue-indifferent, amoral; demonstrated by different evidence than the value-weighing techniques that are today normally used to illustrate morality or immorality. Nonetheless, amoral "custom" is often confused with morality and argued to be binding in "law."

A fifth category is of particular significance today, although its roots are very ancient indeed. That involves blending various conceptions of "natural law" into a single whole, neglecting the inconsistencies among the various sources and their "natural" consequences, and asserting the rule purportedly illustrated by that blend to be of universal validity. An early example is reported by Thucydides in the form of a speech to the Spartan ruling assembly by representatives of Athens in 432 BC:

It has always been a rule that the weak should be subject to the strong; and besides, we consider that we are worthy of our power . . . For example, in lawsuits with our allies arising out of contracts we have put ourselves at a

---

aliens are residents and not transients. The Latin original either implies a technical legal meaning to "peregrinos" not relevant to this investigation, or states an incomplete legal proposition. Zulueta notes that the first lines of I, i up to the "quae" in "quisquae" appear to be interpolations. There are other minor variations in the various surviving texts. Without disputing Zulueta's translation, it is possible to question whether "statute" is a precise equivalent of "legibus" in the first line, and whether "iure" can meaningfully be translated as "law" throughout.

[25] Justinian, *Institutes* (T. C. Sandars, translator and notes) (7th edn., 1922, reprinted 1970), II, i repeats Gaius *Institutes*, I, i, 1 almost *verbatim*.

disadvantage, and when we arrange to have such cases tried by impartial courts in Athens, people merely say that we are overfond of going to law.[26]

This sort of jurisprudential model has been much used by advocates for "human rights" in recent years, finding their own perceptions of such "rights" to be binding on others as a matter of "law" without differentiating among the sources of the asserted rule of law and the cultural and territorial limits to their value systems.[27] It has also been much used by American and other political leaders in recent years and represents views that are always an undercurrent of "realist" criticism of the entire discipline of public international law. It preceded the war in which the Athenians acted on their model of the legal order and met disaster at least in part because that model discounted the "natural" facts of allied and "neutral" resistance to the submission that the Athenians thought "natural."

It seems clear that within the general category of "naturalism" in law, there are contending normative orders, subcategories, and agreement even as to a definition of "law" is unlikely to survive the particular argument for which the definition is posed. This notion of competing normative orders, all of which contribute to the international order, some or all of which influence some actors in that order, sometimes leading them to inconsistent or vacillating policies, is analogous to the notion of competing normative orders in daily life. That is a notion familiar to serious readers of the Bible and writers of major English fiction since at least the time of Shakespeare, the essence of most of the writings of Jane Austen and Anthony Trollope, perhaps most forcefully stated by a contemporary British (his name, at least, is Irish and not English) writer immersed in the literature of the late enlightenment:

I am coming to believe that laws are the prime cause of unhappiness. It is not merely a case of born under one law, required another to obey . . . it is born under half a dozen, required another fifty to obey. There are parallel sets of laws in different keys that have nothing to do with one another and that are even downright contradictory . . . the moral law, the civil, military, common laws, the code of honour, custom, the rules of practical life, of civility, of amorous conversation, gallantry, to say nothing of Christianity for those that practise it.

---

[26] Thucydides, *History of the Peloponnesian War* (Rex Warner, translator, 1954, 1972, Penguin, 1985) I, 76–77 at 80–81.

[27] *Cf.* Herodotus, *The Histories* (Aubrey de Sélincourt, translator, 1954, Penguin, 1986) III, 38 at 219: "[I]f anyone, no matter who, were given the opportunity of choosing from amongst all the nations in the world the set of beliefs which he thought best, he would inevitably, after careful consideration of their relative merits, choose that of his own country."

All sometimes, indeed generally, at variance; none even in an entirely harmonious relation to the rest; and a man is perpetually required to choose one rather than another, perhaps (in his particular case) its contrary.'[28]

And, lest the point be misunderstood, it must be mentioned in this place that it applies as well to the positive law. Under that law, a person is frequently subject to the inconsistent and often conflicting human, discretionary laws promulgated under the written and unwritten constitutions of his or her country, locality, municipality, private and public organizations, like schools, non-divine-law adjuncts to religious organizations, clubs, etc.

"Positivism"

"Positivism" is the system preferred by the legislators of modern society. It emphasizes human discretion as the source of law. To the degree that moral values or religious convictions are embodied in rules that a "positivist" would agree deserve to be called rules of "law," the positivist would tend to emphasize the discretion exercised by the human who pronounces the rule, whether purporting to interpret rules originating outside himself or herself, or simply exercising an authority conferred on him or her by the political order to interpret the rules of "law," whatever the ultimate source of those rules.

Pure positivism is no more a complete or logical system than pure naturalism in any of its guises is an objective one. The constitution of any society rests only in part, if at all, on an exercise of discretion that can be analyzed separately from nondiscretionary historical processes (i.e., historical processes in which the exercise of human discretion is only a remote factor in the evolution of mass culture). An asserted rule that makes "consent" to the legal order a constitutive fact is itself either a natural law rule or a rule that rests on prior consent, thus introducing an infinite regress.

Clearly, there are problems relating both positivism and naturalism to reality, and extreme advocates of subcategories deriving from either view have difficulties in communicating their insights to people outside the circle of the convinced. Indeed, it is a common problem of all jurisprudential writing, including this, that different readers will attach different meanings to key words and phrases. Communicating insight, even where true insight exists (and the writer who is sure that his or her insights are

---

[28] Patrick O'Brian, *Master and Commander* (1970, Norton Paperback, 1990) 318–319.

widely valid is probably wrong),[29] is notoriously tricky and possibly impossible.

Early syntheses

Apart from problems of communication, these logical problems and the difficulties of meshing any basic model with perceptions of reality were well appreciated by thinkers of all times when not involved in polemical model-building themselves. There were three common approaches. The first was to distinguish legal orders geographically or by ethnic or other perceived characteristics. Greece and Persia were seen as two very different legal orders even though Aristotle identified true natural law as the physical law that made fire burn in both places. As noted above, traces of this sort of distinction on a very sophisticated level exist in writings as early as about 1000 BC. It is reflected in the Bible, where followers of Jesus are adjured to "render unto Caesar the things that are Caesar's, and unto God the things that are God's."[30]

The second was to divide the law into functional areas, special jurisdictions within the overall legal order to handle special kinds of problems; to divide criminal law and procedures from torts; the frankly discretionary judicial function (equity) from the theoretically non-discretionary (common law), etc.

The third was to analyze the law according to the contending overall jurisprudential models and specify which model was being discussed, allowing for the likelihood that an action that conformed to some variation of the naturalist model might well violate another variation or the positivist model, thus be praiseworthy in the moral sphere and be subject to dire consequences at the hands of physical nature or human institutions.

The simplest, possibly most eloquent, and probably, for European-derived models, the most influential effort in that third line was by St. Thomas Aquinas. He distinguished four fundamentally different types of

[29] "I wish I was as cocksure of anything as Tom [the great historian Thomas Babington] Macauley is of everything," William Lamb, Viscount Melbourne (*c*.1845?) as retailed in *The Oxford Dictionary of Quotations* 335:13.

[30] *The Bible*, Matthew 22:21. The answer by Jesus was apparently convincing to the Jews of the time and in Western civilization since at least the time of Gratian in the middle of the twelfth century. See Harold Berman, *Law and Revolution* (Harvard University Press, 1983) 143, 144–148. It has been suggested that this notion of overlapping normative orders was rejected in the Islamic world, with enormous consequences for social order in today's Middle East. See Toby E. Huff, *The Rise of Early Modern Science* (Cambridge University Press, 1993) *passim*, especially 116–118.

legal order: eternal Law (the "law" in God's mind), natural law (including both the laws implied by physical nature and the laws derived by "right reason" using mankind's inborn, natural capacity to think, or at least to perceive values and try to weigh them against each other), divine law (the law stated in holy scripture, revelation and other products of the Church organization under its God-given authority) and human law (what we have called positive law). In his famous definition of law, St. Thomas suggests that the word should properly attach only to rules that lie in the intersect of all four special sets, that "Law is nought else than an ordinance of reason for the common good made by the authority who has care of the community and promulgated."[31] Thus, since moral imperatives in Cicero's sense are promulgated in our individual minds, they bind only those in whose minds they exist unless God or nature has placed them in the minds of all. Reason is the tool by which that mine is excavated, but no individual has the capacity to reason for another, so no personal insight is binding as law on another without more. Clearly, this simple definition conceals complexities of extraordinary subtlety.

It also elides various important issues. For example, how do we determine *who* is the authority who has care of the community? Suppose there is a dispute as to authority: *who* determines it? On what basis? Who determines who determines it? Is constitutional law or the customary law of inheritance, including inherited authority in the thirteenth century, not "law" to St. Thomas? Is the authority of some secular law or Germanic tribal or primitive divine law leader simply to be presumed? Or does the Church have ultimate authority to determine questions of the civil community's authority by virtue of the Church's divine-law-based authority to make oaths to God binding, or to absolve oath-breakers in a feudal system where a social contract was literally a contract long before it became an abstract model?[32] Are all questions of authority ultimately questions of divine law? If not, how is the Church's authority to carry over to the human-law arena when St. Thomas's definition involves differ-

---

[31] St. Thomas's four definitions are in the *Summa Theologiae* 1a2ae, Q. 91, 1–4. The overall definition is in Q. 90, 4: "Et sic ex quatuor praedictis potest colligi definitio legis, quae nihil est aliud quam quaedam rationis ordinatio ad bonum commune, ab eo qui curam communitatis habet, promulgata."

[32] This is in fact the position the Church took in Europe. See the Deposition of the Holy Roman Emperor Henry IV by Pope Gregory VII, February 1076, in *Documents of the Christian Church* (Henry Bettenson, ed., Oxford, 1943, 1956) 144; deposition of Frederic II by Innocent IV, July 1245, in Ehler and Morrall, *Church and State Through the Centuries* (London. 1954) 79*ff.*

entiating the four spheres of law? Clearly, this synthesis of the high middle ages could not stand the secularization of society or the loss of confidence in the divine-law basis of the authority of the Church as an institution; the Reformation's perception of the Church as a human institution with fallible officers.

"Reality" and the evolution of theory

It is the plan of this work to trace these two main lines of jurisprudential thought, naturalism and positivism, from their formulation for purposes of the international legal order of the seventeenth century through the great intellectual reorganization of the nineteenth century, when jurists finally began to accept into their own domain, the special world of law, the implications of the Peace of Westphalia. That settlement of 1646–1648 is, with good reason, usually taken to signal the end of divine law, religious and dynastic conceptions, as the basic model for statesmen and scholars analyzing the structure of multi-ethnic, multi-tradition, politically hydra-headed society, and its replacement with the notion that the political world is organized into "states" whose relations with each other are secular, not based on the acceptance of any particular religious writings or institutions as the source of authority or substantive rules of law; and on the equality of those states before the "law."[33]

Of course, "equality before the law" was not intended by either "positivists" or "naturalists" to relate to any other law than the positive law. But in polemical writings or where some national advantage has been sought, states have used economic, military, moral, political and any other "superiority" to achieve, consolidate or at least argue for legal advantage. Normally, the argument involves referring to some perceived moral or political "responsibility" as a "duty"; then equating the moral or political "duty" to a "duty" in the legal order; then arguing that the "duty" implies a "right" or "authority" to discharge it; then concluding that this "right" or "authority" implies a legal "duty" in somebody else to submit. Normally, the argument is unpersuasive to those outside the

---

[33] The writings on the Peace of Westphalia are endless. Indispensable introductions are Leo Gross, "The Peace of Westphalia, 1648–1948", 42 AJIL 20 (1948) and Harold Berman, *Law and Revolution* (Harvard University Press, 1983). Berman's brilliant book deals with the "Papal Revolution" of AD 1075–1122 that followed the rediscovery of Justinian's Code of Roman Law in Europe and the evolution of legal doctrine implied by its acceptance by statesmen and scholars as a useful model of secular rationality and system.

group that perceives itself advantaged by it.[34] This search for legal advantage is found in scholars, lawyers and statesmen of all societies at all times and is not a basis for differentiating among either societies, times, or careers.

The two major schools, "naturalist" and "positivist," follow different intellectual paths. Rather than follow a chronological order, mixing contending orthodoxies as each interacted with others, it seems to lend to clearer exposition to begin the discussion of each school with its dominant figures and focus on the evolution of their ideas as they were adopted or rejected in practice. Little attention is given to the many technical variations and elaborations of doctrine within each school, interesting as some of them are. This is not a text on jurisprudential ingenuity.

My conclusion is that positivism, obsessed with authority and contemptuous of moral balancing, dominates the thinking of statesmen and has so dominated since the seventeenth century regardless of the naturalist models adopted by the publicists whose writings seem to have survived with greatest reputation. Nearly all of those publicists elaborated their variations of natural law models of international society as if any alternatives were evil as well as intellectually shoddy. The great shift in thinking came when what were in Europe universally perceived (by both statesmen and jurists) as the undoubted social evils of piracy and the international slave trade were sought to be rendered "criminal" as a matter of "international law," with practical consequences flowing from that categorization. The natural law arguments were opposed not on moral grounds, but on the positive law ground that the international legal order did not give authority to any one state or group of states to make law for any other or to enforce the universal conceptions of morality against any persons or institutions not somehow brought within the municipal legal order that gives enforcement authority to individuals

---

[34] The unequalness of "equality before the law" is wittily noted by Anatole France, who wrote that "The law, in its majestic equality, forbids the rich as well as the poor to sleep under bridges, to beg in the streets, and to steal bread": *Bartlett's Familiar Quotations* (14th edn., 1968) 802 (*Le Lys Rouge*, 1894). For a formal statement of the argument equating moral or political "responsibilities" with legal "rights" see *Parliamentary Papers*, Cmd. 3302, *Report of the Indian States Committee, 1928–9*, tracing the origin and use of the British conception of "paramountcy." Many examples of the argument in practice, but only against smaller, weaker "states," are analyzed in Alfred P. Rubin, *International Personality of the Malay Peninsula* (Kuala Lumpur: University of Malaya Press, 1974) beginning at 194–195; Alfred P. Rubin, *Piracy, Paramountcy and Protectorates* (Kuala Lumpur: University of Malaya Press, 1974) 54–80.

or organizations; that the enforcement authority of any municipal agency does not extend beyond the reach of the municipal legal order that gave it authority, even if that order were itself subject to a larger, international, legal order.

The identical dispute, with similar rhetoric and similar results, is occurring today with regard to "terrorism," "war crimes" and "human rights." The major thesis of this work is that true advance towards a more humane world and an increase in the influence of humanitarian notions will be achieved by toning down the traditional rhetoric and differentiating moral indignation from legal argumentation; that the law is a very powerful tool, but cannot be used effectively by those who argue in however sophisticated terms that humanitarian rules are legally binding on others primarily because humanitarian and regardless of the distribution of human discretion to transform those moral rules into legal rules with human enforcement agencies.

If one thread dominates this study, it is the search for "authority." Naturalists tend to presume that the authority to make law, located outside of human will, merely allows human institutions or even individuals to interpret or apply that "law" without importing their own discretion; positivists tend to disregard the underlying moral, practical or other sources of substantive rules and to end the search for rules when they have examined the promulgations of the person or institution in which the positivist jurist finds the authority to make the applicable rules. Municipal legislators in states that clearly differentiate between the legislative function and the judicial function have no doubt that it is their discretion alone, exercised in ways directed by the constitutions of their legal orders, that "makes" law. In municipal orders that do not clearly distinguish between legislation and adjudication, or where the functions overlap, as in the United States and England, the rôle of judges as legislators has been subjected to a great deal of soul-searching.[35]

To summarize the distinctions and approach taken here, it might be useful to relate two parables. The first, or naturalist-mocking, parable is of the violinist whose fiddle had only one string, whose finger remained in the same place on that string and who played the same note to all who could hear. When asked why other violinists used four strings and moved their fingers about, the reply was: "They are looking for the note. I have found it." In my view, 3,000 years of people insisting on the validity of a

---

[35] E.g., Benjamin N. Cardozo, *The Nature of the Judicial Process* (New Haven, CT: Yale University Press 1921); Aharon Barak, *Judicial Discretion* (New Haven, CT: Yale University Press, 1989).

single insight and denying the validity of the insights of colleagues who view the world differently demonstrate the futility of the one-string approach to jurisprudence. The world is full of music to those who would listen.

The second, or positivist-mocking, parable is of the person who argued from a presumption of the authority to attach a word for reasons of human choice, policy, to a fact or relationship; the person who believes that a "terrorist" is whatever the legislator defines as one, and the emotive word binds all within the legislator's legal order, come what may. It is a limerick:

> There once was a person of Deal
> Who said, "Although pain is not real,
> When I sit on a pin
> And I puncture my skin
> I dislike what I fancy I feel."

Mislabeling for the sake of a policy goal does not illustrate the perceptiveness of the mislabeler. Nor is it an effective way of changing reality when real skin is punctured by real pins; when "*de facto*" regimes and "terrorists" must be dealt with in the interest of stability and order, regardless of the reasons why the legislator prefers to avoid the words "*de jure*" and "soldier."[36]

Adjudication and legislation

Common law systems
Rules inherent in social organization
The common law can be usefully defined for purposes of this study as the law inherent in the social, commercial or political orders, or established by custom, pronounced by judges and administrators and subject to modification by later pronouncement and analysis by the same or other judges or administrators. There is a tendency in many jurists to identify it as itself a form of legislation. This "law" is seen as existing independently of more formal legislation, i.e., independently of enactments of constitu-

---

[36] The point seems obvious to "naturalist" jurists and is rationalized by modern "positivists" pointing out that it is "practice accepted as law" that determines the legal effect of labels attached for policy reasons. See Hans Kelsen, "Recognition in International Law," 35 AJIL 604 (1941). Thus, to positivist jurists today, an "unrecognized" regime or "terrorist" that is treated identically with a "recognized" regime or "soldier" makes that treatment the legal result of the pejorative label as well as of the more traditional legal category.

tionally designated "legislators." It is frequently seen at least as a sort of law morally superior and perhaps more persuasive than formal legislation, even if superseded by formal legislation under constitutional rules that allow for such supersession. Many analyses of "law" presume that all legal orders are based on social values applied by judges and administrators, and perhaps enacted into positive law by the exercise of discretion based on values determined by legislators reasoning together; that human discretion is, if not absent from the process of law-finding and applying, at least so restricted by social and cultural pressures, or "reason," that the element of discretion is unimportant. They identify "law" with what others call morality blended with practical policy by wise people primarily concerned with maintaining a virtuous society.

That view strikes me as unrealistic. It violates Occam's Razor and ignores the common experience analyzed in Aristotle's *Rhetoric* by assuming that people, whether judges, administrators, scholars or formal legislators, acting in a legislative capacity will focus on issues of ethical judgment and social value that are drowned in emotion when the same people act outside of a legislative arena. It ignores the historical evidence of absurd judicial, administrative, or formally promulgated "legislation" actually produced in times of emergency by real people. It ignores the capacity for hypocrisy and thirst for authority, wealth and station that have marked mankind's political actions both individually and in groups since earliest records. For reasons like these, common law judges mistrust legislation by others. But true common law systems, where the judges themselves function without outside direction except such as they find in their own experience and analyses of social needs, are subject to the same weaknesses; and it is doubtful that any true common law system can exist without a superior legislator in a real human society. A common law system that did not permit to formal legislation a rôle superior to judicial opinion would be a customary law system or a system possibly similar to that of ancient Israel under the "Judges,"[37] whose legislator-judges fill a very different place than those in modern American or British orders, or in the international legal order.

Another anomaly must be faced. Not all legal questions are submitted to adjudication. Indeed, there is a question as to whether a tribunal should or, in the existing international legal order, can properly adjudicate questions even if the legal order of which the tribunal is a part has a

---

[37] *The Bible*, Judges 1:16, 4:4ff. It is not at all clear that the "Prophetess" Deborah and others called "judges" in the usual English translations of the Bible were any more than poetically inspired interpreters of Israelite divine law: priests.

recognized basis for proscribing or prescribing the conduct which gave rise to the dispute, applying those prescriptions to the actors in the dispute, and jurisdiction to enforce those prescriptions. An example might involve a person of the nationality of the prescribing system in the current international legal order, subject on the basis of nationality to a prescription, performing acts abroad against a foreign victim that have no impact at all on the prescribing legal order, then coming "home" for a visit and being sued civilly or even arrested. With all the evidence abroad and no legal interest in the civil case or criminal prosecution, it would be technically possible to conceive of a successful suit or prosecution but not very likely.

In civil matters today, the tribunal's escape valve from legislators' exaggerated notions of prescriptive jurisdiction is in choice-of-law rules, and the escape valve from exaggerated notions of adjudicatory or enforcement jurisdiction is in the rules relating to *"forum non conveniens,"* the doctrine that permits tribunals to dismiss cases that, in the opinion of the judge or administrator, lie outside the legal interest of the forum state.[38] The basic rule in the United States requires the tribunal to weigh various factors before assuming its exercise of authority is appropriate: "A state may exercise jurisdiction through its courts to adjudicate with respect to a person or thing if the relationship of the state to the person or thing is such as to make the exercise of jurisdiction reasonable."[39] Eleven specific ties to the municipal legal order are specified as significant, although probably not intended to be exclusive. They all involve some territorial or nationality link, including a vaguely worded "foreseeable effect within the state" criterion.[40]

In cases of so-called "universal" crimes, despite broad assertions of jurisdiction to adjudicate, a state court of the United States "may exercise jurisdiction to enforce universal and other non-territorial offenses [only] where the United States has jurisdiction to prescribe," and even there, the "state court's jurisdiction to adjudicate in such cases is effectively limited by constitutional safeguards for the accused, for example, the right to be confronted by witnesses and to have compulsory process."[41] The same limitations would seem to apply to federal courts and, by the normal

---

[38] See *Restatement (3rd) of the Foreign Relations Law of the United States* (adopted by the American Law Institute, 14 May 1986) (Philadelphia, 1987) sections 421–423.

[39] Ibid., section 421(1).

[40] Ibid., section 421(2). The "foreseeable effect within the state" condition is listed in section 421(2)(j).

[41] Ibid., section 423 Comment *a* at 318–319.

application of conceptions of human rights and other notions of fairness, to any tribunal interested in doing "justice."

Limitations on the reach of a state's authority to require its own public policy to be the governing law in a real transaction were analyzed by the Permanent Court of International Justice in *The Lotus* (1927).[42] A Turkish statute provided that:

> Any foreigner who . . . commits an offence abroad to the prejudice of . . . a Turkish subject, for which offence Turkish law prescribes a penalty involving loss of freedom for . . . not less than one year, shall be punished in accordance with the Turkish Penal Code [with some modifications].

The court held by the narrowest of margins (six to six, with the President's casting vote determining the "majority") that the exercise of prescriptive jurisdiction by Turkey was permissible in the circumstances, where "the offence produced its effects on [a] Turkish vessel and consequently in a place assimilated to Turkish territory," while refusing to discuss "passive personality" jurisdiction to prescribe, i.e., jurisdiction based on the nationality of the victim alone. In an eloquent and oft-cited dissent, actually concurring in the court's conclusion, Judge John Bassett Moore divided prescriptive jurisdiction into five categories: (1) territory; (2) nationality of the actor; (3) effects; (4) universality; and (5) passive personality. The first two he believed were amply supported by state practice and theory; the third less obvious, but supportable; the fourth possible, citing "piracy" but expressing considerable hesitation in the absence of precedents;[43] and the last unacceptable to all. In recent years, there has been a major movement by many states to expand their jurisdiction over "universal" offenses.[44]

Authority: who makes law?

It appears that many jurisprudential quarrels about the nature of the international legal order, like many about the nature of partially or wholly unwritten municipal constitutional orders, conceal a struggle for authority. Do judges and arbitrators make law, or are judges and

---

[42] *The S.S. Lotus (France v. Turkey)* PCIJ Ser. A, No. 10 (1927); 2 Manley O. Hudson, *World Court Reports* 20 (1935).

[43] That hesitation is certainly well founded. The "conventional wisdom" supporting the universality of prescriptive jurisdiction over the offense of "piracy," and the assumption that if there were universal prescriptive jurisdiction over what each state would define as "piracy" there would necessarily also be universal jurisdiction to adjudicate and jurisdiction to enforce, seem to have very little support in practice or positivist theory and that lack of support is one of the factors leading to this study. See pp. 84*ff.* below.

[44] See pp. 176*ff.* below.

arbitrators mere administrators of law made in society by the forces of history and conscience, flowing through society's tribunals for practical application? If the latter, then the selection processes for these powerful administrators, those with the authority to determine which rules should be applied, and even what the rules are in the absence of some record of agreement as to the hierarchy of social values, becomes the key to understanding the law. The deeper the analysis of this model, the more removed common law seems to become from the ideal of inherent social and moral values; the more the word "law" rests on an analysis of authority rather than the social and moral values the model is supposed to enshrine. Indeed, in 1881 Oliver Wendell Holmes, already recognized as a major scholar of the common law, wrote: "The life of the [common] law has not been logic; it has been experience. The felt necessities of the time, the prevalent moral and political theories, intuitions of public policy, avowed or unconscious, even the prejudices which judges share with their fellow men . . ."[45]

Similarly, if judges necessarily exercise fallible human discretion, can legislators who are not judges or administrators do better to identify morality with "law"? The question can be broadened to cover "divine law" systems as well. If the law flows from outside human discretion, through whom, through what pipeline or channel, is the divine revelation or moral insight entrusted? Even if to a priestly caste reading the augurs, it would be naïve and violate Occam's Razor to presume that the function of the priest or legislator was solely reportorial, with no interpretation involved. And when interpretation is involved, it is equally naïve to suppose that if we reason together there would be no disagreement among similarly trained and equally conscientious and insightful people. And if reasonable people can disagree, then discretion is involved in selecting and interpreting the rule; the process cannot be solely reportorial or ministerial, the administrator cannot be a mere channel or pipeline for a rule promulgated elsewhere.

In theory today, even with parts of the Anglo-American legal orders that are overwhelmingly left to the common law, such as torts (civil wrongs), the pronouncement of a judge binds only the parties before him or her, and only with respect to the particular case presented. Generalities about the law on which a decision is argued to rest might be persuasive to other judges in other cases, but cannot bind them unless the legal order makes the pronouncement of a particular tribunal the equivalent of legislation

---

[45] Oliver Wendell Holmes, *The Common Law* (1881) (Howe, ed., Boston, 1963) 1.

for all others. Even then, the dominant tribunal, like a legislature, can change its opinion, thus change the law, on rehearing or in a later case. In a case involving another party, that new party must be given a day to argue his or her version of "morality," "law" or "justice," but a common law tribunal can overrule itself even if the later case involves the same parties unless legally prevented by whatever rules of *res judicata* exist in the legal order. Those rules do exist, but not to assure "justice" by any usual definition. They exist to require a final decision in the social interest of terminating the dispute regardless of other values, such as the social value of administering substantive commutative justice.

The progress of the common law is evolutionary and cannot be stopped, although at times precedent, stability and certainty are given such high values by the common law judge-legislators that change in the substantive rules is anathema. There is no way to predict a direction of movement with confidence although assertions of inevitability, direction and evolutionary movement often accompany legal argument for change.

Legislation has a different meaning in a common law system to the meaning it conveys in a system that differentiates the legislator from the judge. Legislation is by definition static until a change in the legislated rules is decreed by the legislator. Judges in a system that subordinates judges' discretion to the formal will of the legislator, when the limits of "interpretation" are reached, are bound at least in theory to apply as law the legislated rules, even if the judges feel that the rules violate ethical or political sense either as applied in particular cases or in evolving societies as a whole.

This poses something of a dilemma for those systems. The resolution in the United States, where authority is distributed by a positive constitution modified by common law traditions, has been to allow a wide scope for judicial interpretation of statutory language: to incorporate some vague limits on legislative authority, like "due process of law," and allow the judiciary to interpret the phrase. Legislation that violates the political or moral convictions of properly authorized judges can then be refused application either in particular wrenching cases or in general when those judicial convictions can be categorized to the satisfaction of the authorized courts as consistent with substantive statutory or authority-distributing constitutional language.

"Equity"

Great attention has been given by many jurists to the special authority Aristotelian analysis and European judicial traditions give to "equity";

the scope given to judicial discretion under the guise of a special authority in judges to apply "equitable," as distinguished from "legal," rules.[46] Such exceptions are frequent in a system that does not clearly distinguish between the rôle of a judge as an applier of the law and his or her rôle as a legislator for an evolving system. Those who would like judges to have legislative authority frequently assert that the authority to do "justice," apply "equitable principles" and the like are inherent in the judges' function. The move is resisted by the non-judicial legislators of the legal order, who prefer not to share legislative authority with judges selected for other purposes; who view judges as mere administrators of "law" made by human discretion exercised by others elsewhere. And even when "equitable" solutions are permitted to be applied by judges in disregard of positive law, the "law" applied under the guise of "equity" is binding only on the parties and only in that case; to hold the "precedent" persuasive on others is to move towards making the system into a thorough common law system in which judges replace legislators, and the problem becomes to decide how these powerful judges receive authority; what the precise scope of that authority is and how and by whom the judges are selected. The same applies to tensions between judges and political leaders who are not legislators. Quarrels over whether a "pardon" is an act of mercy or justice, whether "mercy" is part of "justice," thus become questions of the distribution of authority; the issue is *who*, which constituencies' evaluation of social benefits and detriments best reflects the hypothetical will of the society, and other jurisprudential rhetoric and appeals to "justice" quickly prove to be empty. An amusing example of exactly this is an exchange by Ernest van den Haag, a lawyer with political connections in New York, responding to assertions by Professor Alan Dershowitz of the Harvard Law School. Dershowitz had argued that no pardon should be considered by an administrator that could not be rationalized as "just." Van den Haag denied the need for administrators to consider "justice" when exercising their authority to pardon an offender. The underlying, unstated issue is

---

[46] Aristotle, *The Nichomachean Ethics*, V, x, 5 (1137b): "When the law states a universal proposition, and the facts in a given case do not square with the proposition, the right course is to . . . say for him, [the legislator] what he would have put into his law if he had only known": Barker, *Aristotle* 368. But there are many other definitions of "equity" and in England "equitable remedies" were applied by special courts set up under the Crown's prerogative in derogation of the normal common law enforcement system. The subject is far too complex for deeper analysis here. For a beginning, see George Burton Adams, *Constitutional History of England* (revised edn., Robert L. Schuyler, ed.) (New York, 1921, 1934, 1949) 111–114.

who is best situated to decide whether a pardon should be issued: academics and lawyers like Dershowitz trying to influence judges and administrators, or administrators prepared to defend their actions to their constituents who might or might not care about abstractions relating to "justice"?[47]

The international legal order as a common law system

The international legal order is essentially a common law system without a compulsory tribunal; without a priestly or "judgely" caste. Attempts to envisage an invisible college of international jurists, from this perspective, seem to be part of a struggle for authority, with the scholars of the law, or some of them, arguing that their own insights are somehow binding on statesmen. To this school, difficulties in determining the opinions of the "college" should be resolved presumably by listening to their debates. In fact, the scholars' debates, like all legislative sessions that do not end with a formal summary act, like a vote, are usually polemical exercises in group-think or amorphous and inconclusive. And history can give the "college" a different perspective and new biases to make some arguments seem more convincing than others that might have persuaded statesmen earlier. Again, the subject is too complex for a deeper analysis in this place but will become more clear as real situations are examined in the text below. For the present, it is enough to be aware that the central theme of the following jurisprudential discussion is *who* decides, rather than *what* is the rule of substance. In the examples chosen, piracy and the international slave trade, the existence and even the strength of the natural law rules, including moral and divine law commands, were not doubted by either the statesmen trying to enforce them as if rules of "law" or by the statesmen resisting that enforcement.

Sources and language

Jus and *lex*, justice and law?

Because primary sources are the only data that are not tainted by the prejudices of interpreters and selectors, in what follows I have used primary sources wherever possible. The reader will have to rely on my own prejudices being kept under as much control as feasible, and if tempted to disagree with my selection of documents is encouraged to search the same sources and try to find others more congenial to his or

---

[47] *New York Times Book Review*, 6 August 1989, 31.

her own prejudices. I have tried very hard to be balanced even though my conclusions seem inconsistent with today's conventional wisdom. Of course, my deepest research is in English and American sources because those were the most readily available and familiar to me. People approaching the same questions from other linguistic and national experience perspectives might (but might not) come to different conclusions.

Much of the early jurisprudential material is in Greek or Latin. Where this is so, I have used the more or less standard translations of the Carnegie Endowment or, where pertinent, the Loeb Classical Library with occasional comments regarding what seem tendentious errors. To guard against my own errors, I have reproduced the original Latin (and other languages, where appropriate) in notes. Occasionally I have quoted foreign languages at great length, partly because at some periods a discursive style was used, partly to assure the accuracy of the context against which pertinent quotations must be measured. One of the great hazards of research into intellectual history is to read a few words or sentences as if delivered free of intellectual context into today's world. Scholars who read these texts differently should have no difficulty checking their and my interpretations against the original sources. Where the original language was French or German, again I have quoted the original in too-long notes and in most cases used more or less standard English translations in the text. Where the translation is my own, I have said so.

A final caution about translations is necessary. The Latin *"jus"* has several meanings and evolved in meaning over time and place. The closest equivalent familiar to modern linguists might be the French word *"droit,"* which can be translated as "right," "legal right" or "law" in English depending on the context. The word "right" in English, like *"Recht"* in German, has many other meanings and implications in the moral world absent from the French and in most contexts from the Latin (such as, "you are right" or *"Sie haben Recht"* to mean what in French would be *"vous avez raison,"* not *"vous avez droit"*). *"Jus"* does not necessarily imply "justice."[48]

Similarly, the Latin *"lex"* does not necessarily imply amoral positive

[48] Fortunately, it is unnecessary to define "justice" in this work. The classical distinctions among distributive, commutative, retributive and other forms of "justice" are very useful but are frequently disregarded or misapplied in rhetorical debate these days. See Alfred P. Rubin, "Are Human Rights Legal?", 20 IYBHR 1990 45 (1991) at 67–70. See also Rubin, "Enforcing" *passim*.

"prescription" as in the English "legislation." As noted above, to Cicero the unwritten moral law that binds conscience regardless of the acts of a legislator, the Senate of Rome, was the *"vera* [true] *lex."* The English word "law" does not come directly from this word, but originally from a different root relating to "lay," as in "lay down the law" or, for that matter, "lay out a military encampment," in German, a *"Lager."* But the similarity in sound and usage compressed the meanings of the Middle English "lay" and the Latin-rooted *"legis lator"* (he who lays the law on the table) and *"legislatio"* (the laying of that "law"), words introduced into English by clerical scribes in the fourteenth century (*"legis"* is the genitive singular of the Latin *"lex"*).[49] The word used by Cicero in a natural law sense, the *"vera lex,"* has, via its association with positive "legislation," overtones of the positive law in some English and Latin contexts, but not in all. Significantly, in Cicero's writing "lex" has precisely the opposite meaning; it refers to personal moral conceptions derived through "right reason in harmony with nature" by introspection and is independent of the will of the Senate as legislator.

The confusions that flow from this shifting usage have been many. An example can illustrate the complex process and the intellectual risks involved in quoting classical sources as if the word usage were consistent with current usages in all their implications. St. Thomas Aquinas gave the title *"De Lege"* to the section of his *Summa* that dealt with all four categories of "law." When the seventeenth-century Dutch Protestant Hugo Grotius wrote his great work the title in Latin was not *"De Lege,"* but *"De Iure Belli ac Pacis,"* usually translated "Of the Law of War and Peace," although occasionally, and more accurately translated as "Of the Rights of War and Peace." In discussing declarations of war, Grotius wrote that public declarations were necessary in order for the war to be *"bellum justum."* But he obviously did not mean "just war." He probably meant "legal" or "formal" war. He clarified the point by noting that the positive laws of war applied to the *"bellum justum"* and the natural laws of war applied under the law of nature even if the war were not declared.[50] It seems as clear as language can make it that his use of the phrase *"bellum*

---

[49] See *American Heritage Dictionary* (1969) 741 (*Law*), 747 (*Legislator*), Appendix of Indo-European Roots 1525 (leg-, legh). For the earliest uses in English, see *Oxford English Dictionary* (Compact Microtext edition, 1971) 1600, which refers the word "legislative" to the fourteenth century and calls it a back formation from "legislator" and "legislation," although giving as the earliest uses of those latter two words texts published in the early seventeenth century!

[50] Hugo Grotius, *De Iure Belli ac Pacis* (1625, 1646) (F. W. Kelsey, translator) (Carnegie Endowment Classics of International Law, 1925) III, iii, 5 and 6.

justum" is entirely different from the same phrase deriving from the scholastic notion of "just war," involving "just cause," "just object," and "just intention." (St. Thomas adds "lawful authority," and does not differentiate between just object and intention; but this is not the place for a disquisition on classical "just war" theory.)[51]

Authority

The notion that "law" is fundamentally associated with "authority" did not reach the forefront of modern scholarly consciousness until the beginning of the twentieth century. In Wesley Hohfeld's analysis of the use of legal terms, a legal "power" is the ability to alter legal relationships as by legislation or private act, such as making an offer (endowing the offeree with the "power" that he or she had not had before, by acceptance to change the legal relationships of the offeror and offeree from strangers in the legal order to contracting partners). A "right" is something else. It involves the capacity in the holder of the right, at his or her discretion to call on the public enforcement institutions of the law to act.[52] Hans Kelsen and H. L. A. Hart applied the same distinction to public law, positing separate categories, "primary" and "secondary" rules, to distinguish the rules that distribute authority from rules that operate with an immediate impact on their objects.[53]

---

[51] St. Thomas Aquinas, *Summa Theologiae* 2a2ae, Q. 40.1: "Dicendum quod ad hoc aliquod bellum sit justum, tria requiruntur. Primo quidem, auctoritas principalis, cujus mandato bellum est gerendum . . . Secundo, requiritur causa justa . . . Tertio, requiritur ut sit intentio bellantium recta. [Three things are required for any war to be just. The first is the authority of the sovereign on whose command war is waged . . . Secondly, a just cause is required . . . Thirdly, the right intention of those waging war is required]."
St. Thomas's use of *"jus"* as a word in the moral order in this context is consistent with his use of the word *"lex"* to mean "law" in general.

[52] Wesley Hohfeld, *Fundamental Legal Conceptions* (New Haven, CT: Yale University Press, 1923) *passim*. Hohfeld's work, and others' derived in part from Pufendorf's distinctions to be discussed below, is very difficult to read, partly because aimed at an audience accustomed to the pomposities of judges more than the jargon of linguistic philosophers. A useful summary of the Hohfeld terms, derived from the law-review articles that were later reprinted to form his great book, is Arthur L. Corbin, "Legal Analysis and Terminology", 29 YLJ 163 (1919), excerpted usefully in Jerome Hall, *Readings in Jurisprudence* (Indianapolis, IN: Bobbs-Merrill Co., Inc., 1938) 471–484.

[53] Hans Kelsen, *The Pure Theory of Law* (1934, revised edn., 1960, Max Knight, translator, 1967) (hereinafter cited as Kelsen, *Pure Theory*) 134–137, where "rights" are reduced to being a special kind of legal "power." To Kelsen, the state itself is neither more nor less than a legal order; a distribution of authority, with a constitution (perhaps written; in primitive, customary law societies, not) establishing the static, primary, norms under which dynamic, secondary, norms can be made and enforced. Secondary

On closer analysis, the ability to bring a defendant into court or to require the performance of an official act, for example change title to land, is itself a legal "power." So to a positivist adopting the models of Hohfeld, Kelsen and others, the entire structure of "law" seems to come down to a question of discretionary authority.[54]

Discussion of "rights" as distinct from "authority" has some value on a superficial level, but, because the word "rights" has meaning in many different orders and sub-orders, both moral and legal (and, indeed, amoral and pre-"legal" political orders as well), there are pervasive confusions in the literature relating to "rights." For example, it is common in the United States to refer to individual "rights" under the "Bill of Rights" contained as amendments to the Constitution of 1787. Using the Hohfeld language, the Constitution does not confer rights at all: it distributes authority. The Bill of Rights is a list of authorities withheld from the federal government of the United States, some of which are reserved to individuals or the states of the Union and some, under the Fourteenth Amendment, yielded to individuals even by the states. In England, the untouchable reserved "unalienable rights" (to borrow the evocative phrase of the American Declaration of Independence of 1776) of the individual are called "liberties." The word "liberty," not being one of Hohfeld's key words, is not part of the usual jurisprudential vocabulary of American scholars, whatever its use in rhetoric.

In what follows, I have tried to step through these swamps of terminological confusion on stepping stones of Hohfeld and Kelsen, occasionally using my own words where they seem clearer, for example preferring to use the word "authority" for "power" wherever the awkward phrase "legal power" would be required by Hohfeld. In that way it is easier to avoid confusing the legal conception with political or military influence (as in "balance of power") when discussing writings which themselves do not focus on the distinctions which are vital to this work. On the other hand, I claim no originality. Nearly everything to be noted below (indeed, probably everything without the qualifier "nearly") derives from the

---

norms are the rules promulgated within the legal order which prescribe the duties and rights of those persons and institutions subject to the order which the institutions of the order will enforce. See ibid, 286–290. H. L. A. Hart, *The Concept of Law* (Oxford, 1961), reverses Kelsen's terminology by labeling as "primary" the norms with a direct impact on those subject to the law, and "secondary" the rules that distribute authority. There is no need in this place to delve further into the language used by Kelsen or Hart (or other modern jurists) in their analyses of the models of law and society each found most useful.

[54] The point is made at some length in Kelsen, *Pure Theory* 145*ff*.

writings of others. Where I have based my analysis on primary sources, those sources express or imply models of the international legal order which have been acted on or commented on (sometimes derided) by many others. Whenever I have researched deeply enough into the history of an idea I had thought was original in myself, I have found that others had been there first. The object of this study, therefore, is not to express originality, but to question a current conventional wisdom that seems to me wasteful of the intellectual energy, moral courage and insight of very able people.

The slippery slope

One final caution. It is impossible totally to set one's mind back to a time before current vocabulary and current conceptions impinged on the operative jurisprudential model. It is very difficult today, for example, to imagine the confusion caused by choice-of-law theory, the idea that a court should, in the exercise of its own discretion consistently with the legal order that gives it authority to exercise that discretion, apply and enforce a body of law promulgated by a foreign legal order. Before the middle of the eighteenth century it was the hazard of the unwilling defendant appearing physically within the territorial reach of English municipal courts to have the local law applied to his or her transactions by what the tribunal considered the foreigner's constructive consent. The inequities this produced were resolved by establishing special juris- dictions, special courts, to handle the cases in which foreigners were likely to be involved. So in England "staple" courts were established in 1353 to apply what was conceived as a reason-based "law merchant" that might be different from the reason-based "common law" applicable to commercial transactions occurring outside the context in which foreign merchants were encouraged to participate. Admiralty tribunals were separated from common law courts for many reasons, but from early days were conceived as applying a special body of law to ships of any flag that might enter English admiralty jurisdiction.[55] To naturalist jurists, the basic notion before "conflict of laws" and "choice-of-law" theory were popularized involved the Ciceronian notion that certain "natural law"

[55] The first Statute of the Staple in England was 27 Edw. III St. 2 , c. 13 (1353); a separate admiralty jurisdiction and tribunals were first erected in England under the statute 13 Richard II, c. 5 (1390). A complete rundown of the many special jurisdictions and legal sub-orders of England as of the middle of the seventeenth century is in Sir Edward Coke, *Fourth Institute of the Laws of England* (1644) (hereinafter, Coke, *Fourth*).

rules are universal and that any legal order that applies a rule different from that which would be applied in the forum itself must be unreasonable; that there is no theoretical room for applying any foreign law because the law of the forum, based on natural law principles, must be part of the universal law that all reasonable people would apply. Indeed, the publication of Joseph Story's great book, *Commentaries on the Conflict of Laws*, in 1834 helped work a revolution in legal thought whose implications were not fully worked out in the American Constitutional order until the Supreme Court in 1938, over a century later, ruled that federal courts sitting in some private cases (so-called "diversity jurisdiction" where state courts have concurrent jurisdiction with the federal) are bound by the Constitution to apply the law of the state in which they are sitting.[56] It is a notion that few of the framers of the Constitution would have understood.[57]

[56] *Erie RR Co. v. Tompkins*, 304 US 64 (1938). This decision is not grounded on the Full Faith and Credit clause of the Constitution (Article IV, section 1), where current choice-of-law theory would probably place it, but correctly for its time, as a twist on the jurisdictional reach of the Supreme Court under Article III, section 2. It seems likely that there are other areas of federal–state relations within the United States, and there are certainly areas in transnational transactions, that have not been fully analyzed by experts in choice-of-law theory even today. For an influential "legal realist" critique of the entire subject, arguing that lawyers will argue for whatever choice-of-law rule will help their client win a case, and that judges are more influenced by the arguments of lawyers in real cases before them than by abstract theories and the value of consistency in the system, see David F. Cavers, "A Critique of the Choice-of-Law Problem," 47 HLR 173–208 (1933) (hereinafter cited as Cavers, "Critique").

[57] And few contemporary Americans, judging by the literature spawned by the revival through a particularly badly reasoned decision of a federal Circuit Court of Appeals of the provision of the Judicature Act of 1789 giving federal District Courts concurrent jurisdiction with state courts over "causes where an alien sues for a tort only in violation of the law of nations or a treaty of the United States": 1 Stat. 73, 28 USC section 1350. The case is *Filartiga v. Peña-Irala*, 630 F. 2d 876 (2nd Cir. 1980). The reasons for this very harsh characterization of the decision despite the enthusiasm it has aroused in much current literature are set out in Alfred P. Rubin, "US Tort Suits by Aliens Based on International Law," 18(2) FFWA 65–75 (1994) (hereinafter cited as Rubin, "Alien Torts"). This article revises and updates an earlier critique of the case in 21 *International Practitioner's Notebook* 19 (1983).

2   The international legal order

Introduction

The international legal order has its own complex history and traditions; its own legislative process; its own reflections of the conceptual antagonism between those who find "natural law" and those who find "positive law" models to be more congenial. As noted in the tale of Wen-Amon, recited above, the antagonism surfaces with the first known records of legal discussion. In its current form, however, it is not necessary to trace the tensions back further than the rejection of universal divine law theory in Europe and the intellectual restructuring of the system after the Peace of Westphalia in 1648. This reordering actually was a resurfacing of conceptions that had never wholly been lost since the days of Wen-Amon, although overlaid by various imperial and divine law theories. The division of divine law into positivism and secular amorality on the one hand, and "morality" on the other, can be fairly easily seen in the events of the early sixteenth century, when the rulers of Spain and Portugal found ways to by-pass the authority of the Pope in dividing between the two of them the "rights" that flowed by secular conquest in the Western Hemisphere and the trading points South and East of the Azores.[1] But it was really the second half of the seventeenth century that saw the articulation of modern international jurisprudence, although, it should be mentioned at the outset, the natural law theories that dominated the writings of the most influential publicists until theory caught up with practice in the first third of the nineteenth century, make the period from the Peace of Westphalia in the middle of the seventeenth century to the great reordering after the Napoleonic

---

[1] For an analysis of this evolution, see Alfred P. Rubin, "International Law in the Age of Columbus," 39 NILR 5 (1992).

Wars in Europe seem more like the adolescence of modern thought than its maturity.

The naturalist model

Law as moral principle

Great theorists of the law and society, like Thomas Hobbes, had much to say about the characteristics and legal position of the "state" as a creature of history and the supposed inborn needs of human beings. But the towering figure in what many scholars regard as secular legal naturalism coming out of the Thirty Years War was Samuel von Pufendorf, a Protestant native of the German state of Saxony born in 1632. His brilliant book, *Elementorum Jurisprudentiae Universalis* (Elements of Universal Juris-prudence)[2] earned him a newly established Chair of Natural and International Law at the University of Heidelberg in the Palatinate (*Pfalz*). In 1670 he accepted an invitation to Lund, Sweden, where in 1672 he published the eight volumes of his work, *De Jure Naturae et Gentium* (On the Law of Nature and Nations).[3] He moved to Berlin in 1686 at the invitation of Frederick William, the Great Elector, and died there in 1694.[4]

Categorizing Pufendorf as a "naturalist" seems simplistic to the point of being glib. Pufendorf anticipates on the basis of value-based morality the distinctions brought back into jurisprudential analysis by the value-free positivism of Wesley Hohfeld some 250 years later,[5] and preserves the basic orientation towards the international legal order set out most memorably by Grotius a generation before and the demolition by Francisco Suarez two generations earlier of the logic of *jus gentium* theory as the basis for substantive rules in the international legal order.[6]

---

[2] Samuel von Pufendorf, *Elementorum jurisprudentiae universalis* (1660, Cambridge edn. of 1672 reproduced photographically by the Carnegie Endowment for International Peace with an English translation by W. A. Oldfather in 1931) (hereinafter cited as *Elementorum*).

[3] Samuel von Pufendorf, *De jure naturae et gentium* (1672–3, Amsterdam edn. of 1688 reproduced photographically by the Carnegie Endowment for International Peace with an English translation by C. H. and W. A. Oldfather in 1934). An epitome of this long work was issued separately in 1673 as *De officio hominis et civis prout ipsi praescribunter lege naturali* [*On the Duty of Man and Citizen According to Natural Law*]. A photographic reproduction of the 1682 edition of this short volume and a translation by Frank Gardner Moore was published, also by the Carnegie Endowment, in 1927.

[4] These details of Pufendorf's life are taken from the introductions by Hans Wehberg, Walter Simons and Walther Schücking to the three works cited in notes 2 and 3 above.

[5] See chapter 1, note 52 above.

[6] On the model and influence of Suarez, see text at pp. 50–51 below.

Book I of the *Elementorum* consists of twenty-one Definitions, and Book II of two Axioms and five "Observations" on Axiom II. Definition I divides all human actions into those which have moral content because voluntary, and those produced by forces of nature regardless of human will and thus have no moral content. A "right [*jus*]" is defined in Definition VIII as authority over things legally acquired and has moral content:

In addition to those meanings by which the word right (*jus*) [*sic* in the Oldfather translation] is used for law, and for a complex or system of homogeneous laws, as also for a judicial sentence, or the sentence of laws applied to deeds . . . the most frequent use is to employ it for that moral quality by which we properly either command persons, or possess things, or by which things are owed to us. Thus, under the name of right comes commonly authority over persons as well as over things which are our own or another's; and that authority which regards things is in a special sense called "the right in the thing" . . . [R]ight [*recte*] properly and clearly indicates that this authority has been acquired properly and is now also properly held.[7]

The "*jus*" Pufendorf then further subdivides into two categories: "perfect rights" and "imperfect rights." The first are those which are subject to vindication in courts of law or by direct action; the second are called "aptitudes," and have not reached the level at which legal action would be successful or self-help morally justifiable.

Now right is either *perfect* or *imperfect* [italics *sic* in the Oldfather translation]. He who has infringed upon the former does a wrong which gives the injured party in a human court ground for bringing action against the injurer . . . Now it is an imperfect right, which is called by some an aptitude, when something is owed some one by another in such wise that, if he should deny it, he would, indeed, be acting unfairly, and yet the injured party would by no means be receiving a wrong which would furnish him with an action against the injurer; nor would he be able to assert for himself that right, except when necessity does not admit of any other means to secure his safety.[8]

---

[7] *Elementorum*, Definition VIII, section1, at 58 (English), 66 (Latin): "Praeter illas significationes, qua vocabulum juris usupatur pro lege, et complexu seu systemate legum homogenearum, ut et pro sententia judiciali seu sententia legum factis adplicata . . . frequentissimum est, ut sumator pro qualitate illa morali, qua recte vel personis imperamus, vel res tenemus, aut qua eadem nobis debentur. Sic communiter juris nomine venit potestas tam in personas, quam in res nostras aut alienas; et quae res spectat peculiariter jus in re dicitur . . . Jus autem proprie et perspicue indicat, recte eam suisse adquisitam, et iam recte obtineri . . ." Note that Pufendorf carefully distinguishes between a "right" in general (whether perfect or imperfect), calling it "jus," and the legal subcategory of "right" which a human (positive law) court will vindicate, calling it "recte."

[8] Ibid., Definition VIII, sections 2, 5 at 58, 59 (English), at 66–67, 68 (Latin): "Et autem jus

The correlatives of "rights" are called "obligations," which arise either from the law of nature or from the civil (human) law; if the latter, then the legal machinery of the civil law, the supreme authority of the state, furnishes the means of enforcement. If those means fail for any reason, the injured individual cannot vindicate his rights directly because, through the act of civil subjection (which seems to involve a social contract conception not fully explained by Pufendorf in this place), individuals are considered to have yielded up to the state their natural law authority of self-vindication.

Now the force of obligations arises either from the law of nature or from the civil law. Also concerning obligations of the latter kind, indeed, it is beyond controversy that the efficacy of the same in bringing to bear upon both sides the necessity of furnishing that about which the agreement had been made, ultimately resolves itself into the force or the faculty of compulsion which inheres in that which wields the supreme authority in the state.[9]

As to those who are not subject to a common civil law, Pufendorf argued that they are bound to their pacts with each other by natural law; those who violate it, since they have not violated a law that can be enforced by human agency, commit a sin (*peccare*), presumably implying divine law or other enforcement.

Now among learned men it has been a matter of dispute, as to just what strength of obligation there be in pacts which have been joined upon the law of nature alone, such as are the pacts between those who do not recognize a common judge in a human court of law, or the pacts about which the civil law makes no disposition . . . To us the matter does not seem to have so much difficulty about it, if you suppose at the outset, that men have been made by nature to cultivate social relations with one another, and that no one at all ought to bring upon a second person that which can furnish a cause for discord and war . . . it is certainly apparent that men are altogether bound by the law

---

vel perfectum vel imperfectum. Illud quilaeserit, injuriam facit, quae laeso in foro humano actionem adversus laedentem dat . . . Jus autem imperfectum, quod nonnulis aptitudo vocatur, est, quando alicui ab altero quid debentur, ita ut, si illud deneget, inique quidem faciat, haudquaquam tamen laesus accipiat injuriam, quae ipsi adversus laedentem actionem pariat; nec vi adserere sibi istud possit, nisi ubi necessitas aliam expedeindae salutis rationem nonadmittit."

[9] Ibid., Definition XII, section 14 at 84 (English), at 95–96 (Latin): "Oritur autem vis obligationum vel ex jure naturae vel ex jure civili. Ac de posterioribus quidem extra controversiam est, quod efficacia earundem necessitatem adferendi ad praestandum utrinq; id de quo conventum est, ultimo sese resolvat in vim seu facultatem cogendi, quae summam potestatem in civitate gerenti inhaeret."

of nature to keep their pacts, and that men who violate those pacts are sinning against the same law.[10]

This last category, in his view, applied equally to states as subjects of the *jus gentium*: the category of Roman law relating to both the coinciding civil laws of nearly all "nations [*gens*]" (by which he meant legal orders, not necessarily "states") and to "states [*civitates*]" as "moral persons." Aside from this version of natural law, to Pufendorf it seemed that there is no law properly so called that restricts the actions of states in the international legal order.

Something must be added now also on the subject of the *Law of Nations* [emphasis *sic* in the Oldfather translation], which, in the eyes of some men, is nothing other than the law of nature, in so far as different nations, not united with another by a supreme command, observe it, who must render one another the same duties in their fashion, as are prescribed for individuals by the law of nature. On this point there is no reason for our conducting any special discussion here, since what we recount on the subject of the law of nature and of the duties of individuals, can be readily applied to whole states and nations which have also coalesced into one moral person. Aside from this law, we are of the opinion that there is no law of nations, at least none which can properly be designated by such a name. For most of those matters which the Roman jurisconsults and others refer to the law of nations, for example, matters having to do with modes of acquisition, contracts, and other things, pertain either to the law of nature, or to the civil law of individual nations, which, in matters of that kind, coincides with the civil laws of most peoples. These, however, do not rightly constitute a special species of law, since, forsooth, the nations have those rights in common with one another, not from some agreement of mutual obligation, but they have been established by the special order of the individual legislators in the individual states, and so can be changed by one people without consulting others, and are frequently found to have been so changed.[11]

---

[10] Ibid., section 15 at 86 (English), at 97, 98 (Latin): "Quinam autem obligandi vigor insit pactis solo naturae jure coalitis, qualia sunt inter eos, qui communem judicem in foro humano non agnoscunt, aut de quibus jus civile nihil disponsit, inter eruditos controversum est . . . Nobis non ita magnam habere res difficultatem videtur, si illud initio supponatur, homines a natura conditos esse, ut societatem inter se colant . . . adparetsane, omnino jure naturae homines add servanda pacta obligari, et illa violentes in idem peccare."

[11] Ibid., Definition XIII, section 24 at 165 (English), at 190–191 (Latin): "De Jure Gentium ninc quoq; aliquid addendum, quod quibusdam nihil aliud est, quam jus naturae, quatenus illud inter se summo imperio non connexae gentes diversae observant, queis eadem invicem suo modo officia praestanda, quae singulis per jus naturae praescribuntur. De quo non est, quod heic peculiariter agamus, cum ea, quae de jure naturae, deq; officiis singulorum tradimus, facile possint adplicari ad civitates et gentes integras, quae in unam quoq; personam moralem coaluerunt. Praeter isthoc nullum dari jus gentium arbitramur, quod quidem tali nomine proprie possit

Even the laws of war he seems to have regarded as a special class of the *jus gentium* applicable in each legal order as a matter of municipal law applied to regulate its own soldiers, and compelled only by a sense of national honor common to many individual states; it might be derived in each order from notions of natural law, but does not create legal obligations between states.

Finally, there are wont to be listed under the name of the law of nations among most nations (at least those which claim the reputation of being more civilized and humane), those customs which, by a certain tacit consent, are habitually employed, especially in regard to war. For, after these more civilized nations came to regard it as their greatest honour to seek glory in war (that is to say, to exhibit their superiority over others in this, namely, that one was bold enough to kill many men, and skilful enough to do it dexterously), and so unnecessary or unjust wars were entered into; under these conditions, in order to avoid exposing their ambition to excessive ill will, if they exercised the full licence of a just war, most nations have seen fit to temper the harshness of war by some humanity and a certain show of magnanimity . . . And, if any one in legitimate warfare disregard these exemptions, in cases, of course, where the law of nature allows such an act, he cannot be said to have contravened a valid obligation; he is merely, as a general thing, accused of barbarism, because he has not conformed to the customs of those who regard war as one of the liberal arts . . . If, therefore, a man wage just wars, he can conduct them by the law of nature alone, and he is not bound by any law to these customs just mentioned, unless of his own accord he so wish, in order to obtain some advantage of his own.[12]

designari. Pleraq; enim, quae apud JCtos Romanos, aliosq; ad jus gentium referuntur, puta, quaedem circa modos adquirendi, contractus et alia, vel ad just naturae pertinent, vel ad jus civile singularum gentium quod istis in rebus cum legibus civilibus plurimorum populorum coincidit. Ex quibus tamen peculiaris species non recte constituitur, quippe cum ista jura gentibus inter se sint communia non ex aliqua conventione aut obligatione mutua, sed ex placito peculiari singulorum legislatorum in singulis civitatibus constituta, quaeq; adeo ab uno populo inconsultis aliis mutari possint, ac saepenumero mutata deprehendantur.''

[12] Ibid., section 25 at 165–166 (English), at 191–192 (Latin): "Solent deniq; sub nomine juris gentium venire illae consuetudines inter plerasq; gentes saltem quae cultiorum et humaniorum sibi samam vindicant, potissimum circa bellum tacito quodam consensu usurpari solitae. Postquam enim inter cultiores istas gentes maximum fuit decus habitum, bello gloriam quaerere, i.e. in eo praestantiam suam prae caeteris hominibus ostendere, quod quis multos homines auderet, et dextre calleret perdere, adeoq; in non necessaria aut injusta bella est procursum; ne ambitionem suam invidiae nimis exponerent, usurpata omni licentia justi belli, humanitate nonnulla et quadam magnanimitatis specie bellorum atrocitatem temperare pleriq; populis est visum . . . Quae si quis legitimum gerens bellum neglexerit, scilicet ubi per jus naturae recte fieri possunt, nulli obligationi validae contravenisse dici potest, nisi quod ruditatis vulgo arguitur, quia non ad consuetudinem eorum, queis bellum inter artes liberales numeratur, sese composuerit . . . Igitur si quis justa gerat bella, solo naturae

But this approach, which seems to lead in the positivist direction, Pufendorf found shallow. Dismissing the municipal law common to all known societies (i.e., the *jus gentium*) as capable of being anything more than presumptive evidence of the rules of an underlying natural law, in his mature work, *De Jure Naturae et Gentium*,[13] Pufendorf goes back to Greek sources and Cicero to define natural law. In so doing, he returns not to the purported insight contained in man's supposed reason, but to Aristotle and the moral implications of physical facts:

For such an animal [man] to live and enjoy the good things that in this world attend his condition, it is necessary that he be sociable, that is, be willing to join himself with others like him, and conduct himself towards them in such a way that, far from having any cause to do him harm, they may feel that there is reason to preserve and increase his good fortune ... And so it will be a fundamental law of nature that "Every man, so far as in him lies, should cultivate and preserve toward others a sociable attitude, which is peaceful and agreeable at all times to the nature and end of the human race" ... [B]y a sociable attitude we mean an attitude of each man towards every other man, by which each is understood to be bound to the other by kindness, peace, and love, and therefore by a mutual obligation.[14]

The "law" that flows from the application of this great moral principle in real life is then the "law" that is the subject of Pufendorf's further analysis. But, by his own orientation, it is a law consisting of imperfect rights and imperfect obligations; a law of nature enacted and enforced by the legislative and enforcement processes of nature itself (like the law of gravity or the "laws" of economics) and not referable to the legislative and enforcement processes of human law unless authority be given by

jure ea regere potest, nec ullo jure ad istas consuetudines, nisi sponte ob commodum aliquid suum velit, tenetur ..."

[13] Cited note 3 above.

[14] *Elementorum* II, iii, 15 at 208 (English), at 142–143 (Latin): "Quanduam autem usus multorum populorum efficacius paulo videatur allegari ostendendum, aliquid este licitum, quam jure naturae praeceptum: tamen ut ne illud quidem semper tuto liceat concludere, faciunt instituta discrepantia aut contraria celebrum populorum ... Ejusmodo animali, ut salvum sit, bon seque fruatur, quae in ipsius conditionem heic cadunt, necessarium est, ut sit sociabile, id est, ut conjugi cum sui similibus velit, et adversus illos ita se gerat, ut neisti ansam accipiant eum laedendi, sed potius rationem habeant ejusdem commoda servandi, aut provendi ... Inde fundamentalis lex naturae ist haec erit: 'builibet homini, quantum in se, colendam et conservandam esse pacificam adversus alios socialitatem, indoli et scopo generis humani in universum congruentem.' ... [P]er socialitatem innuimus ejusmodi dispositionem hominis erga quemvis hominem, per quam ipsi benevolentia, pace et caritate, mutaque adeo obligatione conjunctus intelligentur." The English translation by C. H. and W. A. Oldfather is in Volume II of the Carnegie Endowment edition.

human law to some human administrator who is inclined to enforce it by human means. To use the terminology of positivist jurisprudence, it is not law at all, but morality based on nature and a value system posited by the analyst without demonstration.[15]

A great development in Northern European naturalist jurisprudential thinking came about fifty years later with the explicit realization that the *jus gentium*, the private law, which many naturalist jurists believed reflected moral and perhaps legal principles common to all mankind although varying in detail from place to place, was not the only arena for natural law analysis. The distribution of authority, what might be called the unwritten constitutional law of the international order, was also part of the concept of natural "law." It existed quite apart from the discussion of substantive rules, i.e., law *versus* morality, "perfect" *versus* "imperfect" rights.

The rise in the early seventeenth century of "social contract" conceptions as the basis for authority, the notion that authority and responsibility were part of an exchange tacitly bargained for,[16] created the need to consider what "law" made such a contract binding on the public authority. Aside from various political theories posing models of more or less persuasiveness for various municipal legal orders, the notion arose that international society could be deemed a "supreme State" with its own distribution of authority and its own law-making processes apart

---

[15] "Forsooth," indeed! I cannot resist concluding this section on Pufendorf by noting that the more or less standard Carnegie Endowment translation by the Oldfathers, while accurate enough for present purposes, is awkward and hard to read. Pufendorf was a major figure in jurisprudential history and his writing deserves to be much more widely known. Since very few jurists can read Latin with any facility today (and I include myself in that condemnation), a more lively and colloquial English translation would be a great gift to American scholarship. A new translation has recently been published: Craig L. Carr (ed.), *The Political Writings of Samuel Pufendorf* (Michael J. Seidler, translator, Oxford University Press, 1994). The Oxford catalogue says that it contains "selections" from the *Elementorum* and *De Jure Naturae et Gentium*; I have not yet seen it.

[16] Not always tacitly. Not only was the Magna Carta resurrected in seventeenth-century England as an explicit distribution of authority, withholding from the Crown some elements of the total "sovereignty" which absolutist legal theory claimed, and attributing to Parliament the residue of authority, but the Mayflower Compact of 1620 was itself an express "social contract" under which the English colonists of New England on the *Mayflower* by writing did "combine our selves together into a civil body politick . . . to enacte, constitute, and frame such just and equall lawes . . . unto which we promise all due submission and obedience": William Bradford, *Of Plymouth Plantation* (Morison, ed., 1975) at 75–76. Thomas Hobbes's great work, *Leviathan*, published in 1651, thus set out in nearly poetic language a train of thought already transformed into practice at least a generation earlier and lying at the roots of American national experience.

from the express agreements that would turn "imperfect rights" into "perfect rights" of states.

Today, the best known example of this trend of thought in a work of theory directed towards the international legal order was published in 1749. Its author was Christian Wolff, a German-speaking prodigy from Breslau (now Wroclaw, Poland).[17] Wolff began by arguing that the "law of nations" is originally nothing except the law of nature applied to nations.[18] This law of nations reflects the "society" that nature has established among all nations. That society Wolff then analogized to a "state":

For nature herself has established society among all nations and compels them to preserve it, for the purpose of promoting the common good by their combined powers. Therefore, since a society of men united for the purpose of promoting the common good by their combined powers, is a state, nature herself has combined nations into a state . . . The State, into which nations are understood to have combined, and of which they are members or citizens, is called the supreme State.[19]

The law of this supreme State rests on the will of its members, but they are in turn bound by natural law to agree upon the rules derived by right reason in accordance with nature; "Hence it is plain . . . that what has been approved by the more civilized nations is the law of nations."[20] Wolff then divides the *jus gentium* into four parts: the "voluntary law of nations," meaning that law which reflects the will of the fictitious "ruler" of the supreme State and is therefore discoverable by right reason from natural law precepts; the "stipulative law of nations," by which he means the law derived from voluntary contracts binding on only the parties to

---

[17] Christian Wolff, *Jus Gentium Methodo Scientifica Pertractatum* (1749) (edn. of 1764 reproduced photographically by the Carnegie Endowment for International Peace, 1934). The details of Wolff's life are set out in the Introduction by Otfried Nippold. The translation of the basic work by Joseph H. Drake appears in Volume II of the Carnegie Endowment set.

[18] Ibid., section 3, at 1: "Gentes quoque originarie non alio utuntur jure nisi naturali, consequenter Jus Gentium originarie non est nisi Jus naturae ad Gentes applicatum."

[19] Ibid., sections 9, 10: "Ipsa enim natura instituit inter omnes gentes societatem & ad eam colendam eas obligat communis boni conjunctis viribus promovendi causa. Quamobreni cum societas hominum communis boni conjunctix viribus promovendi causa contracta civitas sit; ipsa natura in civitatem consociavit Gentes . . . Civitas, in quam Gentes coiviss intelliguntur, & cujus ipsae sunt membra, sue cives, vocatur Civitas maxima."

[20] Ibid., section 20: "Cum tamen in statu populari necesse sit, ut declarent . . . gentes autem omnes per totum terrarum orbem dispersae inter se convenire nequeant, quod per se patet; pro voluntatae ratione recte utantur, consequenter patet, quatenus admittendum, id esse Jus Gentium, quod gentibus moralioribus placuit."

those contracts; the "customary law of nations," resting on tacit consent expressed through habitual behavior and is binding only on those states which render that consent in that way; and the "positive law of nations," by which he said he includes all of the foregoing, including the "voluntary law."[21] The rest of Wolff's work focuses not on the *jus gentium* as defined here, but on the "rights" and "duties" of "Nations" under the true law of nature:

Since every Nation is bound to preserve itself, since, moreover, the law of nature gives to men the right to those things without which they could not perform their obligation, every Nation has the right to those things without which it cannot preserve itself.[22]

From this position, all sorts of "rules" flow which derive from the "true law of nature [*lex vero naturae*]," and not at all from the positive law in its usual definition. On the other hand, in elaborating these arguments, Wolff differentiates between these truly natural rights and duties on basically the same ground as Pufendorf, distinguishing between "perfect" and "imperfect" rights. For example, he considers external commerce to be a "right," but one which cannot be exercised without the consent of another, and repeatedly asserts that that consent can be given only voluntarily, but seems not to argue in any place, as a true "law of nature" approach would seem to require, that commerce necessary for the life of a state can be pursued regardless of the consent of the partner.[23]

---

[21] Ibid., sections 22–25. Section 22 defines the "voluntary" *jus gentium*: "Jus Gentium voluntarium . . . quod ex notione civitatis maximae derivatur, consequenter quasi ab ejus Rectore ficto definitum, ac ideo a voluntate Gentium profectum intelligitur." The "positive law" definition is in section 25: "Jus Gentium positivum dicitur quod a voluntate Gentium ortum trahit. Quamobrem cum facile pateat, Jus Gentium voluntarium, pactitium & consuetudinarium a voluntate Gentium ortum trahere; Jus istud omne jus Gentium positivum est. Et quoniam paro patet, Jus Gentium voluntarium niti consensu Gentium praesumto, pactitium expresso, consuetudinarium tacito, alio autem modo jus quoddam a voluntate Gentium proficisci posse non concipitur; Jus Gentium positivum vel voluntarium, vel pactitium, vel consuetudinarium est."

[22] Ibid., section 32: "Quoniam quaelibet Gens se conservare obligatur, lex vero naturae dat hominibus jus ad ea, sine quibus obligationi suae satisfacete non possunt; Genti unicuique competit jus ad ea, sine sibus se conservare nequit."

[23] Ibid., sections 73, 74, 58–64, 187–228. The closest Wolff comes to arguing that the natural right of self-preservation includes a perfect right of commerce with an unwilling partner is in section 58: "To every nation belongs the right to purchase for itself at a fair price the things which it needs from other nations, which themselves have no need of the same . . . [Cuilibet Genti competit jus res, quibus indiget, ab aliis Gentibus, quae ipsaemet iisdem opus non habent.]" But in sections 190 and 191 the contrary seems to be asserted in absolute terms: "[Section 190] Since no nation can compel another to engage in commerce with itself, although it may be bound by

Thus, the main stream of naturalist thought seems consciously to have devoted its attention to the "law" as it exists in the moral sphere, but enforcement of that "law" required "positive" action. "Duties" could be established only by the consent of the subject of the law undertaking them; "rights" existed without correlative "duties," as "imperfect rights" existed in Pufendorf's model. As to community enforcement, under Wolff's system, because rules that flow from principles accepted *a priori* are implemented only when consented to by the discretionary act of an authority able to implement them by the means allowed it under the legal order of the "supreme State," the model posed is an order under which consent is the basic, if not the only, means of translating community values into rules binding the state itself in a way enforceable in a "legal" sense.

The same fundamental orientation appears in the most influential writings of Wolff's great successor, Emerich de Vattel. Vattel was Swiss. His most influential work, *Le Droit des Gens*, usually translated as *The Law of Nations*,[24] was written in the vernacular (French) and published in 1758. It became by far the most widely read and cited work dealing with the law that applied between states during the period from its first publication until three decades or so into the next century.[25]

---

nature to do so . . . since, moreover, no one is bound absolutely to another . . . nations are not bound absolutely to engage in commerce with each other. [Section 191] No nation can bind another absolutely to itself to engage in commerce except by stipulation, nor can a perfect right to engage in commerce be otherwise acquired. For nations are bound only imperfectly to engage in commerce with each other, consequently that which is due on that obligation is due only as an imperfect obligation. [[Section 190] Cum Gens nulla alteram cogere possit, ut commercia secum exerceat, esti naturaliter obligetur, si in potestate sit, perfecte autem nemo alteri obligetur, si non habeat jus illum cogendi, ut obligationi suae satisfaciat; Gentes quoque ad commercia invicem exercenda sibi invicem perfecte non obligantur. [Section 191] Gens nulla alteram perfecte sibi obligare potest ad commercia nisi per pacta, nec aliter jus perfectum ad ea consequi datur.]"

[24] Note the French word "droit" in this context is usually translated as "law" rather than "right." The reader should be warned once again of the dangers of misrepresenting Vattel's thought by ignoring the original French text, ignoring the philosophical, legal and political context of Vattel's work, reading the English as if parsing divine writ and not appreciating the ambiguity in English itself of the word "law."

[25] The statistics comparing citations to Vattel in common law courts with citations to other major publicists in the late eighteenth and early nineteenth centuries appear in Edwin Dickinson, "Changing Concepts and the Doctrine of Incorporation", 26 AJIL 259, note 132 (1932). They are retailed in Arthur Nussbaum, *A Concise History of the Law of Nations* (revised edn., 1954) (hereinafter cited as Nussbaum, *History*) 162. A more general but no less emphatic appreciation of Vattel's influence is the Introduction by

The mere fact of expressing the fundamental ideas in French instead of Latin shifted some fundamental conceptions. The phrase *droit des gens* appears throughout the work. There is no distinction stated between the *jus gentium* and the *jus inter gentes*.[26] Instead, Vattel defined the *droit des gens*, the law of nations, as consisting solely of what in Latin would be called the *jus inter gentes*: "The Law of Nations is the science of the rights which exist between Nations or States, and of the obligations corresponding to these rights."[27] The sources of these "rights" Vattel found in the "necessary Law of Nations [*Droit des Gens nécessaire*]" which he defined as identical with the "natural law of nations [*Droit des Gens naturel*]"[28] and distinguished from the "voluntary, the conventional, and the customary law, [which] form together the positive Law of Nations" because proceeding from the agreement of nations.[29]

The relationship between municipal law and international law is elevated to a very high level of generality:

As men are subject to the laws of nature, and as their union in civil society can not exempt them from the obligation of observing those laws, since in that union they remain none the less men, the whole Nation, whose common will is but the outcome of the united wills of its citizens, remains subject to the laws of nature and is bound to respect them in all its undertakings.[30]

Albert de Lapradelle to the Carnegie Endowment reprinting of *The Law of Nations* (1758, 1916) at xxxiv*ff.*

[26] This distinction, clear enough in Latin, was brought to English consciousness by 1650 when it was prominently asserted by Richard Zouche, an Admiralty judge accustomed to distinguishing between individuals' property rights in vessels brought before his tribunal, and the public law of the flag state which applied on board those vessels unless English public law were applied to change the ownership of the vessel itself or to supersede the flag state's law in particular cases: Richard Zouche, *Iuris et Iudicii Fecialis, Sive Iuris Inter Gentes, et Quaestionum de Eodem Explicatio* (Oxford, 1650, reproduced photographically by the Carnegie Institution, Washington, 1911) (hereinafter cited as Zouche, *Fecialis*) 1.

[27] Vattel, *The Law of Nations* (1758) (Charles G. Fenwick, translator, Volume III of the Carnegie Endowment set, 1916), Introduction, section 3 at 3. In the original: "Le Droit des Gens est la science du Droit qui a lieu entre les Nations, ou Etats, & des Obligations qui répondent à ce Droit.": Ibid., Volume I, at A.

[28] Ibid., section 6.

[29] Ibid., section 27: "Ces trois espèces de Droit des Gens, Voluntaire, Conventionnel, & Coutumier, composent ensemble le Droit des Gens Positif. Car ils procèdent tous de la Volonté des Nations."

[30] Ibid., section 5: "Les hommes étant soumis au Loix de la Nature, & leur union en Société Civile n'aiant pu les soustraire a l'obligation d'observer ces Loix, puisque dans cette union ils ne cessent pas d'être hommes; la Nation entière, dont la Volonté commune n'est que le resultat des volontés réunies des Citoiens, demeure soumise au Loix de la Nature, obligée à les respecter dans toutes ses démarches."

But this natural law is immediately divorced from the obligations of individual conscience:

This society may be regarded as a moral person, since it has an understanding, a will, and power peculiar to itself; and it is therefore obliged to live with other societies or States according to the laws of the natural society of the human race, just as individual men before the establishment of civil society lived according to them; with such exceptions, however, as are due to the difference of the subjects.[31]

The bulk of the book that flows from this introduction is devoted to deriving rules of conduct from the moral precepts presumed to be inherent in the nature of man's political organization, such as that "[E]ach Nation should contribute as far as it can to the happiness and advancement of other Nations."[32] As in the writings of Pufendorf and Wolff, the "rights" and "obligations" that flow from precepts such as this are denominated "imperfect," with rights being perfected either by treaty or by the operation of natural law itself. An example of this last is the assertion that "All the rights of a belligerent are derived from the justice of his cause,"[33] bringing killing done to defend perfect rights, such as rights of true self-defense, within the natural law. Vattel expressly refers his conception of "right [droit]" to the world of morality; for him there is no clear line between morality and law as far as concerns states interacting with each other.[34]

Since there is no right of self-defense against a second state which is exercising its own right to use force to avenge an injury,[35] and there is no

---

[31] Ibid., section 11: "Cette société, considerée comme une personne morale, puisqu'elle a un entendement, une volontée & une force qui lui sont propres, est donc obligée de vivre avec les autres Sociétés, ou Etats, comme un homme étoit obligée avant ces Etablissements, de vivre avec les autres hommes, c'est-à-dire suivant les Loix de la Société naturelle établie dans le Genre-humain; en observant les exceptions qui peuvent naître de la différence des sujets."

[32] Ibid., section 13: "La première Loi générale, que le but même de la Société des Nations nous découvre, est que chaque Nation doit contribuer au bonheur & la perfection des autres tout ce qui est en son pouvoir."

[33] Ibid., Book III, chapter xi, section 183: "Tout le droit de celui qui fait la guerre vient de la justice de la cause."

[34] Ibid., Book II, chapter iv, section 49: "Le Droit n'est autre chose qu'une faculté morale d'agir, c'est-à-dire de faire ce qui est moralement possible, ce qui est bien & conforme à nos devoirs." The use of the word "droit" in a context that identifies morality with law is common in jurisprudential writings. It easily leads to confusions and logically insupportable conclusions. See Rubin, "Enforcing".

[35] Vattel, The Law of Nations, Book III, chapter iii, section 35: "La Guerre défensive est juste, quand elle se fait contre un injuste aggresseur. Cela n'a pas besoin de preuve. La défense de soimême contre une injuste violence, n'est pas seulement un droit, c'est un devoir

clear acknowledgment that reasonable people might disagree over the responsibility for the first injury or the adequacy or excess in a military action to avenge that injury, the entire structure seems to presume an objective moral order, but its precepts are determined subjectively, by assertion only. The basic precepts for that order are expressed in terms of general principles, as has been seen, but Vattel sets out no objective basis for determining those principles or for establishing a hierarchy among them in cases of apparent conflict.

Jean Jacques Burlamaqui (1694–1748) was not a major jurist, but in the generation of the American Constitutional debates at the end of the eighteenth century, he was the philosopher of law most prominently quoted by the American Founding Fathers. Like Vattel, he wrote in French. Also like Vattel, he defined the "law of nations" as identical with the "natural law of states," and considered that law to be a law between states, the *jus inter gentes*, describing it as "a general law of sociability, which obliges all nations, that have any intercourse with one another, to practice those duties, to which individuals are naturally subject."[36] He did not draw a clear analogy between this law and the *jus gentium* except to attribute the rules of both to an adherence traced to Aristotelian roots in the physical needs of mankind presupposing an underlying moral code obliging (but not enforcing except by natural means) human societies, like individuals, to behave decently towards each other.

The illogical roots uncovered; glimmers of positivism

While this subjective line of juristic thought was developing in Europe, another line existed which attempted to find an objective basis for "natural law." It is most influential in models deriving from Aristotelian arguments equating the ethical rules that are enforced as law in different societies with the physical attributes ("laws" of physics) that bind mankind together as a creation of nature, and separate men and women, masters and slaves, on the basis of supposed abilities and inborn "natures."[37]

As noted above, the jurisprudential writings of St. Thomas Aquinas, which were among the works most influential on Catholic and educated

---

pour une Nation . . . Mais si l'Ennemi qui fait une Guerre offensive a la Justice de son côté, on n'est point en droit de lui opposer la force, & la défensive alors est injuste."

[36] Jean Jacques Burlamaqui, *The Principles of Natural and Politic Law* (1751) (Nugent, translator, 5th edn., 1807) (reprint 1972) chapter VI, section vii, at 136. This influential work was published posthumously.

[37] See pp. 7–8 above.

Protestant jurists in the sixteenth century, suggested that "law" in its essence consisted only in those rules at the intersect of four special categories of legal order: eternal law, divine law, human law and natural law. Since to be "law" the demands of natural law had to be satisfied (along with the others), no command could be called "law" that was not "just" by natural law criteria:

A command has the force of law to the extent that it is just. In human matters we call something "just" from its being right according to the rule of reason. The first rule of reason is natural law.[38]

But whether this natural law is to be found in the coincident positive laws of different societies, whether there is an objective way of determining the natural law once it is acknowledged that man's reason is fallible, remained, as in Aristotle's day, a disturbing question. Those who had serious doubts found it impossible totally to dismiss the idea, even when trying to diminish its utility. For example, among the principal arguments adduced by Francisco de Vitoria, the humane and highly respected Spanish sixteenth-century jurist, to justify the Spanish conquest of Mexico was the "natural" right of trade to the degree it was, in his view, violated by the Indians. The source of this natural right he found partly in the coincident practices of European states to permit free movement of foreign merchants.

[I]t is an apparent rule of the *jus gentium* that foreigners may carry on trade, provided they do no hurt to citizens . . . [I]t would not be lawful for the French to prevent the Spanish from traveling or even living in France, or vice versa, provided this in no way inured to their hurt and the visitors did no injury. Therefore it is not lawful for the Indians.[39]

But a major flaw, equivalent to the hesitations already expressed by Aristotle,[40] was restated by the Spanish Jesuit Francisco Suarez nearly a

---

[38] St. Thomas Aquinas, *Summa Theologiae* 2a2ae, Q. 95, 2. St. Thomas says that he is quoting from St. Augustine, *De libero arbitrario* I, 6. PL 32, 1229; and I, 5. PL 32, 203; and Q. 95, 2: "[I]nquantum habet de justitia intantum habet de virtute legis. In rebus autem humanis dicitur esse aliquid justum ex eo quod est rectum secundum regulam rationis. Rationis autem prima regula est lex naturae." I have not been able to find an edition of *De libero arbitrario* to confirm St. Thomas's use of St. Augustine's language.

[39] Vitoria, *De Indis* (1532) (Carnegie Institution edition, E. Nys, ed., J. P. Bate, translator, Washington, 1917), section iii, Prop. I, proof 1: "Quia etiam hoc videtur ius gentium, ut sine detrimento civium peregrini commercia exerceant" and section iii, Prop. II, proof 4: "[N]on licet Gallis prohibere Hispanos a peregrinatione Galliae, vel etiam habitatione, aut e contrario, si nullo modo cederet in damnum illorum nec facerent iniu riam. Ergo nec barbaris." These passages are taken from pp. 151, 152 (translation); 257, 258 (Latin); 387, 389 (photographic reproduction of text of 1696).

[40] Passages quoted at pp. 7–8 above

century after Vitoria's lectures.[41] Suarez re-examined the entire conception of *jus gentium* and its relationship to natural law. He concluded
that the *jus gentium* differs fundamentally from natural law first because
the *jus gentium* is not derived from reason or the "nature of the case," but
from other sources; second because the *jus gentium*, being the positive law
of many different communities, remains mutable at the discretion of
each community's legislator; and third, because no single precept of the
jus gentium has been found to be universal and therefore the rules of the
jus gentium usually cited cannot be said to come from the universal nature
of mankind. He then divides the *jus gentium* into two parts: The law that
"ought to be" observed by all people and nations in their interactions
with each other, and the law which many individual states observe within
their own borders. The latter he then calls "civil law," reserving the *jus
gentium* phrase for most of what today some naturalist scholars would call
international law, deriving its rules not from nature, but from custom!

On the other hand, the *ius gentium* differs from the natural law, primarily and
chiefly, because it does not, in so far as it contains affirmative precepts, derive
the necessity for these precepts solely from the natural principles . . . The
precepts of the *ius gentium* differ from those of the civil law in that they are not
established in written form; they are established through the customs not of
one or two states or provinces, but of all or nearly all nations . . .

[I]f it has been introduced by the customs of all nations and thus is binding on
all, we believe it to be the *ius gentium* properly so called. The latter system, then,
differs from the natural law because it is based upon custom rather than upon
nature; and it is to be distinguished likewise from civil law, in its origin, basis,
and universal application . . .

[A] particular matter . . . can be subject to the *ius gentium* in either one of two
ways: first, on the ground that this is the law which all the various peoples and
nations ought to observe in their relations with each other; secondly, on the
ground that it is a body of laws which individual states or kingdoms observe
within their own borders, but which is called *ius gentium* because the said laws
are similar and are commonly accepted. The first interpretation seems, in my
opinion, to correspond most properly to the actual *ius gentium* as distinct from
the civil law . . . For if we are speaking of the *ius gentium* properly so called, that
is in the first of the two senses expounded above, it is easily apparent that this
system of law, simply as the result of usage and tradition, could have been
gradually introduced throughout the whole world, through a successive
process, by means of propagation and mutual imitation among nations, and

---

[41] Francisco Suarez, *De Legibus, Ac Deo Legislatore* (1612) (Carnegie Endowment
reproduction of the original texts, 1944) (translation volume by G. L. Williams, Ammi
Brown and John Waldron).

without any special and simultaneous compact or consent on the part of all peoples.[42]

The objection seems insuperable. Nonetheless, among those who, without being able to answer Suarez's arguments, found them unpalatable, the notion remained strong that there could be a concept of what might be called positive "natural law": a natural law whose binding force could be derived from implied consent demonstrated by parallel practice in different municipal systems.

At the turn of the century, Suarez's contemporary, Alberico Gentili, an Italian Protestant principally remembered for his activities and writings as Regius Professor of Civil Law at Oxford University in the very Protestant England of the aging Queen Elizabeth and the pedant James I, frequently cited Suarez in propounding his own view of international law. That view emphasized the policy reasons for adopting or rejecting various legal propositions. Indeed, in reading Gentili's arguments on behalf of Spanish interests before the highest English tribunals, principally the Royal Council Chamber presided over by James I himself, it is unmistakable that Gentili accepted the notion that the law in England was whatever the King thought it should be. It certainly seems as if Gentili believed that the King was more likely to be swayed by arguments based on English interest than on abstract principles, regardless of James's taste for the appearance of scholarship.[43]

Despite Suarez's elaborate demolition of its intellectual base, the

---

[42] Ibid., Book II, chapter xix, paras. 2, 6, 8; chapter xx, para. 1: "Differt autem primo ac precipue ius gentium a iure naturali. Quia quatenus continet praeceptae affirmativa, non infert necessitatem rei praeceptae affirmativa, non infert necessitatem rei praeceptae ex sola rei natura per evidentem illationem ex principiis naturalibus . . . [P]recepta iuris gentium in hoc differunt a preceptis iuris civilis, quia non scripto, sed moribus non unius, vel alterius civitatis, aut provinciae, sed omnium vel fere omnium nationum, constant . . . Si vero introductum sit moribus omnium gentium, & omnes obliget, hoc credimus esse ius gentium proprium, quod & differt a naturali, quia non nature, sed moribus innititur, & a civili etiam distinguitur in origine, fundamento, & universalitate . . . [D]uobus modis . . . dici aliquid de iure gentium, uno modo quia est ius, quod omnes populi, & gentes varie inter se servare debent, alio modo quia est ius, quod singulae civitates, vel regna intra se observant, per similitudinem autem, & conventientiam ius gentium appellatur. Prior modus videtur mihi proprissime continere ius gentium re ipsa distinctum a iure civili . . . Nam si sermo sit de proprio iure gentium priori modo declaratum, facile constat, potuisse ipso usu, & tradione in universo introduci paulatim, & per successionem, propagationem, & imitationem mutuam populorum sine speciali conventu, vel consensu omnium populorum, uno tempore facto . . ."

[43] Alberico Gentili, *Hispanicis Advocationis* (1613, 1661) (photographically reproduced by the Carnegie Endowment, New York, 1921) *passim*. For some particulars, see the analysis of Gentili's style of logic and the position of King James in Alfred P. Rubin, *The Law of Piracy* (Newport, RI: The Naval War College Press, 1988) (hereinafter cited as Rubin,

seductiveness of "objective" natural law theory to scholars of the seven-teenth century is apparent in the writings of Richard Zouche, holder of Gentili's Chair as Regius Professor of Civil Law at Oxford from 1620 when elected at the age of only thirty-one (Gentili had died in 1608 and his deputy, John Budden, who held the Chair between the two notable incumbencies, seems to have left little behind that has survived the vicissitudes of history). Zouche served as a judge of Admiralty in England from 1641 until 1649, when the Cromwellian interregnum forced him back to Oxonian petulance. Writing at Oxford in 1650 with his Admiralty experience behind him, he achieved the remarkable feat for a work of some scholarly pretention in 1650 of directly addressing the definition of *jus gentium* without citing Gentili or Suarez.[44]

Zouche's approach was to divide the concept of "law" as it applies beyond the control of a single municipal legal order into two categories, both parts of "natural law." The first is the *jus gentium*, which Zouche defined as "the common element in the law [established by natural reason] which the peoples of single nations use among themselves." The second is "the law which is observed in common between princes or peoples of different nations." This latter "law" is the law, according to Zouche, by which "nations are separated, kingdoms founded, commerce instituted, and lastly, wars introduced":

Law of the latter kind I choose to describe as *"jus inter gentes"* or Law between Nations. Among the Romans it was called by a special name, *"Jus Feciale,"* . . . which has to do with the conditions of kings, peoples, and foreign nations, in fact with the whole law of Peace and War.[45]

In the body of his work, Zouche does not address any further the issues under examination here but provides only a handbook of substantive

---

Piracy) 19–20, 23–26. A different view, refusing to term Gentili an early positivist, but without particulars that can be analyzed, is asserted in Nussbaum, *History* 164–165.

[44] Zouche, *Fecialis*, Introduction by Thomas Erskine Holland i–iv. Neither Gentili's nor Suarez's name appears in Holland's *Index to Authors Cited* at 204. In his endnotes to chapter I, section 1, quoted below, Zouche cites Bodin, Conrad Bruno, Dionysus of Halicarnasus, Grotius, Hobbes and Rosin only.

[45] Ibid., translation volume by J. L. Brierly, 1. In the original I, 1 at 1–2: "Quod naturalis ratio inter omnes homines constituit, id apud omnes peraeque custoditur, vocaturq; jus gentium, quasi quo jure omnes gentes utuntur . . . este primum, quo singularum gentium populi communiter, inter se utuntur . . . Deinde quod inter Principes, vel populos diversarum gentium communiter intercedit, cum ex hoc jure, uti refert etiam Jurisconsultus, Gentes discretae sunt, regna condita, commercia instituta, & deniq; bella introducta. Quod est posterioris generis, Jus inter gentes placet appellare, quod apud Romanos, speciali nomine, Jus Foeciale . . . quae in conditionibus Regum, populorum, exterarumq; nationum, in omni deniq; jure Pacis & Belli versatur."

rules derived from Hebrew, Greek, Roman and more recent European practice and the opinions of a few publicists.

Because of this emphasis on actual practice as evidence of the rules believed by statesmen to be binding on them in their public acts, and the ruling out of *a priori* assumptions based on assumed values as significant to the perception of substantive rules, Zouche is occasionally categorized as a founder of modern legal "positivism" in public international law.[46]

These conceptions found their way into practice relating to criminal law in England, where the judge-made, reason-based notion of common law crimes competed with the positivist insistence by royal authority that only statutes signifying the will of the sovereign could define acts that required administrators to impinge on the lives and liberties of otherwise loyal subjects. The history is far too complex to summarize usefully here and such a summary is fortunately not necessary. By the time of the great constitutional struggles of the middle of the seventeenth century, Sir Edward Coke, seeing in the *Magna Carta* of the early thirteenth century a persisting positive, contractual limit on the authority of the Crown, had come to champion the naturalist notion of some acts being so evil in themselves (*mala in se*) that there could be no jurisdictional problems in any tribunal enforcing the natural laws prohibiting those acts. His argument is based bluntly on the underlying conception of the *jus gentium*:

But if [even] a foreign Ambassador being *Prorex* committeth here [in England] any crime, which is *contra jus gentium*, as Treason, Felony, Adultery, or any other crime which is against the Law of Nations, he loseth the privilege and dignity of an Ambassador, as unworthy of so high a place, and may be punished here as any other private Alien, and not to be remanded to his Soveraign but of curtesie. And so of contracts that be good *jure gentium*, he must answer here. But if any thing be *malum prohibitum* by any Act of Parliament, private Law or Custom of this Realm, which is not *malum in se jure gentium*, nor *contra jus gentium*, an Ambassador residing here shall not be bound by any of them.[47]

There are obvious difficulties with this approach, which seems to presume that the *mala in se* committed by the Ambassador (and, presumably, any foreigner) were committed within the territory or other part of the enforcement jurisdiction of the enforcing sovereign, making a discussion of the extent of jurisdiction to enforce and jurisdiction to adjudicate essential to an understanding of the limits to jurisdiction that Coke might have accepted. But those limits were apparently not considered

---

[46] *Cf.* Nussbaum, *History* 164–167.   [47] Coke, *Fourth* 153.

significant to sophisticated jurists yet. They had become obvious a century later.

The positivist practice

Introduction

It is undeniable that by the written evidence scholars have much more fun writing about principles and value systems than about lines of authority; about rules as they would be if the judges or scholarly authors were making them for all rather than about proposing legislation or interpreting the legislative intentions of others, including the councils and parliaments whose words formally uttered represent as "law" a distillation of views probably more misleading than incisive about any moral issues. In sum, what passes for scholarship in jurisprudential writings is usually either naturalist elaboration of principles that are asserted as if self-evident but with no necessary connection to wisdom or truth, or positivist works merely descriptive or empirical. Some judges speaking with grand generality about great principles forget that their opinions function as rules of decision only for the parties and the case before them and invest a great deal of effort in applying their perception of social values and "natural" principles to situations to which the writings of scholars might or might not be more insightful. Other judges dealing with similar situations feel free to overrule, distinguish away or simply ignore the supposed "precedents" if they are not persuaded of their logic or applicability. Legislators ignore all but the most influential scholars' and judges' opinions – those on which actual behavior has relied, even if not persuasive and insightful as legal arguments, when pondering new legislative proposals. Indeed, people contemplating formal legislation frequently ignore all legal argument, even legal argument that is subtle, persuasive and influential on others. Still other judges and legislators cite as influential only those scholars and judicial precedents with whose conclusions they agree, and ignore or misstate and denigrate those scholarly writings and judicial precedents that lead to conclusions which they prefer not to adopt for reasons they prefer not to analyze in open writing.

The development of the common law, that part of Anglo-American law that is pronounced by judges under the extraordinary constitutional arrangements of the common law countries by which vast areas of social intercourse are left for *ad hoc* decision by judges without any particular training in morals or philosophy, seems always to have proceeded in disregard of the more extreme natural law writings. That some particular cases become seen as landmarks of social or moral reasoning and others are relegated to libraries frequented only by pedants is the result of a sort of natural selection by teachers and judges in the Anglo-American system. The eighteenth-century naturalists, Wolff and Vattel among them, writing about the law as it would be if it truly descended from the enunciated principles, seem to miss not only much of the law as it actually was acted on, but, except for the emphasis on the value of consent, on "agreement" as "perfecting" otherwise "imperfect obligations," also to ignore the primary evidence of the value systems of the international legal order in fact; the values and interrelationships involved in international transactions as perceived by the statesmen to whom the naturalist theorists were ostensibly addressing their analyses. As noted above, it was not until 1881 that it was actually written that the life of the law in at least one common law system was not logic but experience.[48]

Thus, to see the development of legal theory during the latter part of the seventeenth century and the eighteenth century, indeed, until positivist writing came back into fashion in the 1830s and later, it is necessary to examine the writings of statesmen and lawyers in real situations; to try to understand their conceptions of law as it actually influenced their behavior and their discharge of public responsibilities.

The early days

A prime example of the sort of analysis engaged in by statesmen in practice that appears to be ignored in much of the naturalist writing can be seen in the opinions, letters and judgments of Sir Leoline Jenkins, another British (in this case Welsh) Admiralty judge who was a child of Oxford. Sir Leoline was, in addition, a Privy Councillor to Charles II and in his time the leading jurisconsult in international affairs in England. In this capacity he was asked for his views on a number of questions involving actual disputes between England and other powers in the 1670s and 1680s, and those views not only frequently penetrated to the jurisprudential depths of the cases, but were in practice accepted as guidance by the statesmen of England.

For example, Sir Joseph Williamson, Charles's Secretary of State charged with relations with the Dutch, asked Jenkins for his opinion regarding the position England ought to take when the Dutch captured some Scots privateers during the Third Anglo-Dutch War (1672–1674). The

---

[48] See p. 25, note 45 above.

Scots appear to have exceeded their commissions, letters of marque and reprisal, but the interpretation of those English legal documents was believed by the English to be more a matter for English or Scottish tribunals than for Dutch. On the other hand, England did not want to concede its own incapacity at law to try Dutch privateers for acts of depredation that were not authorized by Dutch public authority. The Dutch charge against the Scots was "piracy."

Jenkins was a member of the English negotiating team in Nijmegen at the time and responded to Williamson in a letter dated 3 April 1675:

The Truth is, I am much scandalized at them [the Scots privateers] in a Time of War; they are in my poor Judgment great Instruments to irritate the King's Friends, to undo his Subjects, and none at all to profit upon the Enemy: But it will not be remedied: The Privateers in our Wars are like the Mathematici in old Rome, a Sort of People that will always be found Fault with, but still made Use of: I may venture to say the same upon your Question, which is the proper Place of judging these Scots, that it will often fall out, but it will never be decided; because there is no third Power that can give a Law that shall be decisive or binding between two independent Princes, unless themselves shall please to do it (which seldom happens) and then cannot be extended beyond the Cases expressed by that Treaty.[49]

In fact, the Crown did interpose regarding these privateers, but on the ground of an interpretation of a complex treaty (which the Dutch interpreted differently) and an assertion patently self-serving and danger-ous if applied reciprocally, that in cases of overlapping jurisdictions primacy must go to the sovereign whose jurisdiction rested on allegiance (nationality, in modern terms) and the flag of the vessel in which the accused acted. The Dutch rejected these assertions and the matter was apparently resolved through negotiation in a broader context.[50]

To the degree that any issue of "natural law" was implicit in this opinion and the transaction that it was part of, it was an issue of the "natural" meaning of "sovereignty" and jurisdiction. There is no mention in Jenkins's opinion or any other known record of this affair of any overriding international obligation to cooperate in the suppression of "piracy" or "war crimes," or actions in excess of a privateer's commission. Cooperation was not perceived to be an issue by those involved; indeed,

---

[49] 2 Sir William Wynne, *The Life of Sir Leoline Jenkins* (1724) 713 at 714.
[50] There is some evidence that the English finally conceded to the Dutch legal argument under some French pressures. See Cornelisz van Bynkershoek, *Questionum Juris Publici* (1737) (Carnegie Endowment, Washington, 1930), Volume II, 101–103; Rubin, *Piracy* 88–90.

the English and Dutch had just ended their third war in twenty years and the cooperation that was to arise when William of Orange was invited to assume the Crown of England in 1688 was far from the minds of the ministers of government under Charles II. Instead, the issue was one of authority; jurisdiction to adjudicate.

Now, to the degree that "jurisdiction to adjudicate" is conceived to rest on natural law, it is not a question of substantive rules embodying moral principles. It is an issue of the distribution of authority. It is entirely possible to view the current legal order's distribution of authority as the result of "natural" forces, including the physical nature of mankind as Aristotle used that notion to derive a natural law of the *polis* and to underlie the Constitution of Athens, or Plato to derive a model constitution for his *Republic* by assigning to each person the static place in the political structure that his or her supposed natural capacities had destined him or her for. It is also possible to view this distribution of authority as the product of history, which can be considered part of a natural process in which discretion, or the sense of discretion that particular statesmen think they have, plays little rôle. But if that is the approach, then it must be conceded that the phrase "natural law" is being used in a very limited sense and does not support further assertions of substantive content to that supposed law. It is logically impossible convincingly to derive a "just" or "moral" distribution of authority, a constitution, if the concepts of "justice" and "morality" are to be related to substance unless we return to a conception of the state as fundamentally theocratic; a notion of kingship or other leadership, authority, that fills part of nature's or God's unknowable plan for the ordering of mankind. That notion was once nearly universal and still reappears from time to time in isolated cases, and it underlies a great deal of the sense of almost religious conviction that various political movements seem able for a while to express. But until God or history or nature speaks to us all in one voice, or until we fallible humans hear the single voice in identical ways, it is a notion that many reject. When translated into practice it leads to forms of government that surely those Northern and Latin Americans and Western Europeans who hear or interpret the natural or divine law commands differently would regard as unjust, if not contemptible.

The elaboration of substantive rules by states in practice in the seventeenth and eighteenth centuries was not by any conscious adherence to the patterns stated with such assurance by naturalist writers. It was by treaty and practice. The treaties of the time are filled with specific rules which the parties, sovereigns, agreed to implement each in his or her own courts. In the series of treaties that form the Peace of Utrecht in 1713, for example, there are not only terms that relate to general relations between the parties to the particular documents, but detailed legal rules. An example is Article XXXIX of the Treaty of 31 March/11 April 1713 between Great Britain and France:

> But if it shall appear that a Captor [in Naval warfare] made use of any Kind of Torture upon the Master of the Ship, the Ship's Crew, or others who shall be on board any Ship belonging to the Subjects of the other Party; in such Case, not only the Ship itself, together with all Persons, Merchandizes, and Goods whatsoever, shall be forth-with released without further Delay, and set intirely [sic] free, but also such as shall be found guilty of so great a Crime, as also the Accessories thereunto, shall suffer the most severe Punishment suitable to their Crime: This the Queen of Great-Britain and the Most Christian King [of France] do mutually engage shall be done without any Respect of Persons.[51]

It is notable, and to be borne in mind, that in this treaty although torture is termed a "Crime," the legal result of committing it is left to the officials of the sovereign with nationality-based jurisdiction to prescribe over the persons or traditional flag-state jurisdiction over the vessel in which the acts were committed subject only to such limitations on that sovereign's discretion as are contained in the treaty.

There are many provisions in the treaties of the period binding sovereigns to enact or enforce municipal legislation in conformity to the agreed principles. There are also deep inconsistencies among the various treaties, such as contraband lists classifying some items as subject to belligerent seizure from a neutral vessel of one treaty partner which would not be similarly subject to seizure in the neutral vessel of another treaty partner. This makes it impossible to classify the contents of the treaties as the embodiment of any "natural" rules, but rather the use of "naturalist" language in places where the rules set forth had been bargained for with national advantage and political relations primarily in mind. Failure of any particular sovereign to assure that the agreed rules are carried out by his or her officials results in failure of the treaty, a matter to be discussed diplomatically and possibly to be left unresolved, as Sir Leoline Jenkins had written was frequently the case. Whatever moral opprobrium was involved was left to other forums to discuss. The

---

[51] Anon., *Extracts from the Several Treaties Subsisting Between Great-Britain and other Kingdoms and States* . . . (London, 1741) 15. The original French can be found at 28 CTS 1 at 23. Since no subtleties of analysis are envisaged for this study, it is not necessary to set out that version here.

jurisdiction to adjudicate reflected the choice of forum which the political order was willing to accept; the one whose interpretation of the natural law or value-based moral rules was acceptable politically.

The positivist writers

The split between rhetoric and practical action, between the legal theories asserted with vigor by naturalist jurists and ignored by statesmen seeking national advantage and personal advancement, only rarely surfaced. Indeed, one of the notable idiosyncracies of eighteenth-century legal writing was the absence of much attention to the increasingly apparent divorce between theory and practice; between what was asserted by scholars to be the law and what law-makers asserted and administrators practiced under their own conceptions of their authority to "make" and "enforce" the law.

One exception to this situation, a writer achieving some notoriety in later years, possibly more because he was one of the very few publicists focusing on state practice as the essence of the legislative process in public international law than because of particularly deep insight, was Cornelisz Bynkershoek, a Dutchman. Bynkershoek's principal surviving work was published in 1737.[52] Its primary evidence for rules relating to the conduct of princes with respect to each other is treaties and municipal statutes, legal documents whose content is entirely discretionary in human beings with authority determined by history, human habits of subordination and political pressures. For example, addressing "piracy," his definition is simply a recital of municipal law cases in which particular states have hanged as "pirates" persons who committed crimes normally denominated "robbery" in England and equivalent municipal law words in other European languages, but committed within the jurisdiction of national officers whose municipal law authority ran to offenses committed outside the territorial jurisdiction of the normal court system, i.e., the "Admiral." But he adds to that class:

various other persons who are punished as pirates on account of the atrocity of their crimes, though they are not actually pirates, as for instance those who sail too near the land contrary to the prohibition of the sovereign . . . commit frauds in matters of insurance . . . and also those who cut the nets of the herring-fishers.[53]

---

[52] Cited note 50 above.
[53] Ibid., 126. The English translation quoted here is by Tenney Frank and appears in Volume II of the Carnegie reprint at 99.

Why insurance fraud is considered more atrocious than, say, embezzlement by a ship's purser, or barratry by the skipper, is nowhere explained. The evidence that insurance fraud and net-cutting (but only of herring-fishers) is so atrocious must be found in Bynkershoek's citations. The citations are only to Dutch statutes. Under those statutes, the word for "piracy" is not the Latin of learned texts of the time, but "*Zeerovery*," the statutory word of the Dutch legislators.

This approach leads Bynkershoek into the same difficulties noted above in the advice Sir Leoline Jenkins rendered to Sir Joseph Williamson. If the rules of public international law are really only the rules of municipal law generalized, then there can be no such thing as *mala in se*, criminal activity forbidden by international law so-called. The "common law of all mankind" conception of the *jus gentium* has only a theoretical existence, but no practical way of discovery and no practical impact in the world of affairs. If that is so, then there can be no universal jurisdiction over "pirates"; the normal rules evolved from state practice and acquiescence in that practice determine the reach of national jurisdiction even with regard to Admiralty tribunals whose territorial reach is worldwide, but whose actual jurisdiction to adjudicate is restricted (with some exceptions not relevant here) to all vessels within the Admiral's state's territorial waters and vessels worldwide flying the flag of the Admiral's state.

Bynkershoek's conclusion was that in theory any sovereign could assert jurisdiction over "pirates," and that in practice the sovereign in whose hands they are could do so and would reject interposition of the authority of any other sovereign: universal jurisdiction to enforce and universal standing to exercise that jurisdiction. But referring back to what appears to have been the same situation involving Scots privateers exceeding their license that had been the subject of Jenkins's legal opinion quoted above,[54] Bynkershoek indicated that the point was not free from doubt. Apparently that was as far as he could come, as a publicist, to make a full pattern of his fundamentally positivist orientation when the intellectual fashion of his time favored naturalist theory.

The intellectual problem could not be entirely ignored forever, and there is ample evidence that the leading publicists of the time were aware of it even if, like Vattel, they chose not to address it. For example, towards the end of the eighteenth century Richard Wooddeson, successor to Sir William Blackstone's Chair at Oxford as third Vinerian Professor of English Law (Blackstone had been the first), wrote that the "law of

---

[54] See p. 56 above.

nations" was a law "adopted and appealed to by civilized states, as the criterion for adjusting all controversies" in which transnational aspects of the transaction in question made inappropriate the application of a single state's municipal law unmodified by the sensibilities and interests of foreign sovereigns. What he had in mind, he explained, were questions involving "the property of captures at sea," among other things.[55]

This assumed validity to the concept of *jus gentium*, of a universal law given national expression by national tribunals that are somehow harmonized with the laws enforced by other sovereigns' national tribunals, led Wooddeson to the same problem that had bothered Jenkins a century earlier and Bynkershoek in the half century between. Again, the issue was whether privateers acting possibly in excess of the license granted by one sovereign could properly be considered "pirates" by another. Wooddeson recited a 1782 case in which it had been possible to satisfy both the positivist emphasis on valid commissions uttered at the discretion of the human institution with authority, and value-morality and amoral custom-based natural law prohibitions on depredations at sea outside of some presumed natural law of war, such as "just cause"–"just object"– "just motive." A British subject, Luke Ryan, by taking a Dutch commission, had violated the terms of the British anti-piracy statute of 1700.[56] But as a Dutch privateer Ryan seemed to lack the criminal intent, the *mens rea*, that the British version of morality-based natural law would make an essential element of any criminal law conviction. Wooddeson records with evident satisfaction that Ryan was convicted but pardoned; convicted under the positive law of 1700 forbidding those subject to English (shortly to become British) law to take foreign commissions, and pardoned as an act of English (British?) grace applying the moral-value-based natural law.[57]

But if the act of grace was also discretionary in the sovereign, then the problem was *not* solved. The implication remained that the sovereign was "bound" to exercise his "discretion" when the moral "law" beyond his discretion required it. That argument in turn leads back to the fundamental naturalism that statesmen in practice found unrealistic, or at

---

[55] Richard Wooddeson, *A Systematical View of the Laws of England* (1794), Volume II, 421.

[56] 11 & 12 William III, c. 7 (1700). The framing of this statute is analyzed at some length in Rubin, *Piracy* 66–78, 82–86. The statute is reproduced at Appendix I.B, 362–369 of that work. Although nearly always cited as here, in the official British *Chronological Table of the Statutes* it is listed as 11 Will. 3, c. 7 (1698).

[57] Wooddeson, *Systematical View*, note "n" at the foot of 426. For a detailed analysis of the Ryan affair, see Donald A. Petrie, "The Piracy Trial of Luke Ryan," 55(3) AN 185–204 (1995).

least uncongenial to the degree it gives legislative authority to scholars like Wooddeson who have no real responsibilities, and takes it from statesmen whose discretion is tempered by the needs of their constituents and their perceptions of the needs of the state far more than by the moral assertions of others.

In Great Britain, the statesmen had found a practical way out of the difficulty by evolving a dual system of administration. Such cases as by English constitutional law fell to be decided by common law or Admiralty judges, they could decide as their own traditions and the positive law of England required. The law between princes was to be discussed by the ministers of princes and "legislated" by contract and treaty, and impliedly legislated by such behavior as could be construed to be part of a "common law" process among states: practices "accepted as law."[58] The process of accepting a rule of international practice as law to be enforced by the officials of the state was a municipal law process. In Great Britain, guidance was distributed to subordinate arms of government by Orders-in-Council or other means appropriate to the situation in British municipal (constitutional) law, in some notable cases based on legal opinions rendered by the "Civilians" (experts in the Roman or "civil" law) of Doctors' Commons or the Law Officers of the Crown[59] or by Acts of Parliament. The Acts of Parliament could be viewed as adopting into British positive law either a direct view of morality or even mere convenience (thus accommodating the amoral "natural" law posited by Aristotle), or translating the Crown's treaty commitments into municipal law.

A dramatic example of the early use of the Doctors of Civil Law as advisers on international law to British Crown officials, was the case of the Irish privateers (or "pirates") in 1693.[60] The Doctors' opinion that

---

[58] *Cf.* Johann Wolfgang Textor, *Synopsis Juris Gentium* (1680) (Carnegie Endowment, Washington, 1916) 1: "In these extracts two sources of the Law of Nations are indicated . . . (2) the Usage of Nations, or what has been in practice accepted as Law by the nations. [Quibus ipsis equidem duo juris gentium principia exprimuntur . . . (2) usus gentium, sive ut illud ipsum a gentibus pro jure actu sit receptum . . .]" For how this theory of legislation worked out in practice in England and elsewhere, see below.

[59] The role of the Law Officers and the evolution of Doctors' Commons is neatly summarized in 3 Arnold Duncan McNair, *International Law Opinions* (1956), Appendix II at 407; an outline of the system during the eighteenth century is at 415–420.

[60] *R. v. John Golding, Thomas Jones et al.* (eight Irish commissioners), 12 *Howell's State Trials* 1269*ff.*, reproduced apparently from the original documents also in 2 R. G. Marsden (ed.), *Documents Relating to Law and Custom of the Sea* (Naval Records Society) (1916) Volume 50, 146.

"privateers" cannot legally be "pirates," based on principles of the "civil" (Roman) law and "reason" was rejected by the Admiralty Board and the accused "traitors" were tried and reportedly hanged as "pirates" for acting under commissions issued by James II after his purported abdication in 1688.

As noted in discussing the case of Luke Ryan above, in the 1700 Offences at Sea (Piracy) Act,[61] Parliament had adopted a view taken contrary to legal advice, making into "pirates" at English law (British law after the Act of Union with Scotland in 1707) those British subjects who attacked British shipping under a foreign license. Obviously, the statute, as positive law, was binding on British courts while the most learned opinions as to the public international law concerned were relegated to a different sphere. The British never did argue that this key provision of their statute reflected either amoral convenience or custom or moral-value-based natural law, or general principles that bound other sovereigns.

The Law Officers in the eighteenth century used naturalist language but their logic was deeply positivist. In what many regard as their most notable opinion, uttered 18 January 1753 during the Silesian Loan crisis, they argued that although the "Law of Nations" was "founded upon justice, equity, convenience, and the reason of the thing," all but "convenience" being "natural law" concepts, it did not allow reprisals "except in case of violent injuries, directed or supported by the State, and justice absolutely denied . . . by all the Tribunals, and afterwards by the Prince."[62] Their reasoning is solidly "positivist":

Where the Judges are left free, and give sentence according to their conscience, though it should be erroneous, that would be no ground for Reprisals. Upon doubtful questions, different men think and judge differently: and all a friend can desire is, that justice should be as impartially administered to him, as it is to the Subjects of that Prince in whose Courts the matter is tried.[63]

There is, thus, an acknowledgment that "justice" is not an objective concept to be determined by "reason," or by evidence as if a fact, but discrimination against British (or, hypothetically, any country's) nationals can be determined as a fact within the existing distribution of authority that gives discretion in particular cases to the municipal tribunals of particular states. It is then the denial of justice, subjectively determined for its own people in the discretion of the municipal order's own law-makers or adjudicators, that is forbidden by the *jus inter gentes*, not the

---

[61] Cited note 56 above.
[62] 20 BFSP (1832–1833) 889 at 892–893.   [63] Ibid., 893.

departure from some objective standard of substantive morality that the administrators can call "law."

This "dualist" approach, distinguishing the "legal" rules of an international order from the legal rules of a municipal legal order, was never fully accepted by naturalist writers and, as noted above, there was a gap between theory and practice that was not closed during the eighteenth century. The practice divided sharply between the *jus inter gentes* that bound princes and could be violated if the violating prince were prepared to accept the consequences in his dealings with his fellow sovereigns, and the *jus gentium* which was conceived in practice as something like the common law of transnational private transactions. Thus the rules of admiralty and prize which determined property rights in ships and cargo transiting the jurisdictions of many sovereigns were considered part of the universal private law of property analogized to the Roman law's *jus gentium*, the law common to all "nations."

Sir William Blackstone, the most influential common law jurist of the period leading up to the drafting of the Constitution of the United States of America, summarized the situation in all its confusion:

The law of nations is a system of rules, deducible by natural reason, and established by universal consent among the civilised inhabitants of the world; in order to decide all disputes, to regulate all ceremonies and civilities, and to insure the observance of justice and good faith, in that intercourse which must frequently occur between two or more independent states, and the individuals belonging to each . . .

In arbitrary states this law, wherever it contradicts, or is not provided for by, the municipal law of the country, is enforced by the royal power; but since in England no royal power can introduce a new law, or suspend the execution of the old, therefore the law of nations (wherever any question arises which is properly the object of its jurisdiction) is here adopted in its full extent by the common law, and is held to be a part of the law of the land . . . Thus in mercantile questions, such as bills of exchange and the like; in all marine causes relating to freight, average, demurrage, insurances, bottomry, and others of a similar nature; the law-merchant, which is a branch of the law of nations, is, regularly and constantly adhered to. So too in all disputes relating to prizes, to shipwrecks, to hostages and ransom bills, for which is no other rule of decision but this great universal law, collected from history and usage, and such writers of all nations and languages as are generally approved and allowed of.

But though in civil transactions and questions of property between the subjects of different states, the law of nations has much scope and extent as adopted by the law of England; yet the present branch of our inquiries will fall within a narrow compass, as offences against the law of nations can rarely be the object of the criminal law of any particular state. For offences against this law are principally incident to whole states or nations; in which case recourse can only be had to war, which is an appeal to the God of Hosts, to punish such infractions of public faith, as are committed by one independent people against another; neither state having any superior jurisdiction to resort upon earth for justice. But where the individuals of any state violate this general law, it is then the interest as well as the duty *of the government under which they live* [emphasis added], to animadvert upon them with a becoming severity, that the peace of the world may be maintained . . .

The principal offences against the law of nations, animadverted on as such by the municipal laws of England, are of three kinds: 1. Violation of safe-conducts; 2. Infringement of the rights of ambassadors; and, 3. Piracy.[64]

Obviously, the "conventional wisdom" of the seventeenth century and Edward Coke that the *jus gentium* included *mala in se* such "crimes" as treason and adultery had been entirely dropped by the increasing inter-communication among merchants in the century between Coke and Blackstone. "Piracy" remained the only expression of that notion openly maintained by this time. As to civil law, the law merchant, admiralty etc., it was apparently Blackstone's view and that of his contemporary scholars, that the need to know that property and contractual rights will be recognized before tribunals erected by municipal legal orders other than those creating the rights, dictated the existence of something like a natural and universal law of contract and property with municipal discretion reserved only with regard to empowering a tribunal to enforce the natural rights.

Natural law theorists had tried to maintain this model of a universal legal order, but those actually dealing with events, like Sir Leoline Jenkins and the Law Officers of Doctors' Commons, had been forced to abandon this conception of the *jus gentium* under the impact of their sovereigns' assertions of absolute discretion in law-making, supported by the oli-garchies who were taking control of the law-making processes within particular countries in Europe and exercising legislative authority in the name of their sovereigns. But the conception now seems to have survived, indeed in a revivified form, as a rationale used by some articulate lawyers and assertive government officials to maintain the interests of individual and corporate property holders and moral actors before municipal tribunals trying to harmonize the various legislative acts of foreign municipal authorities with the needs of parties to actual cases.

---

[64] 4 Sir William Blackstone, *Commentaries on the Laws of England* (1765), 66–69. The edition used here was published by Rees Welsh & Co., Philadelphia, in 1897. It contains the original text of 1765 with additional notes and citations clearly marked.

Debates abounded concerning the source of the obligation that many statesmen felt (and many "realist" statesmen did not) to have their municipal law conform to the pattern and support the fundamental principles of the municipal laws of other "civilized nations."[65]

It is in this sense that there existed in the late eighteenth century a concept of there being "torts," non-contractual legal wrongs committed by individuals against other individuals, in violation of the "law of nations." It was also in this sense that there was a need to control the litigation that might arise out of such wrongs, as there was a need to centralize control over admiralty and prize tribunals, to assure that the universal natural law would not be perverted by petty local interest and thus bring the entire "nation" or state into war with another. This is the obvious reason for the provision, Section 9 of the United States' Judicature Act of 1789, allowing concurrent jurisdiction between state and federal courts, thus plaintiff's option, "of all causes where an alien sues for a tort only in violation of the law of nations or a treaty of the United States." The alien worried about local biases could engage the good faith of the entire federation in a private tort action based on the integrity of the supposed universal natural law, the *jus gentium*.[66]

As to Blackstone's conception of "offences" against the law of nations, each of his three categories deserves an analysis of its own, but that is impossible within the constraints of a single study. In summary, with regard to the first two, violations of safe-conducts expressly issued by a sovereign or his ambassador to the subjects of a foreign power in time of

---

[65] See, e.g., Barbara W. Tuchman, *The First Salute* (paperback edn., Ballentine Books, New York, 1988) 102: "Burke['s parliamentary] . . . motion [to recompense a Jewish merchant for the confiscation and sale of his goods after the British capture of the West Indian Island of St. Eustatius in 1781] precipitated a vigorous debate about whether there was or was not a recognized law of nations." Unfortunately, Tuchman attributes the assertion to Great Britain, Parliament, *The History, Debates and Proceedings of the Houses of Parliament of Great Britain, 1743–1774*, which cannot possibly be correct for a debate in 1781. Nor is her date, 30 November 1781, reliable because in the more or less standard Hansard, *The Parliamentary History of England from the Earliest Period to the Year 1803*, Volume XXII (26 March 1781–7 May 1782) Burke's motion was recorded as debated on 4 December 1781 (cols. 769–783). Hansard records much of Tuchman's paraphrase, but not any debate on the existence of a "law of nations."

[66] The otherwise excellent historical research set out in William R. Casto, "The Federal Courts' Protective Jurisdiction over Torts Committed in Violation of the Law of Nations", 18 CLR 467 (1986), and Ann-Marie Burley, "The Alien Tort Statute and the Judiciary Act of 1789: A Badge of Honor," 83 AJIL 461 (1989), seem to bypass this rather obvious point. The authors' openly expressed regret that Judge Kaufman's approach in *Filartiga v. Peña-Irala*, cited in chapter 1, note 57 above, is historically insupportable might have colored their perceptions.

war, failure of the subjects of the issuing sovereign to abide by the terms of the pass could lead to reprisals and worse. But since enforcement was, by Blackstone's own analysis, limited to the pass-issuing sovereign to exercise over his own subjects and over foreigners in his own territory (as when third-country merchants despoil a foreign merchant leaving England under such a safe-conduct immediately after the declaration of war), it is not clear why Blackstone found it necessary to attribute the common law crime (later made statutory in England) to some universal law of nations.

The criminal law necessary to enforce in British territory what Blackstone called "the rights" of foreign ambassadors had been enacted in England by statute in 1708.[67] It is not clear why Blackstone found it necessary to find a basis in the *jus gentium* for that statutory crime. Its basis exists on the *jus inter gentes* level; the rulers of states had long been conceived to owe to their fellow "sovereigns" in other states obligations to protect foreign ambassadors, and, since at least legendary Roman times, states have been considered legally responsible to their fellow states for the results that accrue when their emissaries mingle in local politics.[68]

Perhaps Blackstone's reference to the *jus gentium* was a reflection of the influence of Sir Edward Coke, the leading English jurist of the pre-Interregnum seventeenth century. As noted above, with regard to enforcement of the local law against foreign ambassadors, Coke had written that foreign ambassadors were subject to local legal process even with regard to criminal matters insofar as the law they had purportedly violated related to *mala in se*, things evil in themselves, as distinguished from *mala prohibita*, things evil under local law only, thus implying their subjection to the *jus gentium* as applied by any tribunal with territorially based enforcement jurisdiction over the accused, including foreign municipal tribunals.[69]

On the other hand, Coke's analysis of the status of ambassadors puts responsibility for their security squarely on the host state. His logic was based on an assertion regarding a supposed universal *jus gentium*:

Ambassadors ought to be kept from all injuries and wrongs, and by the Law of all Countries and of all Nations they ought to be safe and sure in every place, in

---

[67] 7 Anne, c. 12 (1708).

[68] See R. M. Ogilvie, *A Commentary on Livy Books 1–5* (Oxford, 1965) 716–717, explaining why scholars regard as baseless the recitation in Livy, Book V, 4–36, attributing the war of 386 BC between Rome and the Gauls to the failure of the Fabii as ambassadors to Clusium to observe this obligation.

[69] See p. 53 above.

so much that it is not lawful to hurt the Ambassadors of our enemies: and herewith agreeth the Civil Law.[70]

By 1710, the absolute immunity of ambassadors from local law, even with regard to *mala in se*, was derived from "reason" by the English common law in *The Case of Andrew Artemonowitz Mattueoff, Ambassador of Muscovy*.[71] Thus a distinction was established in English law between the substantive rules of the supposed universal reason-based law, and the enforcement systems erected by municipal legal orders to apply those rules in real cases. By 1710 it had become apparent that limitations on the enforcement authority of a municipal legal order were based on practical needs that were superior to any assertions of the need to accept the substantive law as valid. A distinction was drawn between jurisdiction to prescribe, which a tribunal might assert, tracing its prescription to "nature" and reason, and jurisdiction to adjudicate, which was withheld from municipal tribunals in the case of foreign ambassadors. Both rules of substance and rules limiting jurisdiction to adjudicate were derived through "natural law" reasoning by English common law courts.

The situation with regard to "piracy" is extremely complex and will be discussed below.

The confusion between the *jus gentium* and the *jus inter gentes* implicit in Blackstone's *Commentaries* was noted by Jeremy Bentham in 1786 at the latest, and he suggested replacing the phrase "law of nations" in its *jus inter gentes* sense with the phrase "international law."

Now as to any transactions which may take place between individuals who are subjects of different states, these are regulated by the internal laws, and decided upon by the internal tribunals, of the one or the other of those states: the case is the same where the sovereign of the one has any immediate transactions with a private member of the other: the sovereign reducing himself, *pro re nata*, to the condition of a private person, as often as he submits his cause to either tribunal; whether by claiming a benefit, or defending himself against a burthen. There remain then the mutual transactions between sovereigns, as such, for the subject of that branch of jurisprudence which may be properly and exclusively termed *international* [emphasis *sic*].[72]

---

[70] Coke, *Fourth* 153.

[71] QB, 8 Anne (1710), reprinted in 88 English Reports (full reprint) 598.

[72] Jeremy Bentham, *An Introduction to the Principles of Morals and Legislation* (1789, text that, according to the editor, was "printed but not published in 1780," whatever that means) (Wilfrid Harrison, ed., Oxford 1948) vii, 426 (chapter XVII, section 25). The earliest use of the phrase "international law" in the currently published works of Bentham seems to date to 1786. See 2 *The Works of Jeremy Bentham* (John Bowring, ed., 1838–1842, 1962 reprint) 535–536.

This suggestion was not adopted by European or American jurists generally until after the Napoleonic Wars and later when other jurisprudential developments to be mentioned below encouraged the shift in language. The division between the *jus gentium* and the *jus inter gentes* suggested by Bentham flowed eventually from other reasons than the rather simplistic logic he asserted as if self-evident.

This was the legal tradition received by the United States when the framers of the Constitution of 1787 met in Philadelphia.

3   Theory and practice come together

The United States of America

As in many newly independent countries, the elite that found itself responsible for governing the thirteen British colonies during their war of independence first attempted to preserve their separate political bases by maintaining the separate legal existence of those colonies, now become states in the international legal order. The Articles of Confederation were agreed in a Congress of the separate states' representatives on 15 November 1777. They take the form of an alliance in which "Each State retains its sovereignty, freedom, and independence, and every power, jurisdiction and right, which is not by this Confederation expressly delegated to the United States in Congress assembled."[1]

To satisfy the *jus inter gentes* under which an alliance with France was envisaged, the Articles of Confederation were construed almost immediately to give the thirteen colonies, as "states," a single legal personality with which to face the world. Despite the laggardly ratification by Maryland, which was not produced until 1 March 1781, two treaties in the name of the "Thirteen United States of North America" (listed in the preambles of each to include Maryland) were concluded with France and signed at Paris on 6 February 1778, ratified by the Congress on 4 May 1778.[2]

But the laws of war as they applied to real persons and property fell into the domain of the *jus gentium* by the concepts of Blackstone's contemporaries; they were conceived as the reason-based uniform law of

---

[1] United States Articles of Confederation, Article II, first sentence. The text used here is from 69th Congress, 1st Session, House Doc. No. 398, *Documents Illustrative of the Formation of the Union of the American States* (Washington, 1927) (hereinafter *Documents Illustrative*) 27.

[2] 1 Malloy, *Treaties, Conventions . . .* (Washington, 1910) 468, 479–480.

all civilized countries enforced in disputes among private parties by the municipal courts of all countries. So the authority of each state in the international legal order had to be exercised severally, but in the same way as all other "civilized" states in the "Age of Reason" when the rights of privateers, naval capture in general, military appropriation of private property and similar issues arose. The legal questions involved preserving the separate authority of the states, while requiring a uniform set of laws to resolve questions of property under the *jus gentium* that was conceived to apply in wartime. The forum for argument usually involved the legal effect of the belligerent-licensed taking of "enemy" or "neutral" property at sea: privateering. In the Articles of Confederation, the former colonies, the thirteen contracting states, retained their asserted legal authority to issue "letters of marque or [*sic*: the more usual form was the conjunctive, 'and'] reprisal" but only:

After a declaration of war by the United States in Congress assembled, and then only against the kingdom or state and the subjects thereof, against which war has been so declared, and under such regulations as shall be established by the United States in Congress assembled, unless such state be infested by pirates, in which case vessels of war may be fitted out for that occasion, and kept so long as the danger shall continue, or until the United States in Congress assembled shall determine otherwise.[3]

As to the law of prize and admiralty, the living parts of the reason-based law of nations postulated by Blackstone among other categories of law considered necessarily uniform and universal, the power was reserved exclusively to the central body, the United States in Congress Assembled:

Of establishing rules for deciding in all cases, what captures on land or water shall be legal, and in what manner prizes taken by land or naval forces in the service of the united states shall be divided or appropriated – of granting letters of marque and [*sic*] reprisal in times of peace – appointing courts for the trial of piracies and felonies committed on the high seas and establishing courts for receiving and determining finally appeals in all cases of captures.[4]

The law merchant and other categories of what Blackstone considered to be necessarily universal were left for the final determination of the thirteen states' separate court systems, even in cases involving citizens of other states of the United States and aliens. The possibility that the tribunals of the different states of the American Union might have different notions as to the substance of the supposedly universal law does not seem to have bothered their representatives in 1777.

---

[3] Articles of Confederation, Article VI, last para., *Documents Illustrative* at 30.
[4] Article IX, first para., at ibid. 31.

But at the Constitutional Convention of 1787 the issue certainly did arise. In the draft prepared by a "Committee of Detail" on 6 August 1787, the legislature of the federal government was given the power "To declare the law and punishment of piracies and felonies committed on the high seas . . . and of offenses against the law of nations." In a separate clause, the federal legislature was given the quite different power regarding prize cases, "To make rules concerning captures on land and water." These clauses are distinct from the authority to "make war" and "regulate commerce with foreign nations."[5] The only mention of letters of marque and reprisal appears to be the provision in Article XII forbidding the states of the Union to grant them.

The federal judicial power, most fitting for authority to pronounce universal rules based on reason as distinct from the political legislative process, is extended to:

All cases arising under laws passed by the Legislature of the United States; to all cases affecting Ambassadors, other Public Ministers and Consuls . . . to all cases of Admiralty and maritime jurisdiction; [and] to controversies . . . between a State or the Citizens thereof and foreign States, citizens or subjects.[6]

Clearly, the first notion was the need for universal law and a tribunal that could engage the responsibility of the entire federation in its implementation when foreigners were affected.

On closer analysis in the Constitutional Convention in Philadelphia, problems became apparent with this *jus gentium* approach. The discussion of the pertinent powers of the legislature took place on 17 August 1787. James Madison, whose notes on the Constitutional Convention published in 1840[7] are a principal source for the debates, himself raised the issue in connection with the authority to declare the law and punishment of piracies and felonies on the high seas. He recorded that he had argued that the concept of "felony" at English common law is vague, and that:

No foreign law should be a standard farther than [it] is expressly adopted – If the laws of the States were to prevail on this subject, the citizens of different States would be subject to different punishments for the same offence at sea. There would be neither uniformity nor stability in the law – The proper remedy for all

---

[5] Madison's Notes, reprinted in ibid., 109*ff.* at 471 (Committee Report), 475 (Article VII containing the listed powers of the legislature).

[6] Article XI, section 3, in ibid., 479.

[7] 1 Max Ferrand (ed.), *The Records of the Federal Convention of 1787* (New Haven, CT: Yale University Press, 1937, 1966) xv.

these difficulties was to vest the power proposed by the term "define" in the National legislature.[8]

This rather superficial and wholly "policy oriented," i.e., positivist, rationale for adopting a distribution of powers that might seem to have been more convincingly based in 1787 on a Blackstone-like adoption of the natural law notion of *jus gentium*, seems irrational. How can uniformity with regard to offenses committed by persons of different countries be achieved by each country adopting its own laws? The same argument about uniformity of the laws of different states of the Union which supported reposing the authority to define "offenses against the law of nations" in the federal government, seems to support placing the authority to define and punish violations of the "law of nations" in the hands of the national *executive*, which can negotiate uniform rules with foreign officials, or with the treaty power involving both the executive and the representatives of the States' international personality, the Senate, rather than in the national *legislature*. But that would have been a violation of the theoretical distinction between the authority to be granted to the executive or the executive and Senate on the one hand, and legislative branches of government on the other, adopted *a priori* by the framers of the Constitution. Obviously, Madison was somewhat confused on the jurisprudential issues.

On 14 September 1787, the Convention discussed again the draft clause under which the Congress was to be authorized "To define and punish piracies and felonies on the high seas, and 'punish' [sic] offences against the law of nations." Gouverneur Morris, of the Pennsylvania delegation, moved to delete the word "punish" before the final phrase, thus authorizing the Congress "To define & punish piracies and felonies on the high seas, and offences against the law of nations." The implication was that not only the punishment but even the *definition* of "offences against the law of nations" was a matter for the legislature of the Union, not the courts or the executive. This was objected to by James Wilson, also of Pennsylvania. As recorded by Madison, Wilson argued that "To pretend to *define* [emphasis *sic*] the law of nations which depended on the authority of all the civilized nations of the world, would have a look of arrogance, that would make us ridiculous." Morris replied, setting forth the dualist model which, outside of some academic writings and lower court confusions, has ever since dominated United States jurisprudence in this issue: that the "law of nations" is "often too vague and deficient to be a rule"

---

[8] *Documents Illustrative* 558 at 560.

when it comes to criminal offenses; somebody must have the authority to "define" the crime for American courts to be able to try and punish those accused of piracy and "offenses against the law of nations." Morris's argument was adopted six to five with Pennsylvania and Virginia both voting against it.[9] The final language of the relevant Constitutional provisions gives to the Congress the power: "To define and punish Piracies and Felonies committed on the high Seas, and Offences against the Law of Nations."

Other relevant powers given to the Congress of the Union were the powers "To declare War, grant letters of Marque and Reprisal, and make Rules concerning Captures on Land and Water." Those powers follow immediately after the power to define and punish offenses against the law of nations and immediately before the power to raise and support armies. In addition, the federal judiciary was given exclusive authority with regard "to all Cases of admiralty and maritime Jurisdiction."[10]

Morris's view, successful in the Constitutional Convention, was not understood by scholars in the literature that immediately followed, setting the stage for 200 years of continued confusion. A perusal of the pertinent Federalist Papers confirms the notion that, despite Morris's success regarding Article I, section 8, clause 10, the framers of the Constitution, by adopting Blackstone's simplistic categorizations generally, had assumed an identity between the *jus gentium* and the *jus inter gentes* that flowed from the naturalist language of the time and did not conform to the practical experience of statesmen. And Wooddeson's pleasant reaction to the interplay of concepts of strict law and "equity" that maintained some degree of harmony in the system was not available to statesmen framing a Constitution on the assumption that men were inherently corrupt and needed competition and adamantine legal limits to their power in order to save the state from the kind of tyranny that destroyed the Roman Republic in the first century BC.[11] Madison seemed particularly confused, although as eloquent as usual:

---

[9] Ibid., at 723.

[10] United States Constitution, Article I, section 8, clauses 10 and 11; Article III, section 2. Some state authority was construed despite this language in later cases, but that is another tale. See David W. Robertson, *Admiralty and Federalism* (Mineola, NY: The Foundation Press, 1970).

[11] The notion that the American Founding Fathers lived in a gentler world than ours is patent nonsense. After all, it was the election of 1800 that provoked Hamilton to compare Aaron Burr to Cataline, the leader of the anti-oligarchy party put down with great difficulty by the Roman Senate under the leadership of Cicero in 63–62 BC. In 1804 Burr, then the Vice President of the United States, killed Hamilton, the former

The power to define and punish piracies and felonies committed on the high seas and offenses against the law of nations belongs ... to the general government, and is a[n] ... improvement on the Articles of Confederation. These articles contain no provision for the case of offenses against the law of nations; and consequently leave it to the power of any indiscreet member to embroil the Confederacy with foreign nations. The provision of the federal articles on the subject of piracies and felonies extends no further than to the establishment of courts for the trial of these offenses. The definition of piracies might, without inconveniency, be left to the law of nations; though a legislative definition of them is found in most municipal codes. A definition of felonies on the high seas is evidently requisite. Felony is a term of loose signification even in the common law of England; and of various import in the statute law of that kingdom. But neither the common nor the statute law of that, or of any other nation, ought to be a standard for the proceedings of this, unless previously made its own by legislative adoption. The meaning of the term, as defined in the codes of the several States [of the new Union], would be as impracticable as the former would be a dishonorable and illegitimate guide. It is not precisely the same in any two of the States; and varies in each with every revision of its criminal laws. For the sake of certainty and uniformity, therefore, the power of defining felonies in this case was in every respect necessary and proper.[12]

It seems notable that Madison referred to the law of nations in both senses, as the criminal law, particularly "piracy," applicable to individuals and, as such, part of municipal law which might or might not have some similarity with the municipal laws of other jurisdictions, and the law between states which might be violated by the parochial act of a single tribunal.

A similar overlap of meaning is apparent in Madison's defense of the clause of the new Constitution giving power to the federal legislature to regulate foreign commerce:

In regulating our own commerce, he [the hypothetical representative of a state of the Union in the federal House of Representatives] ought to be not only acquainted with the treaties between the United States and other nations, but also with the commercial policy and laws of other nations. He ought not to be altogether ignorant of the law of nations; for that, as far as it is a proper object of municipal legislation, is submitted to the federal government.[13]

Secretary of the Treasury and candidate for the presidency, in a duel. Politics was a blood sport in those days. And in any list of the most foolish legislation ever passed by the Congress in panic it would surely be necessary to include the Alien, Sedition and Logan Acts of 25 June, 6 and 14 July 1798, and 30 January 1799.

[12] Federalist No. 42 (Madison), in *The Federalist Papers* (Rossiter, ed., Mentor Books, 1961) 265–266.

[13] Ibid., 334, Federalist No. 53 (Madison).

There seems to be an underlying assumption that Morris was right after all; that the "law of nations" binds the United States, but to be given municipal law effect must be translated into municipal law by statute. Unlike treaties, which become law of the land directly on ratification under Article VI of the Constitution,[14] the "law of nations" in its *jus inter gentes* phase was believed to bind the state without directly binding its officers or others within its jurisdiction.

John Jay took the same confused view as Madison of the "law of nations," which he and Hamilton both (but not Madison) referred to consistently in the plural, "laws of nations." Jay wrote that "violations of treaties and of the laws of nations afford *just* [emphasis *sic*] causes of war"; thus it makes sense to give jurisdiction over legal questions involving them to the judicial arm of the federal government and not any other arm of the federal government or to the individual states.[15] Indeed, Jay's view was that it was the "laws of nations" in their *jus inter gentes* phase that were the laws underlying the legal bindingness of treaties:

Others, though content that treaties should be made in the mode proposed, are averse to their being the *supreme* laws of the land. They insist, and profess to believe, that treaties, like acts of assembly, should be repealable at pleasure. This idea seems to be new and peculiar to this country, but new errors, as well as new truths, often appear. These gentlemen would do well to reflect that a treaty is only another name for a bargain, and that it would be impossible to find a nation who would make any bargain with us, which should be binding on them *absolutely*, but on us only so long and so far as we may think proper to be bound by it. They who make laws may, without doubt, amend or repeal them; and it will not be disputed that they who make treaties may alter or cancel them; but still let us not forget that treaties are made, not by only one of the contracting parties, but by both, and consequently, that as the consent of both was essential to their formation at first, so must it ever afterwards be to alter or cancel them. The proposed Constitution, therefore, has not in the least extended the obligation of treaties. They are just as binding and just as far beyond the lawful reach of legislative acts now as they will be at any future period, or under any form of government. [As to treaties procured by corruption,] the case is not supposable . . . [But], if it should ever happen, the treaty so obtained from us would, like all other fraudulent contracts, be null and void by the laws of nations [emphases *sic*].[16]

---

[14] United States Constitution, Article VI, clause 2: "[A]ll treaties made . . . under the authority of the United States, shall be the supreme law of the land."

[15] Federalist No. 3 (Jay), in *The Federalist Papers* 43, 44.

[16] Ibid., 394, 395, Federalist No. 64 (Jay).

Although Jay was an experienced internationalist and lawyer,[17] and served as first Chief Justice of the United States (1789–1795), his notion that treaties automatically bind all within the municipal legal order as well as the international legal order, that a constitution can be amended by treaty, and that the universal scope of the *jus gentium* reflects a reason-based single legal order, a "monist" system, could not stand the test of reality.

The idea that treaties, whatever their continued effects in the international legal order, are not repealable for purposes of municipal law by the federal legislature was the very first to go. The alliance of 1778 with France was repealed as municipal law for the United States by an Act of the Congress on 7 July 1798, precipitating a legal quarrel with France.[18]

Although Jay's logic was not accepted by the Congress to establish treaty law as superior to statute law under the Constitution, it did separate the two and set the stage for the entrenchment in American Constitutional jurisprudence of Morris's dualist model; a sharp distinction was drawn between the municipal law of the Union and the Union's international obligations. Since Jay's logic is unassailable as a matter of the *jus inter gentes* under the conceptions of today as well as of 1787, the result has been to split the American Constitutional legal order away from the international legal order and permit actions consistent with the Constitution to have full effect within the municipal legal order, even if simultaneously placing the United States in violation of its international legal obligations. The implications of this "dualism" are many and grave and frequently misunderstood; the fact of this dualism seems to illustrate one result of the Constitution's framers having adopted Blackstone's ill-conceived model of the relationship between municipal law and the "law of nations," and reflects the linguistic confusion between the *jus gentium* and the *jus inter gentes* that had been worked out in theory by Suarez and Zouche 150 years before, but ignored by the conventional wisdom of "Age of Reason" naturalist writers during the eighteenth century.

Hamilton focused on the *jus gentium* meaning of the "laws of nations," but the same confusion of thought results from the overlapping public

[17] John Jay was one of the three representatives of the United States who negotiated the peace treaty with Great Britain in 1783 (the other two were Benjamin Franklin and John Adams). Jay was the sole negotiator of the succeeding arrangement ("Jay's Treaty") in 1794. He was Secretary for Foreign Affairs under the Articles of Confederation 1784–1789. See Samuel F. Bemis, *Jay's Treaty* (1923) (New Haven, CT: Yale University Press, revised edn., 1962); Leo Pfeffer, *This Honorable Court* (Boston: Beacon Press, 1965) (paperback edn., 1967) 37–38.

[18] 5 John Bassett Moore, *Digest of International Law* (Washington, 1906) 609–610.

and private law meanings. In discussing the jurisdiction of the federal judiciary as against the retained jurisdiction of the states' courts he wrote:

As the denial or perversion of justice by the sentences of courts, as well as in any other manner, is with reason classed among the just causes of war, it will follow that the federal judiciary ought to have cognizance of all causes in which the citizens of other countries are concerned . . . A distinction may perhaps be imagined between cases arising upon treaties and the laws [plural *sic*] of nations and those which may stand merely on the footing of the municipal law. The former kind may be supposed proper for the federal jurisdiction, the latter for that of the States. But it is at least problematical whether an unjust sentence against a foreigner, where the subject of controversy was wholly relative to the *lex loci*, would not, if unredressed, be an aggression upon his sovereign, as well as one which violated the stipulations of a treaty or the general law [singular *sic*[19]] of nations. And a still greater objection to the distinction would result from the immense difficulty . . . of a practical discrimination between the cases of one complexion and those of the other.[20]

There is an underlying assumption that the "law [or laws] of nations" contains substantive rules that all states in the international legal order are obliged to apply in private litigation, and that the failure to apply them will result in tensions between states that might even lead to war. Hamilton does not mention "non-discrimination" as the essence of the matter, as had the British Law Officers in 1753.[21] But apparently accepting something like Blackstone's list of the components of the "law of nations,"[22] Hamilton felt that the need for federal jurisdiction was self-evident:

[19] Hamilton appears to have referred to the "laws" of nations when having the *jus gentium* in mind: the laws common to all "civilized" nations in the concepts of the late eighteenth century; and the "law" of nations when referring to the *jus inter gentes*: the entire body of law that bound sovereigns in a single legal order. But the evidence is too sparse and the subject, the concept in the mind of a single person (even though a major participant in public events of the period), of too limited interest to delve further in this study. The usage should be of some interest to students of the thought of Alexander Hamilton.

[20] *Documents Illustrative* at 476–477, Federalist No. 80 (Hamilton). This conception seems to be the path by which Blackstone's language actually made the transition to positive law in the United States. See the grant of jurisdiction to federal courts of "all causes where an alien sues for a tort only in violation of the law of nations or a treaty of the United States" in section 9 of the Judicature Act of 1789, cited at chapter 1, note 57 above.

[21] See p. 63 above

[22] See pp. 64–65 above. Hamilton was clearly referring not to "offences against the law of nations," but to the transnational property cases, "law merchant," "marine causes" and the like.

The most bigoted idolizers of State authority have not thus far shown a disposition to deny the national judiciary the cognizance of maritime causes. These so generally depend on the laws of nations and so commonly affect the rights of foreigners that they fall within the considerations which are relative to the public peace. The most important part of them are, by the present Confederation, [already] submitted to federal jurisdiction.[23]

Hamilton was so concerned that foreign governments be given no just cause for remonstrance as the result of American adjudication that he even would withhold those cases from juries regardless of the common law traditions regarding tort trials:

I feel a deep and deliberate conviction that there are many cases in which the trial by jury is an ineligible one. I think it so particularly in cases which concern the public peace with foreign nations – that is, in most cases where the question turns wholly on the laws of nations. Of this nature, among others, are all prize causes. Juries cannot be supposed competent to investigations that require a thorough knowledge of the laws and usages of nations ... There would of course be always danger that the rights of other nations might be infringed by their decisions so as to afford occasions of reprisal and war.[24]

Clearly Hamilton was concerned not about cases in which the foreign government was a defendant in a private action before American courts, but cases in which foreign private persons might be deprived of legal rights to property (as can routinely happen in prize and admiralty cases) in a manner that might seem discriminatory or otherwise inconsistent with what seem to have been conceived as universal rules of property law evidenced by the municipal laws and usages of many nations: the *jus gentium.*

Hamilton was obviously also concerned about local jury biases. In this regard, he must have been aware of the widely publicized conviction in Pennsylvania in 1784, under the regime of the Articles of Confederation, of the Chevalier de Longchamps, a French nobleman, for two assaults on the French Consul General to the United States (also accredited as Consul to the State of Pennsylvania). Judge M'Kean, Chief Justice of Pennsylvania, wrote that "the principles of the laws of nations, which form a part of the municipal law of Pennsylvania" was the governing law and that if de Longchamps were convicted of the assault as alleged, he should be jailed. After the jury found him guilty, the sentence was suspended to allow the judges to consider whether the assaults, particularly the first assault, which had occurred in the residence of the French Minister Plenipoten-

---

[23] *Documents Illustrative* 478, Federalist No. 80 (Hamilton).
[24] Ibid., 504, Federalist No. 83 (Hamilton).

tiary to the United States, should not properly be a matter for French rather than Pennsylvania jurisdiction. The Pennsylvania court held that jurisdiction lay in the court with authority in the territory (the tribunal refers to the "county") in which the alleged offense occurred, and that "the law of nations . . . in its full extent, is part of the law of this state, and is to be collected from the practice of different nations, and the authority of writers." Violence exercised against the French Consul was then categorized as "a crime against the whole world." Judge M'Kean called it "an atrocious violation of the laws of nations" not in the assault alone, but in making it against foreign public officials: "the peculiar objects of this law."

In dealing with the obligations of a state to apply its municipal law in such a way as to implement the "laws of nations," Judge M'Kean appears to have identified the "laws of nations" with the "*jus gentium,*" and grounded the authority of the State of Pennsylvania to apply its criminal assault law on it. The issue was not whether the United States was under an obligation to France to try de Longchamps. France had formally requested the United States not to try de Longchamps. The issue was whether a trial by ordinary municipal procedures of a case involving only French people was within the jurisdiction to adjudicate of the State of Pennsylvania, and whether the authority apparently retained by Pennsylvania under the Articles of Confederation was consistent with limits on jurisdiction to adjudicate implicit in the international legal order. It is not clear that criminal assault against a foreign public official who had been received under the laws of Pennsylvania was also a "normal" criminal assault. If not, then to apply the "laws of nations" as a source of law to be determined by judges after the event, even if resting on earlier case law, learned commentary and the perceived needs of the overall system, seems to be the creation of a "common law" crime.[25]

As noted above, the notion that judicial officials, particularly state officials free of the responsibilities of the federation, could determine "common law crimes" against influential foreigners troubled Hamilton.

---

[25] *Respublica* v. *de Longchamps*, 1 US (1 Dallas) 59 (1784). The quotations from Judge M'Kean's opinion are at 62. Judge M'Kean's opinion rests heavily on the 1710 British case of *Andrew Artemonowitz Mattueoff, Ambassador of Muscovy*, cited at chapter 2, note 71 above. He does not cite that case, but refers to it as "the noted case of the Russian ambassador" (at 62). That case supports the English obligation to punish persons subject to English law for their infractions of the "law of nations." Judge M'Kean disagreed with the part of it holding that detention of the English offenders in England was linked to the satisfaction of Czar Peter.

Hamilton also worried about the obligations of the United States as a "neutral power" under the "laws of nations" when he was Secretary of the Treasury. In 1793, an American mariner, Gideon Henfield, accepted a privateering commission from Citizen Genet, the Consul in the United States of revolutionary France. The question facing the new United States was whether the acts of Henfield placed the United States in violation of its obligations as a "neutral power" under the *jus inter gentes* not to support either belligerent, France or Great Britain and its allies, in the wars that followed the French Revolution. Also at issue was the interpretation of the Treaty of 1778 by which the infant United States during its own revolution against Great Britain, in return for French military assistance, had agreed to let French privateers fit out in American ports.[26] Several very long and learned opinions are preserved arguing that American obligations under the "laws of nations" include the obligation not to allow its territory to be used to the injury of any foreign power with which the United States was at peace. But there was no United States municipal statute to that effect yet. The prosecution adopted Jay's views and argued that "the law of nations is part of the law of the land" citing Blackstone and the *de Longchamps* case, pointing out that "the law of nations is enforced by the judiciary," not necessarily involving implementing action by the legislature or executive.[27] (Hamilton wrote some notes to help the prosecution on the issue of neutral obligations; Jefferson's views as Secretary of State seem to have been restricted to certifying the correctness of key documents submitted to the court.)

In their charge to the jury hearing the case, the three judges[28] supported the notion of common law crimes: "[H]e was bound to keep the peace in regard to all nations with whom we are at peace. This is the law of nations; not an ex post facto law, but a law that was in existence long before Gideon Henfield existed." They also found support in United States treaty obligations with the Netherlands, Great Britain and Prussia binding the United States to peace with those powers. Since treaties are "law of

---

[26] *Henfield's Case*, 11 Federal Cases 1099 (1793).

[27] Ibid., 1117.

[28] Judges James Wilson and James Iredell of the Supreme Court joined with Judge Peters in the District Court. Under the Judicature Act of 1789 cited in chapter 1, note 57 above, sections 4 and 11, the Districts of the fledgling United States were grouped into three "Circuits" and the Circuit Courts were presided over by a District Court judge and two Supreme Court justices. These Circuit Courts were given original jurisdiction over "all crimes and offences cognizable under the authority of the United States" with some irrelevant exceptions.

the land" under the American Constitution[29] it was asserted that they bound all American citizens directly.[30]

Nonetheless, Henfield was acquitted. It was asserted by Jefferson, in directing the American Ambassador to explain the matter to the British authorities, that the acquittal did not flow from American confusion regarding the law, but from the jury not being convinced of Henfield's guilty intent.[31] What is the basis for Jefferson's assertion is not clear from the published record.

Partly as a result of Henfield's case, the question of which acts by individuals should be made criminally punishable so as to avoid complaint by foreign governments of American violation of the *jus inter gentes* relating to neutral obligations was resolved by statute a few months later.[32]

The impact of reality on theory

Introduction

It was related above how naturalist theoreticians, always a bit uncomfortable with the *jus gentium* as a subject for analysis on the basis of comparative law, had concluded by the time of Pufendorf that Cicero had been correct; that "natural law," the "true law [*vera lex*]" rested on principles that could be perceived by introspection and that judges and statesmen had the authority to apply their own conclusions regarding that "law" to whomever the legal order placed under their authority to define or apply the "law." The pattern of argument rested on *a priori* assumptions of relative values; in cases of conflicting values the theorists

---

[29] Quoted at note 14 above.   [30] *Henfield's Case*, 1120.

[31] Ibid., 1121. Chief Justice Marshall reported many years later that "the verdict in favor of Henfield was celebrated with extravagant marks of joy and exultation": ibid., 1122, quoting from 2 John Marshall, *Life of Washington* 274. The learned compiler of the case appends his own notes in which he indicates his sympathy with the notion that the "law of nations" authorizes judges to define and authorize punishment for "Common Law crimes." He notes that *US* v. *Hudson and Goodwin* (3 US (7 Cranch) 32 (1813)) and *US* v. *Coolidge* (14 US (1 Wheaton) 415 (1816)), which seem to challenge that view, might be read to detract from his opinion regarding the legal force of *Henfield's Case*, but: "How far this opinion is to be considered shaken [by those later cases] is yet to be determined": ibid., 1121. See below.

[32] The Neutrality Act of 5 June 1794, 3rd Congress, 1st Session, chapter 50, 1 Stat. 381. This Act has been repeatedly amended and extended; it is the statutory basis for the current American criminal law relating to neutrality. For a summary of the history with citations, see Alfred P. Rubin, "The Concept of Neutrality in International Law", 16(2,3) DJILP 353 (1988) (hereinafter cited as Rubin, "Neutrality") at 366–371.

tried to find which were the ones which intuition or analysis of the impact of alternative rules on other values of the social order indicated to be the ones to govern a particular dispute.

It was also shown how the decision-makers of at least the Dutch and British political orders acknowledged the language of naturalism, but actually advised each other and made practical decisions and pursued diplomatic correspondence on the basis of assumed positivist, human discretion, exercised on the basis of analyses of interest including the likely reactions of foreign statesmen to various courses of action.

It was then shown how the framers of the American Constitution adopted the naturalist language while revealing considerable confusion and disagreement among themselves as to its meaning and its relationship to the realities of authority in a harshly competitive world.

These last two analyses illustrated also the general pattern of common law logic, building on history, experience, as a law-creating process in general disregard of moral principle. The concept of the *jus gentium* was revived, but not as an expression of morality argued from *a priori* principle. Instead, what dominated the jurisprudential horizon was the very notion that Aristotle and Suarez had rejected: the early sophist and second- to sixth-century AD Justinian-ian notion of an "objective" natural law, to be derived from an analysis of independent municipal law rules, achieved some influence. It was also apparently appealing to "positivist" statesmen to have a moral-free vocabulary that would refer them to the practice of states as a law-making process, and the phrase "law of nations" fitted the bill. Since the phrase was also acceptable to naturalist theorists and could be used to avoid resolving jurisprudential quarrels that did not need resolving in the real world, the phrase became a cover for a lot of notions, many of them incompatible with the others.

This mass of inconsistency was swallowed whole by the framers of our Constitution, but could not be digested. The first issues involved replacing with statutes various judge-made "common law crimes" relating to individual acts that, by violating what was conceived to be the "law of nations" in its *jus gentium* phase, would place the United States in violation of its obligations under an undifferentiated notion of the "law of nations" in its *jus inter gentes* phase. Of particular concern were the obligations of a "neutral" power in time of war among others. But the most enlightening illustration of the confusion rests not on defining as criminal those acts that could easily be translated into statutory crimes. It rests on the areas in which either statutory definition was found impossible to develop, or the consensus of the community could not be found to support legislation regardless of the opinions of judges as to the moral horrors involved in the acts of individuals that did not violate, or were beyond the reach of prescriptions uttered as part of, the municipal positive law. Thus, we now turn to the definition of "piracy," which had been widely thought to be the paradigmatic example of a "crime" under the "law of nations," and attempts to abolish the slave trade by arguing that the "law" must forbid activity so obviously immoral. The resolution of the incompatibilities of jurisprudential models was achieved by yet another legal invention: the conscious development of "choice-of-law" techniques within the elaborated framework of an approach called "conflict of laws." To these things we now turn.

Piracy

In England, the statute of 1700[33] defined "piracy" as a municipal law crime. It did not rest on any assertions of "*jus gentium*." Indeed, in one section the statute clearly departed from any notion of *jus gentium* by including in its definition of the crime the act of any British subject taking a license from a foreign authority to raid fellow Britons:

VIII . . . That if any of his Majesty's natural-born Subjects, or Denizens of this Kingdom, shall commit any . . . Act of Hostility, against others his Majesty's Subjects upon the Sea, under Colour of any Commission from any foreign Prince or State, or Pretence of Authority from any Person whatsoever, such Offender and Offenders, and every of them, shall be deemed . . . to be Pirates.

And the next section defines as pirates those who "shall lay violent hands on his Commander . . . or endeavour to make a Revolt in the Ship." Since "revolt" and "mutiny" occurring entirely within a single vessel have never been adjudged a crime by any law other than the law of the vessel's flag state, it is very difficult to see these sections as codifying any "universal" offense, although it might be supposed that the framers of the statute thought that all civilized states made such acts criminal, thus serving as evidence that they were part of the "law of nations." There is no evidence that such a view influenced the actual wording, passage or interpretation of the legislation. In general, "piracy" was regarded as neither more nor less than "robbery" as defined in English law, but committed within the jurisdiction of English admiralty tribunals.[34] The

---

[33] Cited at chapter 2, note 56 above.
[34] For a review of this entire subject, see Rubin, *Piracy, passim*. The statute is set out in Appendix I.B at 362–369; the background to its passage is set out at 69–78.

definition of "robbery" at English law was, and is now, subject to change at the whim of the legislators of English law: common law judges for common law offenses; Parliament for all offenses.

In the United States, it was pointed out above that in the debates in Philadelphia over the authority of the new federal legislature, the authority of the Congress to "define" offenses against the "law of nations" was proposed by Gouverneur Morris. Morris's proposal was immediately questioned by James Wilson on what seem the solid grounds that no single country has the authority under the "law of nations" in either its *jus inter gentes* or its *jus gentium* phase to define what is already defined by the practice and laws of other nations. Morris's counter-argument, not stated directly in Madison's notes of the discussion in Philadelphia, must have been jurisprudential, asserting that the international legal order and municipal law are not a single system but two legal systems existing simultaneously; that the definition embodied in the "law of nations" in any of its phases must be translated into a definition in municipal law to carry with it effects in the positive criminal law of any country. This dualist approach is implicit in the result; Morris's language passed, even though by the narrowest of margins.

The predicted problem arose immediately when Congress attempted to "define" the one offense that all had thought was unquestionable under the 1787 conception of the "law of nations" in any of its various meanings: "piracy."

The first American federal legislation implementing the authority of the Congress to "define and punish Piracies and Felonies committed on the high Seas, and Offenses against the Law of Nations" was the Act of 30 April 1790. Section 8 of that Act says, in pertinent part:

That, if any person or persons shall commit upon the high seas, or in any river, haven, basin or bay, out of the jurisdiction of any particular state, murder or robbery, or any other offence which if committed within the body of a county, would by the laws of the United States be punishable with death; or if any captain or mariner of any ship or other vessel, shall piratically and feloniously run away with such ship or vessel, or any goods or merchandise to the value of fifty dollars, or yield up such ship or vessel voluntarily to any pirate; or if any seaman shall lay violent hands upon his commander, thereby to hinder and prevent his fighting in defence of his ship or goods committed to his trust, or shall make a revolt in the ship; every such offender shall be deemed, taken and adjudged to be a pirate and felon and being thereof convicted, shall suffer death.[35]

---

[35] 1st Congress, 2nd Session, 1 Stat. 112.

Some anomalies are immediately apparent. The statute seems to borrow English notions of "county" jurisdiction as the limitation on admiralty jurisdiction and the term seems misplaced. Robbery or murder done wholly within a single ship seems to be "piracy," as does mutiny. But there is no evidence at all that such robberies or murders or mutinies have ever had anything to do with the "law of nations" or "piracy" except by the municipal laws of some states, certainly not of all or nearly all. There is no clear meaning to the adjective "piratically" or the conjoined adjective "feloniously." There is no indication how far the jurisdiction of the American tribunals is supposed to reach; if to apply to foreigners in foreign vessels, then there is an assumption of jurisdiction that surely the new country would not have been willing to concede to French or British officials stopping American ships on the high seas when no national interest of France or Great Britain had been affected. If not to reach foreigners in foreign vessels, then just how far was the legislation based on conceptions of the "law of nations" intended to reach? To adopt the universal jurisdiction approach implicit in the notion of *jus gentium* is to imply that a United States tribunal could and should apply an American municipal statutory definition of a "crime" to acts of foreigners abroad whose own country, or the flag state of their ship or any victim's country or flag state, does not define the identical acts as "criminal." And if that is proper, then again the problem of French and British officials extending their jurisdiction into American vessels to enforce French or British municipal law, or municipal versions of some unproved "law of nations," would be raised.

Other, more subtle problems, existed. Was a "privateer" to be considered a "pirate" if operating under letters of marque and reprisal issued by an unrecognized authority? Our very first experience with such things involved the British calling John Paul Jones a "pirate" when acting under license of the Continental Congress in 1779.[36] Many cases involving licensees of unrecognized regimes fighting against Spain for their independence in Latin America were to follow. Were American privateers under revolutionaries' licenses sailing out of Buenos Aires against only Spanish merchants to be hanged as "pirates" by United States tribunals?

The closer the substance of the supposed "law of nations" regarding "piracy" was examined, the more elusive it became. The closer to universal jurisdiction was asserted to enforce criminal statutes of un-

---

[36] 1 Moore, *Digest* at 168–169; 10 *Dictionary of American Biography* 185; Samuel Eliot Morison, *John Paul Jones* (New York: Time Reading Program, 1959) 252–254, 263–267.

certain content and doubtful substantive consensus, the more dangerous the precedent seemed.

An even deeper problem was arising. Between 1810 and 1820, the notion of "common law crimes" was being successfully challenged in all except "piracy" cases. In the 1813 United States Supreme Court case *United States v. Hudson and Goodwin*, Justice Joseph Story had concurred in an opinion by Justice William Johnson dismissing a criminal libel action against a Connecticut newspaper on the ground that no statute had been violated. "[A] majority of this court" (no dissents are recorded, so those who might have been in a minority are not identified; they left no easily available record of the reasons for their differing opinions) concluded that the lower federal courts of the United States had no authority to "exercise a common law jurisdiction in criminal cases."[37] Whether a "common law crime" had been committed was not decided; the issue was one of adjudicatory as distinguished from legislative (prescriptive) jurisdiction.

The issue next arose in *United States v. Coolidge*, an 1816 prize case involving the "rescue" by defendants while *en route* to an American port for adjudication of a vessel captured by American privateers. Justice Johnson, citing the 1813 case, indicated that he considered there to be no jurisdiction in the federal Circuit Court for this one, which he categorized as involving a "common law offense against the United States." Justice Joseph Story is recorded as responding: "I do not take the question to be settled by that case [*US v. Hudson and Goodwin*]." Justice Brockholst Livingston was prepared to hear argument on the point, but the Attorney-General refused to make the argument. Justice Johnson delivered the opinion of the court. He wrote that although there is a difference of opinion, and the court would have been willing to have heard the question argued, since "the Attorney-General has declined to argue the cause; and no counsel appears for the defendant" the 1813 decision will not be reviewed or drawn into doubt.[38] Except for piracy cases, no common law criminal case appears to have ever been heard by a federal court in the United States since that time.

As to "piracy" as a "common law crime" or crime under the *jus gentium*, things reached something of a breaking point when Peter Wiltberger, an American, killed a seaman on board an American ship at anchor in the Tigris River in China, about thirty-five miles upstream from the sea

---

[37] *US v. Hudson and Goodwin* 3 US (7 Cranch) 32 (1813).
[38] *US v. Coolidge* 14 US (1 Wheaton) 415 (1816).

(fourteen miles below Canton). His conviction under the quoted statute of 1790 was reversed by a unanimous Supreme Court in 1820 squarely on the ground that the positive prescriptions of United States criminal law did not apply; that the United States lacked jurisdiction over offenses committed within foreign territory even on board American vessels; that federal criminal law rested wholly on statute and it was irrelevant that the supposed offense might also be an offense under some theoretical *jus gentium*.[39] Indeed, case by case, the American courts found that the notion of a universal *jus gentium* was not sufficient basis to assert a prescriptive, adjudicatory or enforcement jurisdiction for experienced jurists concerned with the limitations of legal authority, a theoretical division between judicial, executive and legislative powers, and the interests of a young nation in establishing and defending its own intellectual and cultural independence as well as its political and legal equality with the older states of Europe.

While the *Wiltberger* case was working its way up to the Supreme Court, other cases leading to the same result were having their impact. The leading cases other than *Wiltberger* are *United States v. Palmer et al.* in 1818[40] and *United States v. Klintock* in 1820.[41] Chief Justice John Marshall wrote both opinions.

In the first, the court ruled *per curiam* that:

[T]he crime of robbery, committed by a person on the high seas, on board of any ship or vessel belonging exclusively to subjects of a foreign state, on persons within a vessel belonging also exclusively to subjects of a foreign state, is not piracy within the true intent and meaning of the [anti-Piracy Act of 1790] . . . and is not punishable in the courts of the United States.[42]

In the second, Klintock was convicted of "piracy" for a fraudulent (nonviolent) taking of a Danish ship. The court held that American prescriptions applied to Klintock as a person "acting in defiance of all law, and acknowledging obedience to no government whatsoever."[43]

Henry Wheaton, widely seen as the most learned American authority on public international law and the *jus gentium* during the age of John Marshall and Joseph Story, in a learned note after the *Wiltberger* case

---

[39] *US v. Wiltberger* 18 US (5 Wheaton) 76 (1820). The opinion by Chief Justice John Marshall was concurred in by Justice Joseph Story, the leading American academic admiralty scholar of the time.
[40] 16 US (3 Wheaton) 610 (1818); 8 *American International Law Cases* (hereinafter AILC) 1.
[41] 18 US (5 Wheaton) 144 (1820).   [42] 16 US 610 at 643; 8 AILC 1 at 18.
[43] 18 US 144 at 152. For more background on these cases, see Rubin, *Piracy* Chapter III, especially 140–141.

argued that it should be interpreted restrictively, held to its precise terms, not to deny that the Congress could make laws to govern the acts of foreigners abroad, including criminal laws to enforce the *jus gentium*, only that the Supreme Court was not satisfied that in its legislation the Congress had done so.[44] But the precedents pertinent to an opinion regarding public international law in its *jus inter gentes* phase relate to state behavior, and not merely to the judicial opinions of national courts. So the very failure of the Congress to make such legislation as Wheaton argued to be within its authority seems evidence that the Congress itself either doubted the proper reach of its prescriptive authority under the Constitution; or doubted that the international legal order would accept that the municipal legal order established by the Constitution could support the extension of United States prescriptive jurisdiction to acts of foreigners abroad when no identifiably American interest was involved. It is also likely that the Congress was concerned more to protect its territorial and nationality jurisdiction over Americans from British, French and other encroachments on the ground of reciprocity, than it was about Wheaton's notions of the social value of suppressing "universal crimes."

Wheaton himself had trouble maintaining the naturalist-monist model of the legal order that he had posed in commenting on the *Wiltberger* decision. When the British proposed various international policing arrangements and tribunals to enforce their notion of the developing law forbidding the international trade in humans, the international slave trade, Wheaton opposed the notion of universal common law crimes and wrote an elaborate brief restricting his broader view to "piracy."[45] By 1836, when Wheaton's great text on international law was published, he had already realized that his earlier views regarding the authority of municipal institutions to enforce a supposedly universal criminal law were not widely acceptable. He maintained that national enforcement could still apply to cases of "piracy as defined by the law of nations," but to little, if anything, else.[46] In fact, it has not been adopted since

---

[44] 18 US (5 Wheaton) 76 (1820) at 106–116.

[45] Henry Wheaton, *Enquiry into the Validity of the British Claim to a Right of Visitation and Search of American Vessels Suspected to be Engaged in the African Slave Trade* (Philadelphia: Lea & Blanchard, 1842) (hereinafter cited as Wheaton, *Enquiry*). I am very grateful to Mr. Jarat Chopra of Brown University for bringing this work to my attention. Brown University is the depository of Wheaton's papers.

[46] See Henry Wheaton, *Elements of International Law* (text of 1836 with commentary by Charles Henry Dana, 1866, and additional commentary by George Grafton Wilson, Carnegie Endowment, Classics of International Law, 1936) sections 124–125 at 162–164.

Wheaton's time even in piracy cases.[47] But a discussion of that evolution will have to wait until after legal aspects of the British anti-slave trade movement are analyzed below.

Later American cases asserting that substantive rules of public international law are part of the law of the United States must be read with these early cases and practices in mind. Prize cases seem well based in tradition when retaining the term "law of nations" insofar as they relate to the likely universal acceptance of their title adjudications. There is a remnant of the *jus gentium* in the judge-made rules administered as the law of prize. Statements by American prize courts that their rules illustrate a much broader proposition, the general penetration of American municipal law by the substantive rules of international law in either its *jus gentium* or *jus inter gentes* phase,[48] seem exaggerations. As applied to prize and some phases of admiralty, they can be supported, but it seems to read *dicta* much further than common law tradition normally allows to treat these statements of prize law principle to illustrate a revival of monistic jurisprudential theories that were rejected by the Supreme Court as part of American Constitutional law from the earliest days when the attention of the court was focused on such issues.

In *US v. Palmer et al.*[49] the Supreme Court denied to the courts of the United States jurisdiction over the acts of foreigners (Palmer and his two associates had English or Irish-sounding names, but were not identified by nationality in the opinions by either Chief Justice Marshall or by Justice William Johnson except to deny that they were Americans) against other foreigners (again, not identified by nationality in this case) outside the United States in the absence of precise direction by the Congress, apprehending openly that if the exercise of enforcement jurisdiction by the United States should bring it into conflict with foreign states, it

---

[47] See Rubin, *Piracy* 162–188, 292–346.

[48] E.g., The *Paquete Habana*, The *Lola*, 175 US 677 (1900). Even here, a close reading of this oft-quoted prize case supports the dualist model the Supreme Court had adopted in the early decisions of Chief Justice John Marshall: "This rule of international law is one which prize courts, administering the law of nations, are bound to take judicial notice of, and to give effect to, *in the absence of any . . . public act of their own government in relation to the matter*" (emphasis added). *Cf.* Phillip Trimble, "A Revisionist View of Customary International Law," 33(3) UCLALR 665 (1986) *passim*, especially 684–687, 723–725. To maintain a "monist" model in the light of this language, it would be necessary to argue that the municipal act superseding an international legal obligation in municipal law also nullified that obligation as a matter of international law. The complexities of any rationalization of such a model, while not impossible, would implicate Occam's Razor.

[49] Cited note 40 above.

should be by direction of the political arms of government, not by the courts asserting a universal jurisdiction to adjudicate or the courts reviving Story's hankering for a continued authority in the courts to define, adjudicate and punish common law crimes. Justice William Johnson dissented from the implication that even the legislature had the authority to extend American prescriptive jurisdiction that way, construing the reach of the legal order established by the United States Constitution to be limited in its own reach by the international legal order.[50]

The response of the Congress was not to draft tighter legislation as the positivists might have preferred, but to go all the way towards adopting the undefined *jus gentium* regarding "piracy" into United States federal criminal law. The Act of 1790 was supplemented by section 5 of the Act of 3 March 1819:

That if any person or persons whatsoever, shall, on the high seas, commit the crime of piracy, *as defined by the law of nations* [emphasis added], and such offender or offenders, shall afterwards be brought into or found in the United States, every such offender or offenders shall upon conviction therefor . . . be punishable with death.[51]

This statute was held valid in *United States v. Smith*, a unanimous opinion written by Justice Joseph Story.[52] The jurisdictional problems that had affected the outcome in *Wiltberger* (an American acting "piratically" in Chinese waters) and *Palmer* (a foreigner acting against other foreign interests on the high seas) were not raised. Smith was an American acting on the high seas. But as to the substantive law, Story's reasoning follows the usual common law pattern: an analysis of the leading "piracy" cases and writings of his time. It ignores the rejection of the notion of "common law crimes" by the Supreme Court against his expressed views in *US v. Hudson and Goodwin* and *US v. Coolidge*;[53] it uses language broader even than Wheaton's notion of "piracy" being exceptional, and supports the notion of a substantive *jus gentium* directly applicable in American courts. Thus, as to substance, it adopts for this piracy case the "monist" position narrowly rejected by the Constitutional Convention. Its effect

---

[50] Ibid., 630–631, 632–633, 641–642.
[51] 15th Congress, 2nd Session, chapter 77, 3 Stat. 510 at 513– 514.
[52] *US v. Smith*, 18 US (5 Wheaton) 20 (1820). This was only the first of a long series of cases that had been held up pending a determination of the validity of the statute. They are reported severally in a series called *US v. Pirates* 18 US (5 Wheaton) 184 (1820). See Rubin, *Piracy* 146*ff.* for a summary of all of them.
[53] Cited at note 31 above.

was to give to judges the authority under a generous statute to define the crime after the fact in particular cases under the usual common law rationale that the "crime" had already been defined by earlier cases and learned writings even though not by legislatures in the municipal order; to revive "common law crimes" in the case of alleged "piracy." But it did not overrule the jurisdictional basis for Wiltberger's and Palmer's discharges.

Story apparently believed that the "law of nations" conceptually served as a reservoir of "common law" crimes, of which "piracy" was one example. But his vigorous and able urging and the acceptance of his view in a few later "piracy" cases were not able in the long run to overcome the inconsistency of this model of the legal order with the distribution of authority into which nearly all other jurists and statesmen felt themselves forced when they had to deal with facts.[54] The substantive prescriptions could not be applied to foreigners acting solely against foreign interests abroad; jurisdiction to prescribe a definition and legal results for what was conceived as a "universal" offense did not necessarily imply jurisdiction to adjudicate, even when the defendant had been properly brought within the court's jurisdiction to enforce.

The statute of 1819 remains in force as municipal law for the United States only. There have been no trials under the statute for over a hundred years, and its continued effect is not clear. In the 1982 edition of the US Code, the following "Historical and Revision Note" appears above the definition:

In the light of far-reaching developments in the field of international law and foreign relations, the law of piracy is deemed to require a fundamental reconsideration and complete restatement, perhaps resulting in drastic changes by way of modification and expansion . . . It is recommended . . . that at some opportune time in the near future, the subject of piracy be entirely reconsidered and the law bearing on it modified and restated in accordance with the needs of the times.[55]

As to the substantive law, all attempts to codify the supposed universal "law of nations" defining "piracy" on the level of treaty have failed to produce a comprehensible definition.[56] Meantime, as to jurisdiction to

---

[54] For the evolution of the piracy cases and Story's persuasiveness, see Rubin, *Piracy* 144*ff*.

[55] 18 USC section 1651. See Alfred P. Rubin, "Revising the Law of Piracy", 21(1) CWILJ 129–137 (1990–91).

[56] Rubin, *Piracy* 305*ff*. includes an analysis of all the proposals that have achieved any degree of significant attention, including the text of the 1982 United Nations Convention on the Law of the Sea. It is not necessary to repeat that analysis here.

adjudicate, there has been no convincing evidence of any change in the restrictions placed by the international legal order on national tribunals with regard to the acts of foreigners against foreign interests outside the territorial or maritime jurisdiction of the forum state.[57]

To summarize, it appears that by 1816 judicial and executive conceptions in the United States had closed serious argument about the authority of lower judges in the federal court system to define "common law crimes" except, perhaps, in the case of "piracy." However, the notion that "piracy" was such a common law crime survived in the guise of using common law techniques to put substance into a statute bringing an otherwise undefined crime of "piracy" into the jurisdiction to adjudicate of the lower federal courts. On the other hand, all attempts from 1790 to the present to codify the supposed *jus gentium* making "piracy" a universal crime have failed. Although the current United States legislation leaves the elements of the "crime" to judges to construe as if part of the common law, it passed against a background that included a limit on American adjudicatory jurisdiction making it doubtful that it could apply to the act of a foreigner against other foreigners in foreign vessels. This jurisdictional interpretation restricts the interpretation of the supposed "crime" under the "law of nations" to a matter of American municipal law, and makes a true test of the conformity of the American interpretations of the supposed *jus gentium* unlikely, if not impossible. In any case, changes in the notion of "due process" and the rôle of judges in defining "crimes," thus "common law crimes," mean that the current American legislation defining "piracy" by reference to the "law of nations" is unlikely to pass Constitutional muster today.

Two other incidents in the earliest grapplings of the American founding generation with the complexities of *jus gentium* theory as applied to accusations of "piracy" must be noted before the impact of the theory on attempts to abolish the international traffic in chattel slaves can be understood. The first is the general view of Chief Justice John Marshall and the Supreme Court in 1804, when a Danish privateer under French

---

[57] This view is denied by some commentators based on two cases in which American and German tribunals have applied their versions of "universal" law to the acts of Middle Eastern "terrorists" whose states of nationality were in no position politically to protest. I doubt that such cases will amount to "precedents" when sought to be applied to American or German or other political activists, but the point will surely be raised. See David M. Kennedy, Torsten Stein and Alfred P. Rubin, "The Extradition of Mohammed Hamadei," 31(1) HILJ 5 (1990) (hereinafter cited as Kennedy, Stein and Rubin, *Hamadei*) esp. pp. 27–35.

license was held not to have violated American legislation of 1800 forbidding intercourse with France during the "undeclared war" of 1798–1800.[58] The second was the handling in the new American constitutional system of the filibustering voyage of *Romp*, where the federal officials seem to have badly misconstrued the authority of the United States under the statutes and *jus gentium* relating to "piracy."[59]

As to the first, the issue as seen by Chief Justice Marshall and what appears to have been a unanimous Supreme Court involved only the construction of American federal legislation. The question was whether under that legislation the construction of the vessel *Jane* in the United States, even though it was then sold to a Danish national who changed its name to *Charming Betsy*, was a sufficient contact with the United States to bring into play an American statute forbidding "all commercial intercourse" with France. If so, then the American captor, Captain Murray of the famous frigate *Constellation*, was entitled to the value of the ship and cargo under the "non-intercourse law." If not, then the value of the vessel and cargo would have to be rendered to its Danish owner and Captain Murray and his people would be entitled only to salvage – the value of whatever services they had performed in rescuing her from French captors who were taking her in to a French prize court to determine whether she was subject to French capture under the French interpretation of the "law of nations" relating to maritime trade at the time; a question that would depend on the French prize court's conclusion as to French relations, belligerent or otherwise, with the flag state, and whether that state were to be Denmark, the United States or some other.[60] Marshall stated what must have seemed a platitudinous rule under the *jus gentium* conceptions of the time:

[A]n act of Congress ought never to be construed to violate the law of nations if any other possible construction remains and, consequently, can never be construed to violate neutral rights, or to affect neutral commerce, further than is warranted by the law of nations as understood in this country.[61]

---

[58] *Murray* v. *The Charming Betsy* 6 US 208, 2 Cranch 64 (1804).
[59] See Rubin, *Piracy* 157–162.
[60] This was not an unusual situation. The anticipation that a French prize court would free a neutral vessel improperly seized by a French privateer lay also at the base of the leading American cases holding the "law of nations" to require all states to apply identical "prize" law when there was in fact organized public military activity even if there were no "declaration of war" as envisaged by the Constitution. See *Bas* v. *Tingy* 4 US (4 Dallas) 37 (1800); *Talbot* v. *Seeman* 5 US 15, 1 Cranch 1 (1801).
[61] *Murray* v. *The Charming Betsy* 6 US 226, 2 Cranch 116.

Under that construction, the Supreme Court held the action by Captain Murray to have been improper. Indeed, he was held to owe a considerable sum to the Danish owner.[62]

The voyage of *Romp* illustrates the confusion implicit in *jus gentium* theory when the "recognition" power of the executive branch of government, the authority to attach legal labels for the sake of foreign policy, conflicts with the authority of the judiciary to attach legal labels based on legal traditions in disregard of political interests. *Romp* of Baltimore sailed against Spanish and Portuguese shipping under a privateering license issued by the unrecognized but effective revolutionary government in "Buenos Ayres" in the second decade of the nineteenth century. In 1817, under the name *Santafecino*, she was seized by a United States naval vessel and the crew charged with "piracy" in an American court. John Marshall, sitting as a federal Circuit Judge in the criminal proceeding,[63] sent the question to the jury as to whether the commissions issued by an unrecognized government were legally effective to relieve the "Baltimore pirates" from the charge of "piracy" under the American legislation of 1790. It took the jury only ten minutes to acquit the crew of *Romp*.[64]

The officers of the Executive Branch were nonplussed. When a similar case involving a license issued by Mexican authorities rebelling against Spain reached the Supreme Court the next year, Marshall summarized the legal situation saving as well as he could the authority of the political branches to attach politically sensitive legal labels:

[W]hen a civil war rages in a foreign nation, one part of which separates itself from the old established government, and erects itself into a distinct government, the courts of the union must view such newly constituted government as it is viewed by the legislative and executive departments of the government of the United States. If the government of the union remains neutral, but recognizes the existence of a civil war, the courts of the union cannot consider as criminal those acts of hostility, which war authorizes, and which the new government directs against its enemy.[65]

Marshall left open a major question: What happens when the legal categories applied by the legislative and executive departments of govern-

---

[62] A note in the end of the official report says that Captain Murray was reimbursed his damages, interest and charges out of the treasury of the United States, by an act of Congress on 31 January 1805: 6 US 229, 2 Cranch 126.

[63] The arrangement by which Supreme Court justices sat in federal Circuit Courts under the Judicature Act of 1789 is mentioned at note 28 above.

[64] *US* v. *Hutchings et al.* 26 Fed. Cas. 440, No. 15,429 (1817).

[65] *US* v. *Palmer et al.* 16 US (3 Wheaton) 610 (1818).

ment depart from the realities demonstrated to the judiciary, as when an unrecognized belligerent acts in conformity with the laws of war under the *jus inter gentes*? Is a revolution "illegal" under the *jus inter gentes* or the *jus gentium* until the defending sovereign concedes that the separating rebels are "belligerents"? What a strange position for the United States to take under a Chief Justice appointed by John Adams, a hero of our own revolution! And European notions of "legitimacy" and the claims of the "Holy Alliance" to authority to determine which "rebels" are criminals and which patriots were never persuasive in the United States.

But under these opinions the *jus gentium* could no longer be (if it ever had been) regarded as a rule of the legal order binding the courts regardless of the wishes of the political branches of the American government. The "dualist" system was effectively established under which the "law" administered by the judiciary of the United States was to be the law of the United States regardless of the *jus gentium*, although the *jus gentium* could still be referred to as a clue to the judicial interpretation of positive legislation by the Congress.

The leading figures of the political branches of government were not at all satisfied with this result. The first attack accepted Marshall's dualist model of the legal order but disputed the court's interpretation of United States municipal law. The question of whether the Neutrality Act of 1794 conformed to the *jus gentium* was not addressed. But on 6 November 1818, just after the ruling came down in the case of *Palmer*, a foreign licensee of an unrecognized authority, William Wirt, the Attorney General in James Monroe's Cabinet, attempted to argue that the American "piracy" statute of 1790 must apply to cases of privateers whose licenses could not have been legally issued in the United States under the prohibitions of the federal Neutrality Act of 1794. If that failed, he advised the federal District Attorney for Baltimore, Elias Glenn,[66] then perhaps it would be criminal under the federal legislation of 1817 forbidding the fitting-out of vessels in the United States for use against a political order or people with whom the Union were at peace.[67] In the case prosecuted by Wirt and Glenn in Baltimore shortly after, these arguments were rejected and the defendants were acquitted without the jury leaving their seats. Secretary of State

---

[66] 1 ATTGO 181, opinion dated 6 November 1818.

[67] Act of 3 March 1817, 3 Stat. 370. The history of the United States neutrality acts as they applied to accusations of "piracy" in the early nineteenth century is retailed in Rubin, *Piracy* at 194–195. Rubin, "Neutrality" sets out a wider analysis of the evolution of American neutrality legislation.

John Quincy Adams was reportedly furious with all involved in the losing prosecution.[68]

The various confusions regarding the place of the "law of nations" in the regime of statute and criminal law applied by American courts were accompanied by a shift in language. Bentham's suggestion that the phrase "law of nations" was more confusing than helpful and should be replaced by the phrase "international law" when the *jus inter gentes* was intended, was slowly being adopted.[69] In several cases in 1815, the United States Supreme Court formally referred to "international law" where "law of nations" had been the phrase that would have been expected under the dominant legal theories of the end of the eighteenth century. Almost all are admiralty and prize cases. There are twenty-seven such uses between 1815 and 1834.[70] Some confusion remains evident until 1834, but that involves factors to be considered later. In light of his writings' later importance to the evolution of language and concept, it should perhaps be mentioned here that Joseph Story joined the Supreme Court in 1811.

While the leading political figures of American government were unhappy that the judicial system did not reflect their view of the *jus gentium*, making criminal whatever activities they felt embarrassed the United States politically, the judiciary were discovering that *jus gentium* theory did not go beyond "piracy" to translate their moral convictions into rules that could make immoral behavior "criminal" under the law applied by American courts. The great arena of debate involved the international slave trade.

The slave trade
American dilemmas
The sale of a person's labor, even for a period of years after the conclusion of the contract of sale, has always been permitted by English law. Apprenticeship and other long-term service contracts, including inden-

---

[68] The entire case is discussed incisively in Walker Lewis, "John Quincy Adams and the Baltimore 'Pirates'" 67 ABAJ 1011 (1981). It is summarized from the perspective of its impact on the evolution of American anti-"piracy" legislation in Rubin, *Piracy*, 160–162.

[69] See p. 68 above

[70] Result of a Lexis search. It seems unnecessary in this place to list all twenty-seven cases and analyze the differences as the vocabulary slowly changed. But it might be significant in light of later confusions to note that as early as 1822 in one brief submitted to the court, counsel argued that the conceptions of "international law" applicable in prize seem different from the conceptions as they might be applied in other areas of the law: *Dorr v. The Pacific Insurance Co.* 20 US 581 (1822).

tures of future service to pay for ship-passage, were well known and enforced. But chattel slavery, the appropriation by law of a person's body to be treated as a chattel at the discretion of another as if a domestic animal or inanimate object, elicited a moral revulsion in the eighteenth century that was quite a different matter. Presumably this revulsion played a rôle in Lord Mansfield's conclusion in England in 1772 that "slavery" was not a status supported by law in England and that therefore a Virginia slave was free when in England and could not be compelled by law to return with his "master" to the West Indies.[71] But the status of a chattel slave was not abolished in the colonies by this decision.[72] That had to await an Act of Parliament in 1833,[73] put into effect at midnight on 31 July 1834 and not fully effective to abolish chattel slavery as a status until 1838.[74]

Meantime, in 1807 Parliament had enacted legislation punishing with a fine of £100 per slave recovered, "all manner of dealing and trading" in slaves in Africa or in their transport from Africa to any other place.[75] The British legislation, including an Act of 1824 analogizing trading in slaves to "piracy,"[76] applied only to British subjects.

In the young United States too, the evils of the slave trade, i.e., the transportation of human beings as chattels across national boundaries, were considered evils of a different and more severe order than the maintenance of a status of chattel slavery, including that status when

---

[71] *Somersett's Case*, 20 *Howell's State Trials* 82 (1772). William Murray (1705–1793) became Chief Justice of the King's Bench in 1756 as Baron Mansfield of Mansfield. He was made 1st Earl of Mansfield in 1776. For an analysis of another of his innovative and far-reaching decisions, see pp. 131–133 below.

[72] The relationship between English common law and the law of the various colonies was from early on categorized in a rigidly positivist mode. See R. T. E. Latham, *The Law and the Commonwealth* (Oxford, 1937, reprinted by Greenwood Press, 1970) 510–520. Legislative powers granted to colonial legislatures were not regarded as subject to review in England by the common law courts applying their conceptions of social-value-based morality as natural law. The Privy Council, which did hear appeals from colonial courts, was an administrative tribunal set up under the Crown and it applied its version of "law" relatively little influenced by the "rule of reason" or other common law expressions of supposedly universal "natural law" although, of course, national pride and the common law training of many judges sitting in Privy Council appeals cases come through in particular choices of language from time to time.

[73] 3 & 4 Will. IV, c. 73 (1833).

[74] The entire tale is too complex to be summarized intelligibly in short compass. See Reginald Coupland, *The British Anti-Slavery Movement* (London, 1933) *passim*.

[75] 47 Geo. III, session 1, c. 36 (1807). This Act was supplemented by another in 1811, 51 Geo. III, c. 23 (1811), raising the penalty for that participation to transportation to Botany Bay, the penal colony in Australia.

[76] 5 Geo. IV, c. 17 (1824).

derived from birth to a slave. Indeed, the American Constitution of 1787 acknowledges the continuance of slavery in the peculiar form of allowing representatives and direct taxes to be determined on a *per capita* basis counting all "free persons, including those bound to service for a term of years [i.e., contract laborers and indentured servants], and excluding Indians not taxed," but including "three-fifths of all other persons" (meaning chattel slaves).[77] The framers of the Constitution acknowledged the especial evils of the trade in slaves between the United States and any foreign country. They provided a compromise between the maintenance of that trade as legal under the positive law of the individual States of the proposed Union, and its abolition as a moral abomination under views widely accepted in the Union as a whole. Apparently, even among those who thought the benefits of the status (benefits to the economic interests of the dominant elites in that time and place and supposed economic and spiritual benefits to the slaves themselves) outweighed its evils, there was some discomfort regarding the international traffic in chattel slaves.

The new Constitution of 1787 provided for sanctity of contract, including contracts of indentured service. It provided that:

No person held in service or labor in one State, under the laws thereof, escaping into another, shall, in consequence of any law or regulation therein, be discharged from such service or labor, but shall be delivered up on claim of the party to whom such service or labor may be due.[78]

As applied to contract labor and indentured service, this provision offended no known eighteenth-century moral scruples. But it did raise questions when applied to a legal status created not by contract between persons of legally equal status, but by operation of legislation independently of contract; legislation that even denied the capacity of one of the parties to make a contract at all. Some people opposed to slavery and the slave trade interpreted the word "service" to exclude "servitude" and found in the Constitutional debates of 1787 a basis for holding only the latter word to refer to the condition of slaves, thereby making this provision irrelevant to the return of fugitive slaves.[79] Others, including Joseph Story, whose moral opposition to slavery and the slave trade

---

[77] United States Constitution, Article I, section 2, clause 2.

[78] Ibid., Article IV, section 2, clause 3.

[79] In another provision (Article I, section 2), "On motion of Mr. Randolph the word 'servitude' was struck out, and 'service' (unanimously) inserted, the former being thought to express the condition of slaves, & the latter the obligations of free persons": 2 Max Ferrand, *The Records of the Federal Convention of 1787*, at 607, Madison's notes for 13 September 1787.

cannot be questioned, interpreted this provision to involve the federal government in upholding that evil institution in the Union as part of the price anti-slavery people would have to pay for the benefits of the overall union.[80] The issue now seems to be moot in the United States.[81]

Whatever the interpretation of this Constitutional provision, the sense of moral outrage at the status of chattel slaves was not sufficient in the thirteen American colonies as a whole to overcome the reluctance in some of them to tamper with what seemed a successful economic and social institution. Even the international traffic in chattel slaves could not be immediately forbidden. Neither could it be maintained in the new Union. The compromise was simply to delay its abolition to a future (but not too distant) time. The new Constitution provided that the Congress of the Union could not enact legislation forbidding the international traffic in slaves, but that that prohibition on Congressional legislation would expire twenty years from the Constitution's entry into force:

> The migration or importation of such persons as any of the States now existing shall think proper to admit, shall not be prohibited by the Congress prior to the year one thousand eight hundred and eight, but a tax may be imposed on such importation, not exceeding ten dollars for each person.[82]

The third and succeeding federal Congresses construed narrowly the Constitutional prohibition on the Congress forbidding the importation of chattel slaves. The prohibitions on Americans engaging in the international slave trade were accomplished with rather evasive language regarding the importation of slaves into the United States, reflecting legal complications involving the authority of individual states of the Union under the new federal system. From 1808 until the Emancipation Proclamation of 1 January 1863 and the 1868 Amendment to the Constitution following the Civil War of 1861–1865, the usual legal formulation was

---

[80] "Historically, it is well known, that the object of this clause was to secure to the citizens of the slave-holding state the complete right and title of ownership in their slaves": *Prigg* v. *Pennsylvania*, 41 US (16 Pet.) 539 (1842) at 611. Whatever the truth of the "well-known" interpretation, it had become unquestionable by the time middle-of-the-century tribunals attributed to the Congress the intention to implement it in the Fugitive Slave Act of 1793 (1 Stat. 302). See *Jones* v. *Van Zandt* 46 US (5 How.) 215, 229 (1847); *Moore* v. *Illinois* 55 US (14 How.) 13 (1853); *Ableman* v. *Booth* 62 US (21 How.) 506 (1859). I am very much indebted to Professor Christopher Pyle of Mt. Holyoke College for much data and argument, correcting some misconceptions of my own on this point.

[81] The Constitutional provision appears to have been impliedly repealed by the Thirteenth Amendment, forbidding "slavery" and "involuntary servitude" in the United States. *Cf. Clyatt* v. *United States* 197 US 207 (1905).

[82] United States Constitution, Article I, section 9, clause 1.

that slavery was inconsistent with universal natural law, but could be permitted by particular positive law, and in the southern states of the American union such positive law was effective.[83]

Although the trade itself could not be forbidden under the new Constitution until 1808, the participation of Americans or American-built vessels in that trade was made both criminal and subject to what looks like a tort action or a form of reward by Act of the Congress in 1794.[84] On 3 March 1800 the Act of 1794 was substantially strengthened by making criminal and subject to two years' imprisonment and a fine of up to $2,000 the act of any citizen or resident of the United States serving on board a foreign slaver. Even holding a financial interest in such a foreign vessel was made subject to a penalty of double the value of the interest in the vessel and slaves and all American vessels involved in the foreign slave trade were to be forfeited, with the value of the vessels when sold to be distributed half to the public treasury and half to the captors as if privateers.[85] To the degree the Congress focused on the point, the statute is restricted in its application to American nationals, American residents, American flag vessels and, in general, to persons and things within the reach of American jurisdiction as the concept existed at the time. Not all the language of the Act is entirely clear, particularly the parts dealing with the distribution of the "prize" money when in fact the laws of war and

---

[83] *Cf.* Opinion of Justice John McLean (Ohio) dissenting in *Scott* v. *Sandford* (the *Dred Scott Case*) 60 US 393 (1857), 529 at 534: "The state of slavery is deemed to be a mere municipal regulation, founded upon and limited to the range of territorial laws." The Emancipation Proclamation, 12 Stat. 1268–1269, applied only in a state or part of a state of the Union, "the people whereof shall then be in rebellion against the United States." It purported to be an exercise of the constitutional power of the President as commander-in-chief of the army and navy as a "war measure for suppressing said rebellion." There are difficulties under the Constitution in the President acting alone to abolish the property rights of slave-owners in the states directly; it was the position of the Union that sedentary property rights are matters for the states alone to decide, that the purported secession of the southern states was a legal nullity and that there was no "war" (there had been no Congressional declaration of war). The key post-war legal adjustment was the adoption in 1868 of the Thirteenth Amendment to the Constitution abolishing slavery as a status for the entire Union: "Neither slavery nor involuntary servitude, except as a punishment for crime, whereof the party shall have been duly convicted, shall exist within the United States, or any place subject to their jurisdiction."

[84] 1 Stat. 347, 3rd Congress, lst Session chapter 11, Act of 22 March 1794. The penalty for violation was the condemnation of the vessel, a fine of $2,000 against the entrepreneurs involved, half to go to the government and the other half to "him or her who shall sue for and prosecute the same," and $200 per slave transported, again divided between the government and the persons who prosecute.

[85] 2 Stat. 16, 6th Congress, 1st Session, chapter 14, Act of 3 March 1800.

letters of marque and reprisal were not applied to the capture of slavers. The enthusiasm of the Congress seems to have outrun its draftsmanship.

On 10 May 1800 another statute forbade Americans or foreigners residing in the United States to have any financial interest in any slaving voyage or voluntarily serving on a slave-carrying vessel even between two foreign ports. Navy vessels of the United States were authorized to seize any slave-carrying vessel, with no stated restriction as to the place or flag of the vessel intercepted. Two years' imprisonment were added to the $2,000 fine as a potential penalty.

On 28 February 1803 it was made a criminal offense to "import or bring, or cause to be imported or brought, any Negro, Mulatto, or other Person of colour, not being a Native, a Citizen, or registered Seaman of The United States" or native of a country "beyond the Cape of Good Hope." But this federal prohibition on the entry of West African natives into the Union was modified by reference to the States; it applied as federal law only with regard to ports or places situated in a state of the Union which by its own law had prohibited the admission of a "Person of colour." Thus it seems to have been calculated to implement in the exclusive federal realm the powers necessary to help enforce State laws as they applied to a special type of foreign trade.[86]

The statute that finally prohibited absolutely the importation of slaves into any place within the jurisdiction of the United States from and after 1 January 1808 was the Act of 2 March 1807.[87]

The jurisdictional issues were posed in their most dramatic form first by Justice Joseph Story, sitting as a judge in the federal District Court in Massachusetts in an 1822 admiralty case.[88] An American naval vessel had seized a French slaver, *La Jeune Eugénie*, off the coast of Africa. Apparently, there were no slaves on board the vessel when it was seized, or, if there had been, they had been set free; in any case, the disposition of the vessel alone was at issue when it was brought into Massachusetts for adjudi-

---

[86] Normally, a state of the United States cannot legally control imports and exports either between itself and another state of the Union or between itself and a foreign country. The evolution of interpretation of the American Constitution's "commerce" and other clauses lies well beyond the scope of this study. The "commerce clause" of the Constitution, Article I, section 8, clause 3: "The Congress shall have power . . . [to] regulate commerce with foreign nations, and among the several States, and with the Indian tribes."

[87] 10th Congress, 1st Session, chapter 22. A convenient reprinting of these statutes except for the Act of 3 March 1800 is in 1(2) BFSP (1812–1814) 984–993 (1841).

[88] The role of Supreme Court Justices in these cases was set out in sections 4 and 11 of the Judicature Act of 1789. See note 28 above.

cation as to title under the American Anti-Slave Trade Act of 10 May 1800 and general admiralty law. The French consul claimed the vessel on behalf of its French owners. He argued that the United States had no jurisdiction over the vessel even if it had been involved in the slave trade in violation of American and French law because American law was inapplicable to a French ship, and French courts alone had the legal authority to apply the French anti-slave-trade statute.

In his decision, Story first pointed out that the ownership of the vessel was very much in doubt, since it was indisputably American built and owned until two years before, and the documents of transfer seemed defective. Thus he was prepared to ground the entire action on the applicability of the American anti-slave-trade laws. But, in his deep detestation of the slave trade, he preferred to go further. Asserting the Blackstone view that the law applied by admiralty courts is part of the "law of nations," he referred to himself as "Sitting . . . in a court of the law of nations" and considered what he would do if that law, rather than the American statutory law, applied.[89]

Acknowledging that the status of slavery existed even in the United States at that time, he differentiated the positive law permitting that status from the natural law that he believed forbade its creation; thus forbidding the African slave trade. He distinguished away the apparently contrary British admiralty precedent of the *Le Louis* case,[90] indicating that even if the distinctions he saw were not persuasive, he would be compelled simply to disagree with the opinion of the British judge, Sir William Scott, in that case. His conclusion was that the slave trade is a trade "prohibited by universal law, and by the law of France, and that, therefore, the claim of the asserted French owners must be rejected." That being said, he nonetheless delivered the vessel to the French consul "to be dealt with according to his own sense of duty and right."[91]

[89] *United States* v. *La Jeune Eugénie* 26 Fed. Cas. 832, No. 15,551 (D. Mass., 1822), reproduced photographically in 1 AILC 144.
[90] To be discussed below. The *Le Louis* (High Court of Admiralty) 2 Dodson 210 (1817) involved a capture by a British naval vessel of a French slaver and its release by the British admiralty tribunal on the ground of lack of jurisdiction to apply British penal law in a French ship or French penal law in a British tribunal, and no right to arrest a foreign vessel in time of peace (i.e., not in the exercise of a belligerent right to visit a neutral vessel and take it in for prize court adjudication under European notions of the "law of nations"). It should be mentioned again that admiralty tribunals were conceived at this time, and indeed, in many cases today, as applying a universal *jus gentium*; that all admiralty tribunals in all jurisdictions should come to the same substantive results in all cases because applying identical, universal rules of law.
[91] 1 AILC 146, 153.

Of course, his handing the vessel over to the libellant (claimant in an admiralty adjudication) precluded any appeal, since the "losing" party actually got what he had wanted from the tribunal, the vessel; apparently the captor of the ship, as an American naval officer, was not entitled directly to prize money under the pertinent statutes, and the Attorney General of the United States chose not to dispute the result.

But the United States precedents did not stop there. Story's approach could not withstand examination by the Supreme Court. Although the *La Jeune Eugénie* decision was not appealed, three years later Story was unable to avoid a full Supreme Court hearing on the substantive issue of whether the slave trade was forbidden as a matter of universal natural law, or whether the laws of the United States and other countries were to be conceived as positive law not subject to the test of referral to such sources of the "law of nations" as might appeal to judges' consciences.

The government of newly independent Venezuela had issued letters of marque and reprisal to a privateer whose officers and most of whose crew were Americans. In the course of her depredations against Spanish and Portuguese vessels as part of the Latin American wars of independence, she acquired their cargoes of African slaves. Various vicissitudes interrupted the voyage, but the upshot was that an American, Captain John Smith (*sic*), and his ship, *Antelope*, were brought into the American port of Savannah by an American revenue cutter. The slaves were claimed by the Portuguese and Spanish Vice-Consuls as the property of their nationals. They were also claimed by Smith as his property in prize under the international laws of war (i.e., the laws applied by the self-defined "civilized" states as part of the supposedly universal "law of nations" in time of war) including the law applicable to privateering. They were also claimed by the United States under the national positive law, the Acts of 3 March and 10 May 1800, to be given their freedom; whether Smith and the other Americans in his ship would be punished under the Acts of 1800 was not submitted to the court in this *in rem* proceeding.

The captain of the revenue cutter filed a claim for the bounty provided by the Act of 3 March 1800 or, in the alternative, to salvage for rescuing the "property" of the Portuguese and Spanish owners under the supposedly universal, "law of nations," maritime law.

Chief Justice John Marshall rendered the opinion of the Supreme Court in 1825. It appears that the opinion was unanimous, thus included Justice Joseph Story, on the major points of interest for this study, although equally divided, thus affirming the decision of the federal Circuit Court in Georgia, with regard to the question, irrelevant to this study, of whether under the Act of 3 March 1800 there should be restitution of the slaves to their owners when the possessors were Americans.[92] That last issue was treated solely as a question of municipal law in which the construction of the intent of the Congress with regard to persons within American jurisdiction was at issue; it did not deal with the legality *vel non* of the slave trade under the *jus gentium*.

Marshall's opinion for the court is a triumph of "dualism" and "positivism." If Story dissented from any part of it, that dissent is not recorded in the official transcript of the case despite the common practice of the time, as now, for dissenting, concurring and partially concurring opinions to be published with the routine publication of the majority opinion.

Finding that the slave trade is morally abhorrent, Marshall also found that it is not forbidden by law as evidenced by the practice of states in his time and "long usage and general acquiescence." Prohibitions had been enacted, he pointed out, but as a matter of positive law by the particular legal orders, states, wishing to forbid the practice within their territories and ships or to persons otherwise within their jurisdiction:

Public sentiment has, in both [the United Kingdom and the United States] . . . kept pace with the measures of government; and the opinion is extensively, if not universally entertained, that this unnatural traffic ought to be suppressed. While its illegality is asserted by some governments, but not admitted by all; while the detestation in which it is held is growing daily, and even those nations who tolerate it in fact, almost disavow their own conduct, and rather connive at, than legalize, the acts of their subjects; it is not wonderful that public feeling should march somewhat in advance of strict law, and that opposite opinions should be entertained on the precise cases in which our own laws may control and limit the practice of others . . . The principle common to [the British] cases is, that the legality of the capture of a vessel engaged in the slave trade, depends on the law of the country to which the vessel belongs. If that law gives its sanction to the trade, restitution will be decreed; if that law prohibits it, the vessel and cargo will be condemned as good prize.[93]

---

[92] The *Antelope*, 23 US (10 Wheaton) 64, 113 (1825) at 126–127: "Whether, on this proof, Africans brought into the United States, under the various circumstances belonging to this case, ought to be restored or not, is a question on which much difficulty has been felt. It is unnecessary to state the reasons in support of the affirmative or negative answer to it, because the court is divided on it, and, consequently, no principle is settled. So much of the decree of the Circuit Court as directs restitution to the Spanish claimant of the Africans found on board the *Antelope* when she was captured by the *Arraganta*, is affirmed."

[93] Ibid., 116, 118.

Marshall then discussed the *Le Louis* case[94] as a British precedent that even the illegality of the trade by the law of the flag state cannot justify interference with the freedom of navigation on the high seas; and no substantive issue can be brought to question if the initial seizure is not conformable with the rules of the positive law of nations. Even if this were not so, he pointed out, as of the time of that case the law of France did not so clearly forbid the slave trade that a British admiralty tribunal could take notice of that prohibition without more evidence than it had before it. Thus, to phrase it in more familiar modern terms, both the jurisdiction to prescribe based on some notion of universal crime or tort, and the jurisdiction to adjudicate a violation of the universal law by French people in a French vessel, were lacking as the *Le Louis* was brought for *in rem* adjudication before the British tribunal. The jurisdiction to adjudicate and to enforce the French version of even a universal law were asserted to lie exclusively in France in time of peace, and arguments based on the universality of the law were rejected.

To return to the *Antelope*'s slave cargo, Marshall, for the apparently unanimous Court, said:

That [the slave trade] is contrary to the law of nature will scarcely be denied. That every man has a natural right to the fruits of his own labor, is generally admitted; and that no other person can rightfully deprive him of those fruits, and appropriate them against his will, seems to be the necessary result of this admission. But from the earliest times war has existed, and war confers rights . . . [to] enslave the vanquished. This, which was the usage of all, could not be pronounced repugnant to the law of nations, which is certainly to be tried by the test of general usage. That which has received the assent of all, must be the law of all . . . Whatever might be the answer of a moralist to this question, a jurist must search for its legal solution in those principles of action which are sanctioned by the usages, the national acts, and the general assent of that portion of the world of which he considers himself as a part, and to whose law the appeal is made. If we resort to this standard as the test of international law,[95] the question . . . is decided in favor of the legality of the trade.[96]

Marshall then made explicit the court's positivist notion that, at least in the United States, international law must be viewed as the product of the discretion of a legislator in a defined legal order; that moralists do not have legislative authority in the international legal order even with regard to common-law-trained judges, who are, after all, the appointees of only single municipal legal orders within the overall international legal order. He was quite explicit:

---

[94] 2 Dodson 210 (1817).   [95] See chapter 2, note 72 and pp. 68–69, 97 above.
[96] The *Antelope*, 23 US (10 Wheaton) 64, 113 (1825).

No principle of general law is more universally acknowledged than the perfect equality of nations. Russia and Geneva have equal rights. It results from this equality that no one can rightfully impose a rule on another. Each legislates for itself, but its legislation can operate on itself alone. A right, then, which is vested in all by the consent of all, can be devested [sic] only by consent; and this trade, in which all have participated, must remain lawful to those who cannot be induced to relinquish it. As no nation can prescribe a rule for others, none can make a law of nations; and this traffic remains lawful to those whose governments have not forbidden it.[97]

The result was the division of the surviving African slaves among the Spanish and Portuguese claimants *pro rata* as they "owned" the original cargo of slaves, as if the slaves were mere property, chattels, distributed under the usual maritime law regarding general averaging of a cargo diminished by the hazards of sea transport. The remaining slaves, those not originally "owned" by Spanish or Portuguese claimants as a portion of the original cargo, were freed by operation of the law of the United States. Which slaves fell into which category was determined apparently by lot.[98]

It might be significant, although anticipating an analysis to be mentioned briefly later, that the referral to foreign law to determine fundamental questions of property and status, "conflict of laws" in its choice-of-law phase, was a fundamental part of this decision. It is possible to speculate that Story's willingness to join in the majority, like his release to French interests of *La Jeune Eugénie*, reflected his intellectualization of the problems after his natural law approach had met the cool and precise positivist attack of Marshall and the United States Supreme Court's majority.

From the time of the *Antelope* case to the present, the jurisprudence of the American Supreme Court has been fundamentally "positivist" and "dualist"[99] in the Marshall mode. Under the *dicta* of *The Charming Betsy*,[100] the municipal courts of the United States may certainly take account of the impact on American legislation of preconceptions of the international legal order in the minds of American legislators. But the rules of the international legal order are not as such binding on the courts of the United States unless made so by the legislature, as in the Piracy Act of 3 March 1819[101] or reduced to treaty, which, after advice and consent by a

---

[97] Ibid., 122.   [98] Ibid., 132–133.

[99] I.e., treating the international legal order and the American municipal legal order as two quite separate systems.

[100] 6 US 208, 2 Cranch 64 (1804).

[101] 15th Congress, 2nd session, chapter 77, 3 Stat. 510.

two-thirds majority in the Senate, can be ratified by the President and thus made municipal law by the operation of Article VI, clause 2, of the United States Constitution.[102]

An illustration, more or less typical in expressing this orientation in the middle of the nineteenth century, was a charge to a jury in another slave-trading case, this time in Philadelphia, in 1855. The case also illustrates the "conventional wisdom" regarding "piracy" and "common law crimes"; a conventional wisdom that was superficial then and has been repeated often enough in judicial and scholarly *dicta* to be almost unquestioned today while still obviously incorrect when subjected to examination by looking at real cases in which the distinctions and categories are in fact pertinent to the result.

An American naval vessel caught a slave ship operated by a syndicate under the American flag, apparently procured by what was alleged to be fraud, as a flag of convenience.[103] The master of the vessel, Captain Darnaud, presented himself as French, although under American law at the time only nationals of the United States could be masters of American flag vessels and he had an American master's license. The question was whether American criminal law, French law, the "law of nations" in any of its phases and, if that latter, whether directly or as part of American law, should be applied to Darnaud if the prosecution could not prove his American nationality or that of his ship. Judge Kane first disposed of the argument that participation in the international traffic in slaves was "piracy" under the "law of nations." Noting that the application of the key word "piracy" to participation in the slave trade derived from legislation and not from widely observed international practice, he concluded that calling the slave trade "piracy" for purposes of American law did not make it so as a matter of the law of nations, so the universal jurisdiction and universal criminality that he believed flowed from the label "pirate" under the law of nations were inapplicable to the case. Since there was no "piracy" case before him by his own rationale, his observations as to universal criminality and universal jurisdiction as they might attach to true piracy cases are unnecessary for his conclusions, mere *dicta*:

---

[102] Quoted in note 14 above.

[103] The criminal statute involved was the Act of 15 May 1820, 3 Stat. 600, 16th Congress, 1st Session, chapter 113, sections 4 and 5 of which made participation in the slave trade into "piracy" as far as American criminal law was concerned. Since this was an admiralty matter, federal law applied.

In a word, no State can make a general law applicable to all upon the high seas. Where an act has been denounced as crime by the universal law of nations, where the evil to be guarded against is one which all mankind recognize as an evil, where the offence is one that all mankind concur in punishing, we have an offence against the law of nations, which any nation may vindicate through the instrumentality of its courts. Thus [pirates] . . . may be punished by the first taker.

This assertion of a universal policing jurisdiction with regard to piracy was common at the time. It was actually exercised only when no state was in a position to object or the state asserting jurisdiction had *jus standi* (nowadays included in the concept of jurisdiction to adjudicate), a particular legally protected interest that could be vindicated by that assertion, like protection of its nationals as victims of the "piracy," or had in mind imperial ventures.[104] Judge Kane found no such basis for universalizing the statutory American crime of involvement in the international traffic in slaves. In general, he instructed the jury that there must be some legal interest, *jus standi*, before a positive law of any state could be applied to foreigners. The rôle of the honest judge under the true law of nations was, in his view, to maintain the limits fixed by the international legal order on any state's authorities' jurisdiction to adjudicate and the jurisdiction to enforce; to restrain the enthusiasm of legislators overreaching their authority under the *jus inter gentes*; not to enforce or permit other judges under any rationale to enforce national versions of the moral *jus gentium*:

But so soon as we leave these crimes of universal recognition [i.e., piracy], the jurisdiction of a State over the acts of men upon the high seas becomes circumscribed . . .

But it is only in the two cases, where the individual accused is himself a citizen, whose allegiance continued while he was upon the common highway of nations, or where the property upon which the individual was found perpetrating a wrong was properly recognized as American, owned by Americans, it is only in these two cases that the United States can make a law which would be binding upon all citizens or which could be en-forced by courts of justice; and I do not hesitate to say, after something of mature consideration, that if the Congress of the United States, in its honorable zeal for the repression of a grievous crime against mankind, were to call upon courts of justice to extend the jurisdiction of the United States beyond the limits I have indicated, it would be the duty of courts of justice to decline the jurisdiction so conferred.[105]

---

[104] The subject is addressed at some length in Rubin, *Piracy*, *passim* and need not be repeated here. The evidence is far too elaborate to present again, and the conclusion is as stated.

[105] *US v. Darnaud* 3 Wallace Cir. Ct. Cases (3rd Cir.) 143 (1855) at 160–163.

Under this charge Darnaud was acquitted. Failure to prove his American nationality or the American nationality of his vessel was apparently construed to take him beyond the range of the courts authorized by American constitutional law to enforce or adjudicate the American Congress's criminal prescriptions.

But this was a charge to a jury, not an appealed decision. The reach of the Congress's authority over the acts of foreigners abroad was not quite so narrowly construed by the Supreme Court in the early nineteenth century, but nearly. As noted above with regard to Story's decision in *La Jeune Eugénie*, ways were usually found to state a broad proposition favoring American moral prescriptions and jurisdiction, but usually ways were also found to structure the legal situation to avoid the possibility of treading on the toes of another sovereign who might want to pursue either issue. In *La Jeune Eugénie*, Joseph Story, acting as a federal Circuit Court judge in an admiralty case, actually awarded the offending vessel to the French claimant. In the *United States v. Wiltberger*,[106] the accused "pirate" was actually let go by the Supreme Court apparently for fear of encroaching on Chinese jurisdiction or setting a precedent with regard to Chinese jurisdiction that would lead to difficulties if applied against British or French jurisdiction, or cited by the British, French or others as a basis for their exercise of jurisdiction in American waters. The farthest the United States was willing to go in the direction of universal jurisdiction in "piracy" cases was to apply the American prescriptions to a person asserted to have no nationality at all,[107] thus indicating the reluctance to press theories of universal prescriptive jurisdiction and universal standing to the point at which a real discussion on the diplomatic level might take place.

The British press the point

The leading British[108] case concerning the slave trade was the *Le Louis*

---

[106] 18 US (5 Wheaton) 76 (1820).

[107] *US v. Klintock* 18 US (5 Wheaton) 144 (1820). For a discussion of the context of this case, see Rubin, *Piracy* 142–144.

[108] The England and Wales that united with Scotland in 1707 to become "Great Britain" united further with Ireland in 1800 (effective 1 January 1801) to become the United Kingdom. 39 & 40 Geo. III, c. 67 (1800). For purposes of this study, England is normally used when English common law is involved; Great Britain is used when admiralty jurisdiction or imperial policy is involved. The term "United Kingdom," although technically correct after 1801, did not come into common use until the twentieth century, and the adjective "British" seems easier to comprehend than "Kingdom-ish," which seems never to have caught on.

case.[109] A French slaver from Martinique was captured by a British cutter and taken to the Vice Admiralty Court in the British colony of Sierra Leone on 11 March 1816. After various movements unnecessary to recount here, the case was brought before the High Court of Admiralty in London and heard before Sir William Scott, the leading British admiralty judge of his time. Sir William Scott found the authority of the British captor to depend on the reach of the British license authorizing him to seize foreign slave ships. Like the American court in the *Darnaud* case a generation later, he based his rejection of that authority on the *jus inter gentes*, the structure of the international legal order: "[N]either this British act of Parliament, nor any Commission founded on it, can affect any right of [*sic*, or?] interest of foreigners, that are [*sic*, is?] consistent with the Law of Nations." As to whether the "law of nations" applied to authorize the British action, Scott focused not on the substantive law that might have been held to forbid the slave trade as part of the *jus gentium*, common to all civilized nations, but on the *jus inter gentes*:

[T]wo principles of Public Law are generally recognized as fundamental. One is the perfect equality and entire independence of all distinct States. Relative magnitude creates no distinction of right; relative imbecility, whether permanent or casual, gives no additional right to the more powerful Neighbour; and any advantage seized upon that ground is mere usurpation. This is the great foundation of Publick Law, which it mainly concerns the peace of mankind, both in their political and private capacities, to preserve inviolate. The second is, that all Nations being equal, all have an equal right to the uninterrupted use of the unappropriated parts of the Ocean for their own convenience . . . I can find no authority that gives the right of interruption to the navigation of States in amity upon the high seas, excepting that which the rights of war give to both Belligerents against Neutrals.[110]

But Scott did find another authority: the law regarding "piracy."

The right of visitation being in this present Case exercised in time of peace, the question arises, how is it to be legalized? And looking to what I have described as the known existing Law of Nations evidenced by all Authority and all practice, it must be upon the ground that the captured Vessel is to be taken *legally* [emphasis *sic*] as a Pirate, or else some new ground is to be assumed on which the Court may conceive itself to be authorized to carry this right beyond the limits within which it has hitherto been legally exercised . . . It is perfectly clear, that this Vessel cannot be deemed a Pirate, from any want of National character legally obtained . . . If, therefore, the character of a Pirate can be impressed

---

[109] 2 Dodson 210 (1817). Quotations are taken from the reprint of the case in 8 BFSP (1820–1821) 281*ff.*

[110] Ibid., at 283, 285.

upon her, it must be only on the ground of her occupation as a Slave-trader; no other act of Piracy being imputed . . . It has not been contended in argument that the common case of dealing in Slaves could be deemed a Piracy in law . . . Be the malignity of the practice what it may, it is not that of piracy, in legal consideration.[111]

Scott went on to examine the possibility that the *jus gentium* might be included in public international law, the *jus inter gentes*, as a basis for universal jurisdiction. His logic in rejecting that argument goes to the structure of the international legal order. That logic is prefigured in the perceptions noted above that had surfaced by the eleventh century BC[112] and had been reiterated since then in terms of increasing subtlety by Aristotle and St. Thomas Aquinas, and bluntly by Suarez most notably among early jurists. It squarely distinguishes the substantive prescriptions of "law" from the distribution of authority to interpret and apply, i.e., to adjudicate and enforce, the law. It prefigures later distinctions among jurisdiction to prescribe, jurisdiction to adjudicate and jurisdiction to enforce as applied to public international law. For its simplicity and eloquence in stating the model, Scott's most influential language is worth quoting at some length:

Piracy being excluded, the Court has to look for some new and peculiar ground: but the first place a new and very extensive ground is offered to it by the suggestion, which has been strongly pressed, that this Trade [in slaves], if not the crime of Piracy, is nevertheless *crime*, and that every Nation, and indeed every Individual has not only a right, but a duty, to prevent in every place the commission of crime. It is a sphere of duty sufficiently large that is thus opened out to Communities and to their Members. But to establish the consequence required, it is first necessary to establish that the right to interpose by force to prevent the commission of crime, commences not upon the commencement of the overt act, nor upon the evident approach towards it; but on the bare surmise grounded on the mere possibility; for unless it goes that length it will not support the right of forcible inquiry and search. What are the proximate circumstances which confer on you the right of intruding yourself into a Foreign Ship, over which you have no authority whatever, or of demanding the submission of its crew to your inquiry, whether they mean to deal in the Traffick in Slaves, not in your Country, but in one with which you have no connection? . . . Secondly, it must be shown that the act imputed to the Parties is unquestionably and legally criminal by the universal Law of Nations . . . and I say *legally* criminal, because neither this Court nor any other can carry its private apprehensions, independent of Law, into its public judgments on the quality of actions. It must conform to the judgment of the Law upon that subject; and

---

[111] Ibid., 286–287.
[112] The pertinent parts of the tale are set out on pp. 1–3 above.

acting as a Court, it cannot attribute criminality to an act where the Law imputes none. It must look to the legal standard of morality; and upon a question of this nature, that standard must be found in the Law of Nations as fixed and evidenced by general and ancient and admitted practice, by Treaties, and by the general tenour of the Laws and Ordinances, and the formal transactions of civilized States . . . [T]here *are* Nations which [still] adhere to the practice [of enslavement] under all the encouragement which their own Laws can give it. What is the doctrine of the Law of Nations relatively to them? Why, that their practice is to be respected; that their Slaves, if taken, are to be restored to them . . . All this, surely, upon the ground that such conduct is no departure from the Law of Nations; because, if it were, no such respect could be allowed to it, upon an exemption of its own making; for no Nation can privilege itself to commit a crime against the Law of Nations, by a municipal regulation of its own . . .

It is pressed as a difficulty; what is to be done, if a French Ship laden with Slaves for a French Port, is brought in? In answer, without hesitation, restore the possession which has been unlawfully divested – rescind the illegal act done by your own Subject, and leave the Foreigner to the justice of his own Country. What evil follows? If the Laws of France do not prohibit, you admit that condemnation cannot take place in a British Court. But if the Law of France be what you contend, what would have followed upon its arrival at Martinique, the Port whither it was bound? That all the penalties of the French Law would have been immediately thundered upon it. If your case be true, there will be no failure of justice. Why is the British Judge to intrude himself *in subsidium juris*, when everything requisite will be performed in the French Court, in a legal and effectual manner? Why is the British Judge, professing, as he does, to apply the French Law, to assume a jurisdiction and direct that the penalties shall go to the British Crown and its Subjects, which that Law has appropriated to the French Crown and its Subjects? . . . [A] Nation is not justified in assuming rights that do not belong to her, merely because she means to apply them to a laudable purpose; nor should she set out upon a crusade of converting other Nations to humanity by acts of unlawful force. Nor is it to be argued, that because other Nations approve the ultimate purpose, they must therefore submit to every measure which any one State or its Subjects may inconsiderately adopt for its attainment. In this very case nothing can be clearer than that the only French Law produced is in direct contradiction to such a notion; because approving as it does (though to a very limited extent) the abolition, it nevertheless reserves to its own authorities the cognizance of each cause and the appropriation of the penalties [emphases *sic*].[113]

Le Louis was returned to its French master, together with its cargo of slaves. Scott did not assess costs and damages against the British seizor of the vessel, as would have been the usual British practice in admiralty, on

[113] *Le Louis* 2 Dodson 210 (1817) at 286–292.

the ground that the case was original, a matter of first impression. A better ground might have been that because the seizor had acted under the authority of the British Vice Admiral in Sierra Leone who had issued his orders, the fault was that of the overreaching magistrate there, who was not party to the case. But that involves issues not directly pertinent to this study.[114]

Scott's opinion started out by finding the analogy to "piracy" to be misplaced, and crime by analogy to be a dubious concept as applied to the "law of nations" unless by "general and ancient practice, by Treaties, and by the general tenour of the Laws and Ordinances, and the formal transactions of civilized States." He disposed of the basic "natural law" argument based on moral principle by finding no prohibition of the slave trade as such in basic moral principle evidenced by the practice of ancients or the highest moral writings universally acknowledged in the culture that produced his court, Christianity. He did not deny that such principle if adopted in practice and evidenced by accepted teachings would be law; indeed, it is fundamental to Anglo-American common law theory that some custom, practice accepted as law, is a source of true binding rules that a judge can rest on when exercising the functions normally given to judges in our society. But he was quite clear in arguing that writings divorced from practice would not carry that burden.

From the point of view of this study, most noteworthy was his argument disposing of the notion that "universal" rules of municipal legal orders somehow convert themselves into rules of the entire international society and can be enforced directly by the community or members of it without

---

[114] As noted in discussing *Murray v. The Charming Betsy* 6 US 208, 2 Cranch 64 (1804), the American response to a similar fact situation was to hold the seizor liable, leaving to the legislature, which has the sole Constitutional authority to issue letters of marque and reprisal, the question of reimbursing him for his obedience to "illegal" orders. See also *Little v. Barreme*, 6 US (2 Cranch) 170 (1804). Oddly, in his decision in that latter case, Chief Justice Marshall did not mention the Constitutional provision that went immediately to the heart of the dispute between the Executive and the Congress, Article 1, section 8, clause 11: "[The Congress shall have power to] grant letters of marque and reprisal, and make rules concerning captures on land and water." The real issue in the case was whether this express grant of authority to the Congress diminished the authority of the President as commander-in-chief of the navy to issue such letters. It seems likely that political factors were involved that the Supreme Court in 1804 chose not to address. Later citations to the case that ignore its political context and the Constitutional provision that expressly addresses the matter seem more argumentative than persuasive. For example, in Thomas M. Franck and Michael J. Glennon, *Cases and Materials on the Foreign Relations Law of the United States* (1987) 5, the editors' note on this case tries to fix the Constitutional context, but does not mention Article I, section 8, clause 11 of the Constitution!

regard for *jus standi* or the limits the international legal order places on the authority of any single legal order, state, to interpret for others the supposed universal rules. His reasoning there precisely parallels the reasoning of Suarez.[115] The law-making process, the constituencies, the function of judges, the fines and other emoluments of successful prosecution, all the incidents of applying the law are, in the existing legal order, reserved to states. And no one state can, since the Peace of Westphalia, claim to be in a position to declare the law binding on all. Scott cannot have read Madison's unpublished notes on the Constitutional Convention of 1787, but his approach seems to be identical to that of James Wilson, confining the law of nations to its *jus inter gentes* phase or its *jus gentium* phase, but not permitting the conceptions appropriate to the one to penetrate the other, and impliedly denying the very existence of any operative *jus gentium*, whatever the value of the conception to building a moral order for international society.

As noted in discussing the American cases above, this opinion had enormous influence, was frequently cited, and no opinion disputing its fundamental reasoning appears to have survived, although, until *Antelope* was decided by the United States Supreme Court, Joseph Story's reasoning in the *La Jeune Eugénie* case stood as a brave attempt to overrule it.[116]

The British try to change the substantive rules of the *jus inter gentes*

Within the British municipal system, Lord Castlereagh was a vigorous opponent of the slave trade. Blocked by what at the time was widely taken to be the unassailable persuasiveness of Scott's opinion in the *Le Louis* case from an approach that would let British courts determine and apply his version of the substantive rules of the "law of nations" as directly binding on the merchants of other countries, Castlereagh tried to have those substantive rules adopted directly into the body of rules acknowledged as part of the *jus inter gentes*.

On 4 December 1817 the Plenipotentiaries of Austria, France, Great Britain, Prussia and Russia met at London. Castlereagh presented Conventions concluded by his Government with Portugal on 28 July 1817 and with Spain on 23 September 1817 under which each power agreed to take steps to abolish the slave trade. He then proposed a general Convention with the same object.[117] The British proposal was rejected primarily

---

[115] The pertinent part of Suarez's analysis is set out at pp. 50–51 above.
[116] See p. 103 above.
[117] 6 BFSP (1818–1819) 23. The two Conventions are in 67 CTS 373 and 68 CTS 45

because of the Portuguese objection that it went beyond the positive commitments Portugal had made earlier. Portugal insisted on continuing to withhold from international control the Portuguese slave trade south of the equator; i.e., between West Africa and Brazil. No moral or other argument was able to overcome the consensus that without the actual consent of all, no general assertion of law could be made.[118]

At the Congress of Aix-la-Chapelle in October and November 1818, when the principal European powers gathered to complete arrangements for the withdrawal of allied troops from France and the establishment of post-Napoleonic order, Castlereagh tried again. But while abolition of the slave trade was high on the British agenda it was much lower on everybody else's.

At the close of the Congress, Castlereagh circulated a minute in the name of the British Government outlining the legal position he proposed to take.[119] Regretting the failure of the Congress to act, Castlereagh took particularly to task the Russian Plenipotentiaries whose enlightened sentiments stopped short of accepting the British proposal that slave traders be agreed to be qualified as "pirates" with all the legal consequences the British felt should flow from that legal quality, including a universal right of visitation on the high seas and universal jurisdiction to adjudicate, i.e., that criminal procedures against slave traders could properly be brought before any state's municipal tribunals without regard for *jus standi* or other restraints placed by the international legal order in operation.[120]

It seems likely that the barely suppressed fury in this part of the British Minute was not only a reflection of the emotion that the slave trade had begun to arouse in the British Government, and frustration over the legal order as expressed in the *Le Louis* and actual piracy cases, as has been seen, but also a reaction to the element of hypocrisy detected in the powers then in the process of forming the Holy Alliance. While denying to

---

respectively. It is not proposed to analyze their terms here, or their place in the tortuous British effort to abolish the international slave trade. See Wheaton, *Enquiry*. An equivalent agreement was reached with France in 1831. See note 143 below.

[118] 6 BFPS (1818–1819) 52, formal Note of the Five Plenipotentiaries to the Portuguese Minister dated 11 February 1818.

[119] The memorandum was apparently written by a British anti-slave-trade activist named Clarkson, but was presented as a British initiative by Castlereagh, and, as shall be seen, was adopted as important policy by Castlereagh's Government. I have called it Castlereagh's Minute for simplicity's sake. See Wheaton, *Enquiry* at 42–43.

[120] Castlereagh's Minute is in 6 BFSP (1818–1819) 77*ff*. The first part, to 80, deals with the Russian Memoir and Portugal.

themselves legislative authority over the evil of slavery, they were speaking loudly about their authority to intervene in the governmental succession of other states.

The two positions are in fact not necessarily inconsistent. "Legitimacy" as a rule of governmental succession in the international legal order, while it can be argued to reflect some moral values such as continuity, predictability, security etc., does not necessarily presume any moral basis; it can be coldly viewed as a political *desideratum* urged by those who gain or retain authority under the Germanic "divine law" of inheritance. Thus, the equation of moral imperatives and "law" implicit in *jus gentium* theory does not operate to forbid revolution as it was believed to operate to forbid the international slave trade. On the other side, since all known legal orders forbid "treason" and *coups d'état*, even those like that of the United States that permit peaceful amendment of the Constitution, *jus gentium* theory in its amoral, Roman law origins could be interpreted to forbid revolution as a matter of agreement among all legal orders including the international legal order. But revolution against the established authority of states in the international legal order was not the object of the Holy Alliance. The Alliance sought to forbid by law revolutions within municipal orders. From that point of view, "legitimacy" as argued by the supporters of the Holy Alliance did not reflect any substantive rules or any particular law-making process within the international legal order. If revolution and *coups d'état* were historically or by state practice "illegal" as a matter of international law, then very few ruling powers of the early nineteenth century could claim clear title to their kingdoms. And treaties that would forbid revolution would surely have been regarded as an impermissible intervention in the internal affairs of a state party seeking to achieve its own government; be seen as evidence that a government relies more on a foreign "friend" than on its own population for support. This is not the place for a deeper analysis, but it can be suggested that if there is any substance to modern notions of *jus cogens*, a rule so deeply part of the legal order that a treaty cannot be valid if inconsistent with such a rule,[121] a treaty that forbids a people to change its own government would be invalid.

---

[121] *Cf.* 1969 Vienna Convention on the Law of Treaties, UN Doc. A/CONF.39/27 (1969), Article 53:

> A treaty is void if, at the time of its conclusion, it conflicts with a peremptory norm of general international law. For the purposes of the present Convention, a peremptory norm of general international law is a norm accepted and recognized by the international community of states as a whole as a norm

Be that as it may, the Russian Memoir merely formulated a position agreed by Russia, Austria and Prussia that until Portugal had agreed to the proposed rule, that rule did not have universal assent and could not be promulgated as a rule of "law" binding on all.

The Russian Memoir had also alluded to the United States and France as two dissenting powers. Castlereagh's response was that the great powers should take the lead and bring along the young and weak United States and the defeated France by the power of their assertions and example. More significantly, faced with the Russian argument based on treating the international legal order as a positive law system, the British lowered their tone of moral preachment. Castlereagh rephrased the problem as one simply of municipal law enforcement by British authority against British subjects, implying that all other countries must have similar problems and mutual concessions of enforcement powers would help solve them even without theories of universal jurisdiction to adjudicate. In modern terms, the problem as he redefined it was one of entrepreneurs establishing corporations of convenience, particularly in countries whose enforcement system was lax: "Many instances have occurred of British Subjects evading the Laws of their Country, either by establishing houses at The Havannah [i.e., in Cuba, Spanish territory] or obtaining false Papers."[122]

No further action was taken at Aix-La-Chapelle.

The British drive reached what seems to have been its diplomatic peak at the Congress of Verona in November 1822. The British representative was the Duke of Wellington himself, a hero but not yet Prime Minister. He acted under the instructions of George Canning, the Foreign Minister. On his way to Verona, Wellington stopped at Paris and reported that he had pressed upon the French Foreign Minister the need for France to enforce its own laws to suppress the slave trade in French vessels. The French reply was that they were doing and would do all in their power to that end as a matter of French law enforcement and French observance of her

---

from which no derogation is permitted and which can be modified only by a subsequent norm of general international law having the same character. This Convention as a whole is usually regarded as codifying general international law, thus expressing rules that are binding as a matter of that law even on states that are not parties to the Convention itself. There are a number of provisions in the Convention for which this "conventional wisdom" can be doubted, including this provision, but this is not the place for further analysis of it.

[122] Castlereagh's Memorandum of 1815, revised and sent to the British Ambassador in Paris on 21 February 1818 for presentation to the French Foreign Minister: 8 BFSP (1820–1821) 299 at 301.

international treaty obligations.[123] Canning was upset by the French refusal to enter into any new engagements, to enforce her own laws more vigorously, or to allow the British to enforce any rules aimed at stopping the slave trade in French vessels. Accepting as a fact that the French public simply did not have the same sentiments as the British about the moral need to suppress that abominable trade, Canning found it "lamentable or incredible" that:

[T]here is no Public Feeling – none, on this subject in France, which responds in the smallest degree to the sentiment prevalent in England; – that no credit is given to the People, or to the Legislature of this Country [England], for sincerity in those sentiments; that our anxiety upon the matter is attributed to a calculation of National Interest.[124]

To pressure the French to act, Canning considered the desirability of proposing that the Verona Congress declare the carrying on of the slave trade to be "piracy," although he doubted that such a proposal would be effective:

But does there appear the slightest probability that the French Plenipotentiaries would concur in a position, qualifying as acts of Piracy, acts which the French are committing every day, and laying open the Ships and Properties of those Subjects, not merely to a right of visit to be mutually exercised, but to sweeping uncompensated capture by the Cruizers of Great Britain?

Even more telling from the point of view of this study:

Would such a Declaration by Powers who have no Colonies of their own, carry great weight? and would not an assumption on the part of the Congress, of a pretension to legislate on matters of Public Law, and to establish a new Principle of Maritime Police, excite, in other Powers, a disposition to demur to its jurisdiction?[125]

He ended by proposing that the participating countries "severally, or by joint compact, prohibit the introduction of Colonial Produce from the Colonies of States which have not legally and effectually abolished the Slave Trade." But the "joint compact" he had in mind appears to have been something less:

A Declaration in the names, if possible, of the whole Alliance; but, if France shall decline being a Party to it, then, in the names of the Three other Powers . . . exhorting the Maritime Powers, who have abolished the Slave Trade, to concert Measures among themselves for proclaiming it, and treating it, as

[123] 10 BFSP (1822–1823) 90, Wellington to Canning, Paris, 21 September 1822.
[124] Ibid., Canning to Wellington, 1 October 1822, at 93.   [125] Ibid., 93.

Piracy; – with a view to founding upon the aggregate of such separate Engagements between State and State, a general Engagement to be incorporated into the Public Law of the Civilized World.

This substitution of a declaration for a treaty, and the substitution jurisprudentially of international engagements, evidences of the *jus inter gentes*, for municipal law which already reflected common abhorrence of the slave trade in each state concerned (except for Portugal and its trade south of the equator), was the effective abandonment of the natural law arguments that had so moved Castlereagh and been so ineffective to move the rest of the "Civilized World":

Such a Declaration, as it assumed *no binding force* [emphasis added], would not be obnoxious to the charges which would attach to a Declaration of new Public Law, by an incompetent Authority; while at the same time its moral influence might materially aid us in our Negotiations with other Maritime States.[126]

At Verona, Wellington proposed a "General Declaration" along the lines of Canning's instructions. He phrased the problem as one of national law enforcement with regard to "contraband trade" (in slaves) and blamed France by name for its continuance "notwithstanding the Measures adopted by His Most Christian Majesty to carry into execution His Treaty with His Allies, His Own Royal Declaration, and the Law of France."[127]

The four other Powers responded almost immediately. Austria indicated that it was prepared to join in a new General Declaration announcing the intention of the Powers to end the slave trade (but with no immediate action promised and no time limit mentioned); would take part in agreements by which the Maritime Powers which have themselves abolished the slave trade by municipal law would cooperate among themselves to declare that trade to be "piracy"; would refuse the protection of the Austrian flag "to individuals born outside His [the Emperor's] territory, if there were any such, who used that flag to cover trading in slaves";[128] but reserved its position with regard to any action affecting France until some common action were agreed that could be supported by the French government.

Lest it be thought that Austria was disingenuous about maritime affairs, it should be remembered that in 1815 the Austro-Hungarian

---

[126] Ibid., 94.

[127] Ibid., 95, Memorandum presented to the Congress on 24 November 1822, at p.99.

[128] Ibid., 102. The quoted language is my translation from the French: "A retirer l'usage et la protection de Son Pavillon, aux individus nés hors de Son Territoire, s'il devait en exister, qui serviraient de ce Pavillon pour couvrir un Commerce en Esclaves."

Empire had recovered Venice and the Dalmatian coast and was itself therefore a Mediterranean power. On the other hand, the Empire had no territories involved in the profits of either the slave trade or the tropical produce of slave labor. Therefore her position involved no serious constituency problems. In these circumstances, the focus on futile actions, the condition of French consent, and the obvious reluctance to interfere with matters clearly regarded as internal to the several European powers, gives some indication of the low importance the leading Austrian statesman of the time, Prince Metternich, attached to moral outrage as part of the law-making process. Since the British had colonies whose elites still profited from the labor of slaves and, by Castlereagh's own analysis, influential constituents involved illegally (by British law) in the trade itself, the moral fervor of the British presents an interesting contrast. But the line between the distribution of authority in the international legal order and its legislative processes on the one hand, and the substantive rules within that order that derive from those processes, could not be breached by moral fervor at least as far as the Austro-Hungarian Empire was concerned.

The response to Wellington's Memorandum by the Russian Empire was prefaced with a rather pompous statement of moral condemnation of the slave trade. But, as to actual steps to stop it, the Russian Cabinet in the name of the Emperor indicated that the problem was essentially one of law enforcement by the maritime powers whose respective subjects were engaged in that trade against their national laws. If those powers wanted to cooperate with each other by agreeing to call that trade "piracy," they should be able to do that, but as to specific actions regarding France, "The Emperor is ready to support them in the negotiations which will be able to take place on that subject," implying no necessary conclusion to those negotiations.[129] The only part of the British proposal that might affect Russia directly, the notion of embargoing trade with colonies that still participated in the slave trade, Russia rejected on the ground that trade with Portugal's African colonies was particularly significant to Russia. But

---

[129] Ibid., 107 at 108–109: "Quant aux autres Propositions faites par Son Excellence Monsieur le Duc de Wellington, et qu'interessent plus particulièrement les Puissances Maritimes, le Cabinet de Sa Majesté Impériale exprimera constamment les voeux que forme L'Empereur pour qu'il puisse s'établir entre ces Puissances un accord qui fournirait à chacune d'Elles les moyens de reprimer, parmi leurs Sujets respectifs, la continuation de la Traité, en la déclarant Acte de Piraterie; et comme, parmi ces propositions, il y en a qui concernent spécialement le Gouvernement de Sa Majesté Très Chrétienne, L'Empereur est prêt à les faire appuyer dans les Negotiations qui pourront s'ouvrir à ce sujet."

Russia did indicate a willingness to participate in such an embargo if, after all the allies of Russia had agreed to impose it and notified Portugal of their intention, Portugal still refused to end that trade. The Russian concern seems to have been less with the morality in substance of the slave trade than with an equal sharing among the powers of the burdens that would result from actual political action to impose that moral view as positive "law" for all.

The Prussians in a short note indicated that they were ready to repeat in a new Declaration pronouncements made at the Congress of Vienna, but as to any enforcement action, political or legal, they had no authority to concur and in any case would want to consider any French arguments before deciding.[130] Obviously, to Prussia the issue was one of the legislative process, and moral fervor was not considered sufficient in itself to create law in the international order.

The response of France was obviously the key to the immediate result of the Congress. After the appropriate moral condemnations of the slave trade and an explanation of the difficulties with which positive law forbidding it had been enacted both in French municipal law and by treaty to bind France internationally, two major points were made. One was to slap at the English, whose new-found depth of moral conviction did not wipe out generations of slave-trading under which the British West Indies had become, if anything, overstocked with slaves giving them what the French obviously felt to be an economic advantage over the French tropical colonies. While it may not be clear why profit and moral conviction should be regarded as necessarily antagonistic to each other, as implied in this part of the French note, it is clear that the French themselves did not feel that moral conviction removed from some financial sacrifice was a very persuasive argument for legislation that would involve others in such a sacrifice.

The second point is more significant for the present argument. The French wrote that they were ready to sign a Declaration which could help suppress an abominable commerce and bring to bear the "vengeance" of the law against those guilty of it.

---

[130] Ibid., 106–107: "Que quant aux Mésures politiques et législatives, que le Gouvernement Britannique juge les plus propres à l'effet de voir reprimer les abus qu'il denonce, ils n'auraient que prendre, ad referendum, une position, dont l'adoption excéderait leur pouvoir: et . . . qu'ils pensent, qu'avant de se prononcer sur ce que le Gouvernement Anglais demande à La France, il sera convenable d'attendre les explications, que Messieurs les Plenipotentiaires de Sa Majesté Très Chr. [sic] tienne vont donner à ce sujet."

But a Declaration which obliged all the Governments to apply to the slave trade the punishments appropriate to Piracy, and which would make of it [the law regarding piracy, which was conceived as municipal law parallel in many countries, but municipal in each] into a general law of the civilized world, is a thing which does not seem to the Plenipotentiaries of France to be within the competence of a political conference. Insofar as it would establish the death penalty, that is a matter which, in the nature of governmental structure, belongs to the judiciary or the legislatures which are called on to make law.[131]

The French note ends with the conclusions to be expected by this positivist, dualist approach. All embargoes against the colonial produce of countries that permit the slave trade are rejected on the ground that Portugal was the only country of Europe permitting the slave trade (south of the equator) and Portugal was not represented at the Congress, so could not present its counter-arguments.

The limited right of visit by British cutters to inspect French vessels for possible violation of French law was rejected in clear terms as inconsistent with principle and French interest:

As to the right of visit, if the Government of France could ever consent to it, there would be the most deplorable consequences. The national character of the two peoples, French and English, are opposed to it; and if there were need to prove that view, it would suffice to recall that in this very year, in time of peace, French blood ran on the shores of Africa. France recognizes the freedom of the seas for all foreign flags, of all legitimate Powers, she claims for herself only the independence which she respects in others and which becomes her dignity.[132]

---

[131] Ibid., 102 at 105: "Les Ministres Plenipotentiaires de Sa Majesté Très Chrétienne sont prêts à signer toute Déclaration collective des Puissances, tendante à fletrir un commerce odieux, et à provoquer contre les coupables la vengeance des Loix. Mais une Déclaration qui obligeroit tous les Gouvernements à appliquer à la Traité des Nègres des châtimens [sic] infligés à la Piraterie, et qui se transformeroit en une Loi Générale du Monde Civilisé, est une chose qui ne parait pas aux Ministres Pleniponiaires de Sa Majesté Très Chrétienne être de la compétence d'une réunion politique. Quand il s'agit d'établir la peine de mort, ce sont la nature des Gouvernemens [sic], les Corps Judiciaires, ou les Corps Législatifs qui sont appelés [sic] à statuer."

[132] Ibid., 106: "Quant au droit de visite, si le Gouvernement Français pouvait jamais y consentir, il aurait les suites les plus funestes: le caractère national des deux Peuples, Français et Anglais, s'y oppose; et s'il était besoin de preuves à l'appui de cette opinion, il suffirait de rappeler, que cette année même, en pleine paix, le sang Français a coulé sur les rivages de l'Afrique. La France reconnait la liberté des mers pour tous les Pavillons Estrangers, à quelque Puissance légitime qu'ils appartiennent; elle ne réclame pour Elle, que l'independence qu'Elle respecte dans les autres, et qui convient à Sa Dignité." It is not known what particular incident in 1822, involving the spilling of French blood on the coasts of Africa, was intended.

The final result of all this in substance was a series of Resolutions adopted on 28 November 1822 stating the existence of international commitments relative to the suppression of the slave trade, and expressing the Powers' continued interest in carrying them out. But to give effect to the Declaration containing these renewed sentiments, all that was undertaken was that "their respective administrations will reexamine all the measures compatible with their [national] laws and the interests of their subjects, to lead to a result that demonstrates to the eyes of the world the sincerity of their views, and their efforts, in favor of a cause worthy of their common concern."[133]

All the British efforts had failed. And the cause of the failure was the conception of all the major powers of Europe which the British could not dispute, and would not dispute in her own interest, that a moral argument alone did not make "law" in the international legal order.

The search for alternatives: a multi-national tribunal?

The legislative process as conceived in the decades following the Napoleonic Wars in Europe involved consent to a proposition as "law," not merely an agreement as to moral principle, no matter how widely and how strongly held. The basic underlying rules of the order were conceded in practice to be not substantive, but constitutional. The *jus gentium* as such was not a source of "law" in the international legal order whatever its weight in the moral order. To conclude this phase of the discussion of the British desire for a right to visit vessels on the high seas suspected of abusing the French flag to cover English crimes, or to reveal to the French the degree to which their own merchants had been violating French law, it should be mentioned that a treaty yielding to the British a limited authority to visit French flag vessels in time of peace was eventually agreed by France, but only a decade later. The Treaty, usually referred to as the Convention of 30 November 1831,[134] itself restricts the British right of visitation to narrowly prescribed areas of the sea; it stops far short of the general authority the British had wanted.

The British did not give up the moral fight because hemmed in by overarching constitutional considerations of the international legal order.

---

[133] Ibid., 109 at 110: "Qu'afin de donner effet à cette Déclaration renouvelée, leurs Cabinets respectifs se livront avec empressement à l'examen de toute Mésure compatible avec leurs droits et les interêts de leurs Sujets, pour amener un résultat, constant aux yeux du Monde la sincerité de leurs voeux, et de leurs efforts, en faveur d'une Cause digne de leur solicitude commune."

[134] 82 CTS 271. The Convention was supplemented in 1833. See note 143 below.

A series of initiatives was undertaken which prompted the most eminent American authority on public international law, Henry Wheaton, to reply in an elaborate legal brief.[135]

In that brief, published in 1842, Wheaton reviewed all the pertinent British and American tribunals' decisions relating to the international slave trade including several not briefed here because rejected as unpersuasive by Wheaton and not cited as significant in international correspondence in later years.[136] He then examined the series of initiatives taken by the British Government beginning at Aix-la-Chapelle in 1818 to find a way consistent with the international legal order to enforce the moral imperatives prohibiting that abomination.

Wheaton regarded Sir William Scott's decision in the *Le Louis* and the United States Supreme Court's decision in the *Antelope* as superseding earlier cases upholding interceptions of slave-trading vessels.[137] Since the earlier cases rested on *jus gentium* theory, the notion that moral abominations universally condemned under the positive law of "civilized" states must be part of the substantive *jus inter gentes*, and applicable against individuals under theories of universal jurisdiction to adjudicate, had now to be rejected. The shift in dominant legal theory was clearly marked.

Wheaton's approach was uncompromisingly dualist. To begin, he was concerned about the integrity of the American Constitution. He notes that there was a substantial United States constitutional question raised in diplomatic correspondence with Castlereagh as early as 1818. Castlereagh had proposed a Convention (i.e., a multi-party treaty) under which the parties, including the United States would agree to multilateral policing of the seas; the capturing vessel (probably a British warship) would haul the slave trader before its own tribunal, which would then enforce the law of the flag state of the captured vessel forbidding the

---

[135] Wheaton, *Enquiry*.

[136] When Wheaton was writing, the fate of those decisions was not yet clear. Wheaton regarded the *Le Louis*, 2 Dodson 210 (1817), and *Antelope*, 23 US (10 Wheaton) 64, 113 (1825), as by far the most persuasive of the slave-trading cases in the common law countries despite their coming to substantive conclusions that he, along with Joseph Story, detested. Indeed, it can be asserted that his (and Story's) ability to rise above moral outrage to see the "law" as necessarily including questions of authority is part of what made them eminent.

[137] Particularly the *Amadie*, 1 Acton's Rep. 240 (1810). Wheaton quotes at some length the opinion of Sir William Grant in that appeals case coming out of the British Vice-Admiralty Court in Tortola. Wheaton, *Enquiry* at 60*ff.* Marshall, in the *Antelope* had also cited it and the other cases discussed by Wheaton when concluding that they were unpersuasive: The *Antelope*, 23 US (10 Wheaton) 64, 113 (1825) at 116–117.

international traffic in slaves. Wheaton records that President James Monroe's Secretary of State, John Quincy Adams, instructed the American Ambassador to reject the idea, questioning the authority of the federal government of the United States under the Constitution to enter into any engagement by which any American could be submitted to "a court consisting partly of foreign judges not amenable to impeachment for corruption, and deciding upon the statutes of the United States without appeal."[138]

The point was carried even further in 1823, when Secretary of State John Quincy Adams replied to initiatives by the British Minister in Washington, Sir Stratford Canning, proposing that the United States become a party to treaties instituting international tribunals with the power to condemn slave traders. Adams again pointed out "the incompatibility of such tribunals with the constitutional rights guaranteed to every citizen of the Union." To his earlier objections, he added the further reference to "those articles in the constitution of the United States which expressly prohibit their constituted authorities from erecting any judicial courts, by the forms of [sic, or?] the process belonging to which American citizens should be called to answer for any penal offence without the intervention of a grand jury to accuse and of a jury trial to decide upon the charge."[139]

Negotiations were held in 1823 and 1824 to get around the American constitutional problems, and a draft treaty was proposed under which the naval vessels of each party were to be authorized to visit and search suspected slavers of the other off the coasts of the United States and British possessions in the Caribbean, but to hand over persons caught carrying on that trade to a competent tribunal of the country to which the accused belonged. When the draft was presented to the Senate of the United States for advice and consent under the Constitution, the provision that permitted British cruisers to visit American flag vessels off the coasts of the United States was stricken out. The American Senate's objection was not to the lesser likelihood of slave-trading vessels being active in the waters of the Gulf of Mexico or the West Indies than in the waters off the British Isles, but to the legal imbalance. Why should British warships be authorized to intercept American vessels off the coasts of the

---

[138] Wheaton, *Enquiry* at 38–39. The correspondence on which Wheaton relied was an instruction from Secretary of State John Quincy Adams to the American Ambassador in London, Mr. Rush, dated 2 November 1818.

[139] Wheaton, *Enquiry* at 80.

United States when American warships were denied the equivalent legal powers off the coasts of Great Britain?[140]

Another objection lay in the provision for the trial of the accused as pirates when they were found in a third-country vessel. Although Wheaton is not clear as to the reasons for this objection, it seems likely that they lay primarily in the inconsistencies implicit in the analogy to "piracy." The participation of American nationals in third-country slave trade was already criminal under American municipal law,[141] and it is hard to understand why a commitment to Great Britain to make it so was anything other than a confusion of the foreign affairs power with the power of the Congress to legislate municipal criminal law for the Union.

A six-months-denunciation clause was inserted, making it clear that in the American Senate the treaty was regarded as positive law only, not a codification of any overarching natural criminal law.

When the British Cabinet refused to accept the American changes, the initiative collapsed.[142]

The British initiative did bear some fruit about ten years later when, in a Convention concluded with France in 1831 and supplemented in 1833, a British right of visitation was conceded by France in specified waters of the West Indies, an East–West band of sea off the west coast of Africa and within twenty leagues of Madagascar on the east coast. Adjudication was to be by the tribunals of the arrested slave-carrying vessel's flag state only.[143]

On the other hand, when Portugal proved impervious to British moral argumentation in the 1830s, an attempt by British municipal law to authorize British enforcement of what was argued to be the natural law forbidding the slave trade even in third-country vessels failed. The initiative proposed in the House of Lords by the Whig Prime Minister,

---

[140] Ibid., 107: "Great Britain is the last maritime power in the world that would consent to the exercise of the right of search, in peace or in war, upon those seas which wash her shores, – those seas over which she has ever asserted the supreme, absolute, and exclusive dominion." Wheaton's history might be a bit exaggerated, but the point is clear.

[141] See pp. 101–102 above.   [142] Wheaton, *Enquiry* at pp. 104–106.

[143] The Convention of 30 November 1831 established the mutual right of visitation for British and French naval vessels to inspect each other's suspected slave-traders in specified areas of the high seas: 18 BFSP (1830–1831) 641 (1833). Some interesting diplomatic correspondence relating to the slave trade and the negotiation of the arrangement is reprinted in ibid., 496*ff*. The 1831 Convention was supplemented on 22 March 1833: 20 BFSP (1832–1833) 286 (1836).

Viscount Melbourne,[144] was supported by the Bishop of London on the ground that:

[T]he British ... nation was especially appointed by Divine Providence, to undertake the task of putting an end to the slave trade, and that her position amongst the maritime nations of the earth, which had given her the power, had at the same time imposed the duty of abolishing this unsanctified traffic.[145]

It was opposed by the Conservatives' former Prime Minister (1828–1830), the Duke of Wellington, on the ground that independent nations, such as the United States (which Wellington referred to by name) must take offense at this arrogation of authority and would successfully press claims for compensation should any American vessel be detained on the basis of British municipal legislation unsupported by a treaty subordinating American vessels to that British authority.[146] The bill passed in the Lords in 1839, but became entangled in British politics and was dropped before it could become law.[147]

It thus appears that in the situations in which moral fervor was strongest, in which there was no dispute about the underlying moral values involved, a distinction was drawn between the substantive rules of law and the rules distributing authority among states. In both its phases, as the substantive rules derived from moral principle, and as substantive rules evidenced regardless of moral principle by the more or less uniform enactments of parallel legal orders, the *jus gentium* was rejected as the basis for action. The *jus inter gentes* which allocates authority among sovereigns was supported as the higher value protected by the international legal order. Rules of substance, even where their moral basis was universally acknowledged in municipal law and by the acquiescence of statesmen, were regarded as possibly fit for legislation binding on sovereigns by treaty, but not by themselves binding in the international legal order.

Perhaps the most revealing aspect of the debates, illustrating the hypocrisy involved when the distribution of authority in the existing legal

---

[144] Melbourne had returned to the office of Prime Minister in May 1839. The initiative was taken in August.

[145] Quoted in Wheaton, *Enquiry* at 113.   [146] Ibid., 111–112.

[147] Sir Robert Peel, Conservative Prime Minister 1834–1835, became Prime Minister again in 1841 and dropped the initiative. It seems unnecessary to review the complexities of British domestic politics of 1839–1841 in this work. William Lamb, 2nd Viscount Melbourne, had been Prime Minister in 1834, again from 1835–1839 and, after a brief bit of electoral turmoil, again in 1839–1841. Obviously, the anti-slave-trade initiative, while important to domestic electoral politics in 1839, was not a major issue for the Melbourne Government as a whole.

order stood in the way of translating these British moral arguments into enforceable rules of law, was the British refusal to concede reciprocal authority to those foreign countries acting under identical moral imperatives to those activating British rhetoric. The British in the middle of the nineteenth century, like many Americans today, trusted their own moral integrity and distrusted the equivalent moral integrity of less powerful states even though all states, whatever their moral, military, economic or social power, were conceived as equal before the law, as all persons under English and American common law are, with only rare and compelling exceptions, legally equal.[148]

The British rejection of the attempt by the United States to import reciprocal authority into the British proposal of 1824 was not unique. In 1839 Haiti passed legislation similar to that which Melbourne had proposed in London except that the Haitian legislation actually provided for adjudication of third-country slave-carrying vessels in Haitian courts (presumably adopting the view that admiralty and prize courts are organs of the universal legal order merely administered by municipal procedures; i.e., that *jus gentium* theory, the basis for so much British argumentation and statements of "conventional wisdom" at the time, really was the basic model for maritime law). In January 1840, Lord Palmerston, Foreign Secretary under the third Government of Melbourne, focused not on the assertion of a universal jurisdiction to adjudicate (which he presumably wanted to continue to assert for British admiralty and prize courts), but on the much broader principles of jurisdiction to prescribe and to enforce. This argument repeats the essence of the American position in 1818 and 1824, and aligns Great Britain also with a view of the international legal order that rejects any state's authority in peacetime to interfere with another's freedom of navigation on the high seas. It adopts the model of the legal order that was so central to Sir William Scott's 1817 decision in the *Le Louis*:

Hayti has undoubtedly a full right to make such an enactment about her own citizens and ships, but her Majesty's Government apprehend that Hayti has no right to legislate for the ships and the subjects or citizens of other states. That in time of peace, no ships belonging to one state have a right to search and detain

---

[148] See pp. 18–19 and comment in chapter 1, note 34. The legal equality of individuals under English law raises other questions better not analyzed in this place. Historically, a trial by a jury of one's peers as provided in cap. 39 of the *Magna Carta* meant that nobility should be tried before a jury of nobles; commoners by commoners. See J. C. Holt, *Magna Carta* (Cambridge University Press, 1969) 226–229. Holt's careful translation raises the question of whether trial by one's feudal equals was an alternative to trial by the different forms of the common law, or part of those forms.

ships sailing under the flag of, and belonging to another state, without the permission of such state, which permission is generally signified by treaty; and if Haytian cruisers were to stop, search, and detain merchant vessels sailing under the flag of, and belonging to another country, even though such vessels were engaged in the slave trade, the state to which such vessels belonged would have just grounds for demanding satisfaction and reparation from Hayti.[149]

In 1842 Wheaton regarded as nearly complete the transformation of civilized state practice to a basically positivist-dualist orientation. He did not use the terms, but his conclusion was that the persistent search for a treaty basis for a right of visitation and search in time of peace (i.e., when not authorized under the customary international laws of war as expressed in practice and diplomatic correspondence in the form usual for the *jus inter gentes*) was conclusive evidence absent express agreement that there was no such right. His review of the adjudications in American and British courts supported this conclusion. Moral imperatives were subordinated to the structure of the legal order and its distribution of authority. He did make one seeming exception: "piracy." But that exception was coupled with a clear assertion that "piracy" meant "piracy under the law of nations," not "trading in slaves" even if that abominable traffic were denominated "piracy" in some texts or by some judges:

It is, therefore, a looseness of language, fatal to all accurate reasoning, to call slave traders "piratical outlaws," and to assert that, for the sake of discovering and punishing these persons as offenders against the law of nations, a general right of search is to be assumed in time of peace, as if cruising against slave traders were to be put on the same footing with public war between sovereign communities.[150]

Conflict of laws

The last legal argument supporting the *jus gentium* as part of public international law rested on the growth of international commerce and the need for property and contract rights granted by the legal process of one country to be valid in another. As early as the fourteenth century in England, a need was felt to free foreign merchants at English fairs, and English merchants visiting foreign fairs with goods for sale whose title derived from English property law, from the technicalities of English common law rules with regard to goods brought into England. Special commercial courts were established by Parliamentary legislation in England, the so-called "Staple" Courts, defining and administering their

[149] Quoted in Wheaton, *Enquiry* 116–117.   [150] Ibid., 144.

own "law merchant."[151] It is not important to this study to trace the history of the Staple Courts or how their law merchant got folded into the English common law. But it is significant for present purposes that by the end of the eighteenth century, a new conception had taken hold: Conflict of Laws. As seen in the tale of the priest of Wen-Amon trading to Dor, its roots lie in the remotest antiquity with the notion that the laws binding the members of one religious worship or political organization did not bind persons outside the perceived legal order, and that the personal law even of traders had to be respected if there were to be any commerce at all between persons construed to be owing obedience to the rules of different legal orders. English commercial enterprise required consideration of the problem, and by the end of the seventeenth century distinctions were being drawn between English law and the law applicable in even British colonies where conditions were different although the settlers themselves were English.[152]

By 1760 the most prestigious English jurist of his time, Lord Mansfield, could refer to a "general rule" under which the law applicable to a contract was the law of the place where the contract is made unless the parties "had a view to a different kingdom."[153] There was considerable difficulty finding an intellectual framework into which this referral to foreign law could be rationalized without appearing to undercut the power of national legislators, and judges in appropriate cases, to make law for all within their jurisdiction. Lord Mansfield's rationale was that the foreign law was in England "established *ex comitate et iure gentium*."[154]

It is an error to attribute Ciceronian meanings to the Latin used by lawyers in non-Ciceronian contexts, and Lord Mansfield's precise notion is better evidenced by context and the jurisprudential mind-set of his time than by linguistic analysis of the Latin classics disregarding intermediate

---

[151] The great Statute of the Staple cited at chapter 1, note 55 above, was 27 Edw. III St. 2, c. 13 (1353), expanded somewhat the next year in 28 Edw. III, c. 12–15 (1354).

[152] That was the situation in *Blanckard* v. *Galdy* (1693) 2 Salk. 411. See also *Smith* v. *Brown & Cooper* (1706) 2 Salk. 666. In many cases the settlers themselves were not English. This raised early "choice of law" questions and provoked some anomalous results. Again, the literature on the point is voluminous. I have attempted a summary of the literature and cases applicable to one colony, where the complexities were typical: Alfred P. Rubin, *International Personality of the Malay Peninsula* (Kuala Lumpur: University of Malaya Press, 1974), *passim*, especially 149–151, 158–167; Alfred P. Rubin, *Piracy, Paramountcy and Protectorates* (Kuala Lumpur: University of Malaya Press, 1974) 81–133.

[153] *Robinson* v. *Bland* 2 Burrow 1077 (1760).

[154] Ibid., Note that the word "*comitate*" is used, relating to a group in attendance, not its derivatives "*comis*" or "*comiter*," which would have related more directly to mere courtesy, kindness and civility.

usages as if the eighteenth-century notion of classical education insulated its best products from legal training and individual thought. The "comity" thus used was distinguished by Lord Mansfield from the *jus gentium* and appears to have been a "naturalist" notion reflecting community obligations saddling England as a member of international society despite the postulated incapacity of foreign sovereigns to make law for English judges, at least as far as the English judges were concerned. The notion to one who was familiar with the writings of Wolff and Vattel appears to have been that all civilized nations in the world formed an informal "committee," or companionship, community, whose common interest and culture engendered a respect for each other's views. This respect was "binding" not because dictated from above but because the system was structured to make it so. The respect owed to foreign views, including foreign legislation with regard to matters within the proper scope of foreigners' discretion, was not so "binding" that it in any degree replaced the discretion of a country's own municipal authorities, who might choose to be discourteous to their neighbors. But it limited to some degree the discretion of the municipal sovereign by social and political pressures without going so far as to appear to subject a "sovereign" to a law to which he had not consented. It is a sociological notion probably derived from Aristotle's well-known analysis of the "natural law" under which the "*polis*" was the form of community to which human beings tended. It has nothing to do with morality or ethics as usually defined. It has much to do with the physical nature of man and mankind's capacity to "reason" in order to gain advantage; to have children; to protect a social organization; and to trade surplus property for what a trader might believe to be the equivalent value of the surplus property of another willing trader.

The notion that "comity," the constraints dictated by wise policy applied to interactions among legal equals, implicitly restricted the authority of statesmen was a brilliant conception for its time. It was a major step in freeing "positivist" jurists from the "naturalist" dogma implicit in the other phrase used by Lord Mansfield, the *jus gentium*.

The foreign law which Mansfield might feel to be the law appropriate to the issue between two private individuals whose case was being heard in an English court would not be directly binding in England. But under the "conventional wisdom" of the time, English common law was based on "reason." If that were so, if the English common law were truly "reasonable," then it should be seen, at least in abstract generality, in the laws, or general principles of law, to be found in other "civilized" legal orders. In sum, English common law in principle should coincide with the *jus gentium*; it should be possible to show that the rules of English common law reflected a version of the underlying natural law which would be binding on all persons without human legislation. Since that underlying law is binding, the enforcement of the foreign transaction under the interpretation and value given it by the foreign law which, by a "natural" distribution of authority, would seem to apply to it, is directly a matter of English law, which incorporates the *jus gentium*.[155] Thus, by the logic implicit in Mansfield's choice of words taken in the jurisprudential context of his time, both "natural law" and, in a sense, "positive law" supported the enforcement in English courts of some "foreign" laws in some circumstances. The notion was rich with implications and ripe for further development.

That development followed a twisting and ironic course which it is impossible to trace here, and is, fortunately, not directly relevant to this study. In brief summary, the notion of "comity" as the basis for legal obligation in a "horizontal" legal order of equal subjects with no common superior but the collectivity of themselves, has survived and to some degree found a rather anomalous place in the literature of public international law, the *jus inter gentes*, where the term has been used to imply that the rules of public international law are somewhat less than binding. The conclusions that flow from this occasional misuse of the term "comity," reflect what seems the usual confusion between the distribution of authority that is the essence of constitutional law in any legal order, and the substantive rules applied in the system. All constitutions are obeyed essentially because those who share authority under them have a political interest in maintaining their position and limiting the assertions of authority by their rivals. But we do call "constitutional law" the study of these relationship established by a constitution. That "law" is binding as law not because enforced by police (although occasionally by armies), but because the alternative is seen as undesirable to those with a place in the constitutional order, in the "community" established or rationalized under conceptions of a "constitutional order." Thus, assertions that "comity" is not a sufficient ground for establishing rules of law seem more polemical than convincing at this time and seem to rest on the assumption that authority structures are issues of right and

---

[155] For a more or less recent reflection of this line of thought, see the opinion of Lord Asquith of Bishopstone in the *Abu Dhabi Arbitration*, reprinted in 1 ICLQ 247 (1952); usefully abstracted in L. C. Green, *International Law Through the Cases* (London: Stevens & Sons Ltd., 2nd edn., 1959) 390.

obligation, rather than issues of right and obligation being issues of authority. This will be considered further below.

In private international law, the term "comity" lost a great deal of its persuasiveness under the impact of the influential synthesis of Justice Joseph Story, whose *Commentaries on the Conflict of Laws* was published in 1834.[156] Story focused on individuals' rights and obligations under the authority structure; he was not addressing constitutional law in any of its phases, but private law. He took basically a "naturalist" position, finding particular references to foreign law by American tribunals to be compelled by "reason" or other sources of "natural law" beyond human discretion. Story assumed that the judiciary was the institution of government charged with defining on the basis of "reason" and the public policy of the legal order erecting the forum, the circumstances under which some foreign law should apply to a case. The substantive question that really interested him was, in cases involving transactions that crossed the boundaries of different legal orders, which foreign law should be interpreted and enforced by the forum. It is not surprising that he found the answer to be in the common law techniques normally used by the tribunals with which he was familiar, subject, of course, to whatever rules governing what he called "conflict of laws"[157] might be enacted for the forum by the legislator of the legal order that authorized the forum to find and apply "law." Thus, he argued that in a real contract dispute before a real tribunal the tribunal should consider the will of the parties, either expressed or implied (normally implied by attributing to them the intention to make the law of the place of contracting the law that determined the validity and interpretation of the contract) to determine the law that makes the contract binding, and the law of the place of performance to be the law that governs interpretations that affect performance. This comports with Lord Mansfield's conclusion as well.

But the most influential and compelling part of the book is its beginning, where Story demolishes the notion of *jus gentium* as an underpinning for substantive rules of law. He does not repeat the logic of Suarez, whose work on the subject does not appear in Story's otherwise

---

[156] Story was by vocation a professor of law. His *Commentaries on the Conflict of Laws* (Boston, 1834, reprinted, 1972) (hereinafter referred to as Story, *Conflict*) records the author not as a Justice of the Supreme Court, which he had been since 1811, but as Dane Professor of Law in Harvard University.

[157] In current legal analyses, "conflict of laws" is usually divided into three parts: jurisdiction, choice-of-law, and enforcement. Story focuses exclusively (or almost) on the second.

long bibliography. Rather, he tackles the question from the point of view of an Anglo-American common law naturalist responding to the European admiration for Roman law and movement towards legislated codification.

Story directly analyzed and rejected the continental European notion that the summary principles collated in Justinian's *Institutes* reflect universal principles approaching the *jus gentium*:

> The jurists of continental Europe have with uncommon skill and acuteness endeavoured to collect principles, which ought to regulate this subject among all nations. But it is very questionable, whether their success has been at all proportionate to their labour; and whether their principles, if universally adopted, would be found either convenient or desirable under all circumstances.[158]

He also downplayed the binding force of "comity" as the basis for the rules of conflict of laws under which a sovereign may choose to apply foreign law to a real case. Misreading the Latin, he reduced "comity" to mere "courtesy," and adopted the "positivist" view that the responsible officials of each state have the discretion to apply or not to apply the foreign law to best meet the public policies of their own municipal order:

> It has been thought by some jurists, that the term, "comity," is not sufficiently expressive of the obligation of nations to give effect to foreign laws, when they are not prejudicial to their own rights and interests. And it has been suggested, that the doctrine rests on a deeper foundation; that it is not so much a matter of comity, or courtesy, as of paramount moral duty. Now, assuming, that such a moral duty does exist, it is clearly one of imperfect obligation, like that of beneficence, humanity, and charity. Every nation must be the final judge for itself, not only of the nature and extent of the duty, but of the occasions, on which its exercise may be justly demanded . . . The true foundation, on which the administration of [private] international law must rest, is, that the rules, which are to govern, are those, which arise from mutual interest and utility, from a sense of the inconveniences, which would result from a contrary doctrine, and from a sort of moral necessity to do justice, in order that justice may be done to us in return.[159]

There is much else in a similar vein.[160]

---

[158] Story, *Conflict* 27.   [159] Ibid., 33, 34.

[160] See Alfred P. Rubin, "Private and Public History; Private and Public Law," 82 PROC 1988 30 (1990). A short analysis of the role of "comity" today in private international law, summarizing some of the evolution of Story's orientation in the 150 years that has passed since then, is Harold Maier, "Extraterritorial Jurisdiction at a Crossroads: An Intersection Between Public and Private International Law," 76 AJIL 280 (1982) at 281–285. For a suggestion that "comity" is a real "glue" holding the international legal order together, see Rubin, "Enforcing", at 159–161. *Per contra*, Cavers, "Critique".

It would be quite wrong to conclude that the movement of mainstream legal thought away from the language of courtesy-"comity" and *jus gentium* itself ended a jurisprudential debate as scholarship adapted itself to the positivist-dualist Westphalian constitution of international society. As always in intellectual life, new generations rediscover the patterns that attracted their intellectual ancestors, frequently with little or no knowledge of the wealth of intellect and energy already expended on the subject. Indeed, contemporary legal literature is filled with "natural law" writings, attempts to replace statesmen, who have real constituents in real legal orders, with scholars and judges seizing on incidental or irrelevant or unconsidered language of earlier decisions or diplomatic correspondence to argue for the "obligation" of statesmen to obey the insights of irresponsible scholars and moralists.[161] But it is not the function of this study to pick quarrels with advocates for any particular model of the current legal order. Rather it has been the aim to expose the intellectual origins of the current international legal order in operation and its evolution into a frankly positivist and dualist system as an implication of the probable inherent structure of human society as demonstrated in correspondence going back 3,000 years, and the facts of the Westphalian settlement of the middle of the seventeenth century.

The Westphalian settlement was the result of the liberation by its own efforts of the Dutch Republic from Spanish legal domination. It produced a radical shift in the description of the legislative process of the international legal order. This was perceived immediately by the active statesmen and scholars of the seventeenth century and pursued with increasing confidence since then, while later scholars of the law played with substantive issues of justice and morality as if inseparable from issues of law in its constitutional distribution-of-authority phases until harsh reality and intellectual honesty brought about a revolution in thought. But revolutions never end, and the issues raised in this study have major implications both for those whose deep moral feelings face the same frustrations, and engender the same enthusiasms, as the British anti-slavery movement of the early nineteenth century, and for those whose notion of international crime parallel the notions of those for whom "piracy" should be the occasion for international tribunals, or at

---

[161] See Mark Janis, "The Recognition and Enforcement of Foreign Law: The *Antelope*'s Penal Law Exception," 20(1) IL 303 (1986), showing that two generations of American lawyers blindly accepted a patently erroneous interpretation created in a 1932 HLR article of a sentence by Chief Justice Marshall concerning foreign penal laws in the *Antelope*, 23 US (10 Wheaton) 64, 113 (1825).

least national tribunals seizing and trying foreigners whose actions implicated only other foreigners on the high seas or in foreign territory. Setting forth a few implications for today should serve to tie things together.

4   Putting it together

The rise of positivism and the naturalist reaction

The development of conflict of laws, with its emphasis on the municipal law bases for jurisdiction to prescribe, to enforce and to adjudicate, and its "choice-of-law" solution to the inconsistencies created by *jus gentium* theory in a world of equal "sovereigns," was accompanied by a great simplification and refinement of basic "positivist" jurisprudence. Joseph Story's seminal book was published in 1834. It is probably evidence of a *Zeitgeist* that John Austin's lectures, *The Province of Jurisprudence Determined*, were delivered in 1832, very shortly before.[1]

In his introduction, Austin divides "law" into four categories: divine law, positive law, rules of "positive morality" and "laws metaphorical or figurative."[2] He defines "natural law" as either a part of divine law, a sort of positive morality, or only figuratively called "law."[3] He goes on:

The positive moral rules which are laws improperly so called, are *laws set* or *imposed by general opinion* ... Some are set or imposed by the general opinion of a larger society formed of various nations ... And laws or rules of this species, which are imposed upon nations or sovereigns by opinions current amongst nations, are usually styled *the law of nations* or *international law* (emphasis *sic*).[4]

Note that to Austin, publishing in 1832, the phrases "law of nations" and "international law" are synonymous, reflecting the shift in concept and language of his time. Indeed, he is quite specific about the shift in language:

---

[1] John Austin, *The Province of Jurisprudence Determined* (1832, Weidenfeld & Nicolson reprint, 1954).
[2] Ibid., 1.   [3] Lecture V, 129–131.   [4] Ibid., 140–141.

Society formed by the intercourse of independent political societies, is the province of international law, or of the law obtaining between nations. For (*adopting a current expression*) international law, or the law obtaining between nations ... regards the conduct of sovereigns as related to one another (emphasis added).[5]

The assumption that municipal legal orders are the only truly "legal" systems in a world of equally sovereign "states," reducing the *jus gentium* to nothing and the *jus inter gentes* to rules of "positive morality,"[6] is in retrospect so naïve and simplistic that it is somewhat surprising that it took yet another century for "positivism" to develop a really useful model of the distribution of authority in the world and the rôle of "law" in both its constitutional and its substantive phases. That model was set out in its simplest and most persuasive form by Hans Kelsen, an Austrian scholar, in 1934.[7]

Kelsen defined the "state" itself as essentially a "legal order." He adopted a "monist" position in which municipal legal orders derived their authority by a metaphysical delegation from the overarching international legal order, thus preserving Austin's vertical conception of law:

[T]he principle of effectiveness (which is a norm of positive international law), determines both the reason for the validity and the territorial, personal, and temporal sphere of validity of the national legal orders; and these, therefore, may be conceived as being delegated by international law and therefore subordinated to it – conceived, in other words, as partial legal orders included in a universal world legal order; the coexistence of the national legal orders in space and their succession in time is then made legally possible by international law.[8]

But the strains and inconsistencies inherent in the dominant train of "positivist" thinking, and their partial solutions in the models of later scholars would take us too far into mere model-building, too far from reality, to be worth pursuing in this place.

One of the great ameliorations of the rigidity of Kelsen's model of the international legal order must be noted. When the Permanent Court of International Justice was established in 1920, a codification of the sources of "international law" was achieved. The founding document of the court, its "Statute," provides:

[5] Lecture VI, in ibid., at 200–201.
[6] Ibid., Lecture V at 127, 141–142; Lecture VI at 200–201.
[7] Kelsen, *Pure Theory*. The first edition was published in 1934.
[8] Ibid., at 336.

38. The Court [, whose function it is to decide cases in accordance with international law such disputes as are submitted to it,]⁹ shall apply:

1. International conventions, whether general or particular, establishing rules expressly recognized by the contesting States;
2. International custom, as evidence of a general practice accepted as law;
3. The general principles of law recognized by civilized nations;
4. Subject to the provisions of Article 59,¹⁰ judicial decisions and the teachings of the most highly qualified publicists of the various nations, as subsidiary means for the determination of rules of law.¹¹

In a final, unnumbered, paragraph, the fundamental positivism of the system to be applied by the court was made unmistakable; moral arguments were distinguished from legal arguments: "This provision shall not prejudice the power of the Court to decide a case *ex aequo et bono*, if the parties agree thereto."¹² Presumably, if the parties did not agree that the court should apply the rules of morality, deciding the case on the basis of equity and the good, the court lacked the authority to intermix those considerations with its analysis of the positive law as set out in the four numbered subparagraphs. To the extent "equity" or other moral considerations could be included in the conception of "law," then the court would have to find those conceptions accepted by states in the usual way for rules of positive law. Of course, various arguments for finding such rules among the "general principles of law recognized by civilized

---

⁹ The bracketed phrase was added to the Statute of the Court when the Statute of the Permanent Court of International Justice was superseded by the Statute of the current International Court of Justice in 1945. Except for the technical amendment noted at note 11 below, the two Statutes are, in all respects pertinent to this study, identical.

¹⁰ Article 59 provides that: "The decision of the Court has no binding force except between the parties and in respect of that particular case." It is a simple statement of the usual "*res judicata*" rule of municipal legal orders, but because phrased in the negative has often been mistaken for a rule denying "*stare decisis*." "*Stare decisis*" is a rule of Anglo-American common law that requires lower courts to adhere to the rules enunciated by courts superior to them in that legal order. Since there is no court in the international legal order either superior or inferior to the Permanent Court of International Justice or its successor of 1945, the current International Court of Justice, and since any court can overrule its own precedents even in the common law systems, the frequent references to *stare decisis* in the context of Article 59 of the Statute of the Court seem to reflect a fairly widespread misunderstanding of the Latin phraseology and the operation of common law systems of adjudication.

¹¹ Statute of the Permanent Court of International Justice, 16 December 1920, PCIJ Ser. D, No. 1, 2nd edn., 8–22. The Statute was revised in 1929 in ways irrelevant to this analysis.

¹² When the current International Court of Justice was established in 1945, the first paragraph with its listing of the permissible sources of law was designated paragraph 1, with the four sources listed in it as a, b, c, and d; this unnumbered paragraph was designated paragraph 2 of article 38.

states" or among the opinions treated as "subsidiary means for the determination of rules of law" exist and are persuasive to those who wish to be persuaded that Article 38(2) was not intended to be meaningful.[13]

Regardless of the place of "equity" in the agreed (thus "positivist") listing of the formal sources of rules of law in the international legal order, the listing can be easily seen to have reduced the naturalist emphasis on learned opinion to a "subsidiary" place in the hierarchy of sources of "law."[14] It emphasizes the "positivist" sources based on discretionary consent by statesmen through accession to "conventions" (treaty) and participation in custom, asserted to be law primarily by diplomatic correspondence and consistent practice against short-term interest.[15] It preserves the concept of a *jus gentium* as municipal law evidence ("recognized by civilized nations") of overarching principles ("general principles of law") assumed to exist as substantive rules also in the international legal order.

What is left of the *jus gentium* was the subject of Sir Hersch Lauterpacht's first great contribution to an understanding of the international legal order. His doctoral dissertation at the University of London in 1925 was expanded and published in 1927.[16] In it, he shows that the "general principles" applied as municipal law in many states are not directly

---

[13] On this point, see Mark Janis, "The Ambiguity of Equity in International Law," 9(1) BJIL 7 (1983).

[14] For an example of a key naturalist jurisprudential writer relying heavily on learned opinion as evidence of true "law" to the exclusion of realities, see Joseph Story's 1820 opinion in *US* v. *Smith*, 18 US (5 Wheaton) 20 (1820); see also Wheaton's long commentary on *US* v. *Wiltberger*, 18 US (5 Wheaton) 76 (1820) at 106–116.

[15] See Anthony A. D'Amato, *The Concept of Custom in International Law* (Cornell University Press, 1971). Chapter 4 of this work (73–102) is the best single analysis that I know of theories that convincingly relate practice (and abstention) to "custom" and some "custom" to "law." In my own opinion, which surely repeats things written elsewhere but not familiar to me, practice or abstention by a state that seems to gain by its action or inaction is not probative of as much in law as in political theory. But when a state acts or fails to act in a situation in which its action or failure seems to cost it some legal advantage, the "precedent" can be persuasively used against other states in an analogous position. The subject admits of too many variations to be elaborated beyond this point in this study. For a start, compare D'Amato's work with Leo Gross, "States as Organs of International Law and the Problem of Autointerpretation," in G. A. Lipsky (ed.), *Law and Politics in the World Community* (University of California (Berkeley) Press, 1953) 59; also in 1 Gross, *Essays on International Law and Organization* (Transnational Publishers, 1984) 367; in the one volume edition (1993) at 167.

[16] Hersch Lauterpacht, *Private Law Sources and Analogies of International Law* (Longmans, Green & Co., London, 1927, reprinted Archon Books, 1970). It is a sobering thought that Sir Hersch was not only writing in a language not his native one, but was only 27 years old when he wrote this and 29 when it was published.

applicable as substantive rules in the international legal order, the *jus inter gentes*, although many such rules have analogies in rules applied in practice and found applicable by arbitrators and judges in the international legal order. For example, the near-universal municipal law rule that makes promises given with a formal seal or "consideration" or "*causa*" binding and invalidates promises made under physical coercion would invalidate many peace treaties. Therefore, the international legal order can accept coercion as invalidating a treaty commitment only with many conditions and exceptions; not as a general principle.[17] Lauterpacht ingeniously (also ingenuously) suggested that the basis for a rule nullifying coerced treaties lay already (in 1927) in Article 10 of the Covenant of the League of Nations, placing treaty-based, positivist, procedural obstacles in the way of legal recourse to force by member states of the League, but not wholly forbidding it. His suggestion was adopted with a naturalist twist in the 1969 Vienna Convention on the Law of Treaties, Article 52:

A treaty is void if its conclusion has been procured by the threat or use of force in violation of the principles of international law embodied in the Charter of the United Nations.[18]

In the light of state practice and the moral desirability of ending even "unjust" wars, by treaty if necessary, it is doubtful indeed that Article 52 of the Vienna Convention sets out a rule that either codifies an existing rule of general international law or creates a viable rule of current treaty law. It can certainly be regarded as an international agreement as to moral principle that should be applied in practice when that application does not diminish to an unacceptable degree other moral values of the international order.

Sir Hersch was not alone as a "naturalist" transforming the focus of scholarship in law from positivist description which, if understood, can help statesmen achieve political goals, to naturalist prescription. Prescribing the law is normally the rôle of a legislator, a person or group authorized by the system to create "law," rather than a lawyer, a person

---

[17] Ibid., sections 73–74 at 161–167. Lauterpacht supports the analogy between municipal law contracts and international treaties in the usual naturalist way, by citing writers who take the position he wants to support and simply asserting them to be a majority without deeper analysis of the number and quality of those taking a different view, or why those he cites take the view he prefers. But he ends by arguing that the analogy must exclude treaties concluded by coercion until the international legal order develops rules that make coercion illegal.

[18] 1969 Vienna Convention on the Law of Treaties, UN doc. A/CONF.39/27 (1969), Article 52.

authorized by the system to argue the law before others. Sir Hersch recognized that judges and arbitrators frequently play a rôle that confuses the two functions by purporting to enforce existing rules that did not clearly exist until the judge or arbitrator said so. But Sir Hersch seems to neglect the corollary that exists in all known legal orders, that the "law" pronounced by a judge or arbitrator in a particular case is posited to exist only for the particular parties and the particular case before the particular judge or arbitrator, however "persuasive" to other judges or arbitrators (or lawyers).

Sir Hersch, in emphasizing the rôle of private law, municipal law, analogies to the rules of public international law that he posits seems to have been trying to revive the *jus gentium*. His basic idea appears to have been that "international law" applies to individuals through municipal legal orders in the usual case, but not necessarily through anything – perhaps in some cases directly; that municipal legal orders are somehow "bound" to conform their municipal prescriptions and enforcement to the universal "rules" of the international legal order discovered by moral analysis based on the acceptance universally of fundamental moral principles and labeling them norms of "law." But that is the very *jus gentium* approach that had failed in the only cases in which it had to be measured against actual action: the criminal law applied to "piracy," "war crimes," and the attempt to translate the moral revulsion at slavery into a legally enforceable system that would supersede municipal law or somehow require the various states' municipal law systems to enforce the supposed international prohibition of at least the international traffic in slaves as chattels.

In the enthusiasm that followed the Second World War, Philip C. Jessup, an American jurist and judge in the International Court of Justice, the successor to the Permanent Court of International Justice, wrote two books trying openly to revive the *jus gentium*.[19] The main theme, that the problems of international society have simple analogies to the everyday problems faced by municipal orders and that it is impossible in the modern world to confine the operation of rules of law to hermetically sealed territorial units, led him to conclude that there must be general rules that require states to harmonize their laws; that there must be a "transnational" law that governs legal relations that cross national boundaries. He bluntly argues that the post-Second World War behavior of

---

[19] Philip C. Jessup, *A Modern Law of Nations* (Macmillan Co., 1946, reprinted Archon Books 1968) and *Transnational Law* (Yale University Press, 1956).

states and the behavior of private parties cannot be clearly distinguished; that capitalism had modified itself and socialism had become the operating system for many municipal orders. He actually proposed that the phrase "international law" be replaced with the "fine Roman expression, *jus gentium*" and chose to call his own work *A Modern Law of Nations* with knowledge of the history of the term. In his view, "positivism" had won the jurisprudential battles of the nineteenth century, so "the hypothesis on which this discussion proceeds involves a break with the past."[20]

To solve the obvious problem of defining a legislator for the desired international legal order, Jessup echoes Aristotle. He concludes that the needs of society, not consent, must be the fundamental law-creating process. To harmonize differing views as to the needs of the increasingly complex and interactive "transnational" society, he argued that the United Nations should be developed until it becomes an effective world government:

[T]he lack of universality of the United Nations presents the problem of the rights of third states. Under the hypothesis of the acceptance of the principle of community interest, the proposed law would be considered to be a law of general application, and non-Member states might be invited to adhere to the conventions embodying the rules. But . . . the rules should be deemed applicable to third states even if they do not adhere.[21]

But Jessup's attractive, idealistic and insightful proposals for an operating model of international (or transnational) society were not, or could not be, made the basis for a living international legal order. I cannot forbear from mentioning that in the early 1960s, when, as a lawyer in the office of the Assistant General Counsel (International Security Affairs) in the United States Department of Defense, I had a long discussion with a Department of State lawyer, later to become dean of a law school, concerning a legal situation in which Jessup's model seemed attractive to both of us and would have made a significant difference in the way a problem was approached officially by the United States Government. In full sympathy with Jessup's ideals, we nonetheless decided that his model could not work in practice; at least not in the specific situation confronting us.

I don't know if Jessup himself ever modified his views significantly. But as a judge in the International Court of Justice he wrote a long separate opinion ultimately concurring with the overwhelming majority (15–1 with the one being the judge *ad hoc* of the losing party) in a case denying

---

[20] Jessup, *A Modern Law of Nations* 17.   [21] Ibid., 221.

recourse to a claimant when Jessup's model of the international legal order would seem to have led to a very different conclusion. Jessup's logic in that opinion was basically that until all the facts relevant to his model's notion of a complete analysis of the case were revealed to the court, the court could not come to a decision and should not permit itself to be used as part of a political bargain among contesting parties with many other interests at play.[22] Given the realities of state involvement in what are presented as private multinational transactions in the late twentieth century, it is very difficult to imagine a real situation in which his model world of a "transnational legal order" would not founder on the same rocks, making judicial recourse under the current order's institutional arrangements all but futile.

The frustration of those who would like their perceptions of community values to be propounded with general legislative effect by judges dealing only with specific cases seems frequently to lead them to assert that their views have already won the consensus of all relevant parties except some "positivist" whose writings are under discussion. It is a polemical view that does not help the clarity of discussion.[23] No doubt this study, if read or cited at all, will be subjected to the same treatment by those unhappy with its conclusions.

The "evolving" world order and "interdependence"

It is frequently asserted that the "victory" of "positivism" in the nineteenth century might have been appropriate to the world of that time, but that universal law is required by increasing interdependence, the enormous expansion of international communications and transportation and the integration of what had hitherto been practically as well as legally segregated societies and economies. There is no doubt that if integrated economies are the highest values in the international legal order, as some believe they are, other values would have to yield place. But such a conclusion should not be accepted without a closer evaluation of the facts and the values to be diminished by such a shift in model.

As to the facts, while the expansion of international (or transnational)

---

[22] See *Barcelona Traction, Light, and Power Co. Case (Belgium v. Spain) (Second Phase), ICJ Reports* (1970).

[23] José E. Alvarez, "Review of Danilenko, Law-Making in the International Community," 15(3) MJIL 474 (1994). I cite only one example, and that only because probably necessary to those who think I exaggerate. Alvarez's article is actually most enlightening and worth perusing for those interested in modern "naturalist" thought quite apart from the technique of argumentation.

contacts seems undeniable, it seems equally undeniable that statesmen have jealously preserved their authority under their municipal constitutions and the authority of their states in the international order. The proliferation of specialized international agencies dealing with international communications, transportation and many other matters reflecting our economic and social interdependence, has not involved any irrevocable delegations of authority to the civil servants or other officials of those agencies. The closest to such irrevocable arrangements recently achieved have been in the European Union, now delayed by the insistence of several of the member states that control over their financial regulations remain matters of state authority and not be delegated to a multinational or independent authority which might endanger the financial stability of particular members in somebody else's evaluation of the interest of the supposed community. The obstacle is the one which the present analysis would have predicted.

Another arrangement argued to represent an irrevocable trend towards world government has been the interpretation of the Charter of the United Nations to expand the bindingness of "decisions" of the Security Council beyond the area of international "peace and security" originally envisaged. To those familiar with European history, it looks like the same rationale that supported the Holy Alliance after the Napoleonic Wars. But the Holy Alliance failed in part because major powers, particularly Great Britain and the regional power of the young United States, refused to join; in part because the pretensions of the Holy Alliance were rejected by the "colonies," particularly the Spanish colonies in Latin America, for whom "legitimacy" as determined by the princes of Europe would block the movement towards local self-government that seemed to them the higher political value. It is very hard to see now that those states which would lose by the consolidation of authority in the Security Council would choose to remain in the United Nations if the authority of the Security Council were interpreted by its members to extend too far.[24] Moreover, the hypocrisies involved are so clear that the entire attempt seems more likely to weaken the structure of the law than to lead to its wider

---

[24] A recent example of the attempt of the members of the Security Council to extend their authority beyond what many would regard as the intended meaning of the phrase "international peace and security" is the so-far futile attempt of the Security Council to force Libya to surrender two of its officials to foreign tribunals in relation to atrocities several years ago for which those officials might or might not have had some responsibility: See Alfred P. Rubin, "Libya, Lockerbie and the Law", 4(1) D&S 1-19 (1993) (hereinafter cited as Rubin, *LLL*).

observance. For example, the current effort to operate an international tribunal under Security Council authority to deal with the "grave breaches" of the 1949 Geneva Conventions and other atrocities occurring in the former Yugoslavia, under the plea that the individuals as "war criminals" are directly subject to international law and whatever processes the community erects to enforce that law, exclude the identical acts committed by officials of the enacting states; the tribunal's writ extends only to the actors in former Yugoslavia, and the ones of most concern, the Bosnian Serb leadership, are not represented in the United Nations at all. But under the analysis above, other ameliorations of the tragedy of the Balkans are possible. One or two will be noted below. Under the pressure of enthusiasts who believe the entire system will change to accommodate their *jus gentium* notions, the alternatives are not being proposed by serious statesmen.

As to values, the most obvious value to suffer by accepting a model of world order based upon universal values and a notion of universal "law" to which municipal systems would have to conform, is the value of self-determination. Who is the "law-maker," the legislator, of the world under the "evolving" system? In the past, judging by Joseph Story's approach in *United States v. Smith* and *La Jeune Eugénie*, the judges, like Story himself, become legislators, informed by the text-writers they choose to rely on in the cases before them. Lawyers, as advocates for rules they perceive resulting from "comity" or selected precedents, participate as direct actors in the law-making process. The result is that the law becomes inherently retroactive; that nobody knows what the law is until a judge has heard all the arguments and made a decision, and that decision operates retroactively on the parties before him or her. As to the prospective operation of the law, in the common law system of law-making familiar to Story, the same judge in a later case, other judges in the appeal of the same case, if there is one, and later judges in the same facts but a different case, or judges in sister jurisdictions in any case, can ignore or overturn the "judge-made" or "judge-found" or "judge-pronounced" rule of "law." Story himself did all of those things. In the circumstances, it appears that the common law rationale for judges' authority to "find" the law operates as "legislation" only in a very attenuated sense, and not at all in the senses proposed by its most vigorous advocates. The key is that even under the usual common law approaches, a judge's decision binds only the parties in the case before him or her.

Worse, statesmen, those who climb to the top of municipal constitutional orders to assume positions of authority in "states," find their actions measured against standards applied by persons selected by other processes. What are those other processes? Who are the "judges" and who licenses the "lawyers"? Would judges selected by municipal legal orders' processes be accepted by the integrated world community as having world interests uppermost in their minds? Would any municipal legal order make expertise in international affairs a qualification for appointment to judicial positions? If so, how? Who would fix the standards? Under whose oversight? Would the "election" of judges be inconsistent with the system? What about election of the people who select judges? Indeed, the closer the conclusion that an increasingly interdependent society requires uniform law and an international law-making process, the more it begins to appear that the argument involves a leap of the imagination that leaves out all the difficult steps. The problem is not new. Proposals for governance by "guardians" specially qualified by hypothetical virtue, insight or intelligence (or all three) have been popular among those who believe themselves possessed of all three since at least the time of Plato. But: *quis custodet custodiens*?; who supervises the supervisors?

Indeed, several models of a more integrated world have been examined by an articulate and experienced international civil servant and these problems, and many more, have been raised.[25] No answers have been given. There appears to be an assumption that the problems will somehow disappear or solutions will be found consistent with the *jus gentium* model of the legal order if the model is pushed hard enough. But the collapse of that model when it was part of the conventional wisdom of all active European statesmen, and its successful replacement by a choice-of-law positivist model, dictate a different conclusion. If a general adoption of the *jus gentium* model is indeed the direction of world political organization, then instead of joyful anticipation, some attention should be paid by lawyers to the values threatened by that movement and, if appropriate and feasible, legal safeguards put in place to protect those values.

Moreover, it is not at all clear that the trend towards greater economic and social integration is not already accompanied by strains that the existing system cannot well handle and that the posited universal *jus gentium* system already failed to be able to handle when the signs first appeared some two centuries ago. The resurgence of ethnic nationalism, of which the Nazi spasm in central Europe in the middle of this century was only the most notorious recent disaster, seems already to have

---

[25] Evan Luard, *Types of International Society* (New York: The Free Press, 1976) chapter 14 ("Future International Societies"), at 345–361.

become a major destabilizing factor in the world. The Nazi spasm seems not to have been an aberration (although its occurrence in Germany, by any measure surely one of the most sophisticated societies of the world in the 1930s, surely exacerbated its effects) but a graphic illustration of the evils to be avoided primarily by accepting the likelihood of many people believing that religious or ethnic or other self-defined "identities" justify atrocities against "outsiders" in the name of "self-defense" of the "group" the "defender" fancies is under threat. From this point of view, it is quite possible to suggest that both models of human nature normally discussed, that which defines human beings as essentially and by nature "benign" and that which defines human beings as essentially and by nature "malign," should be replaced by a different intellectual model. Perhaps it would be helpful to regard human beings as "wired" to defend the extended family against any threat, however remote, as a value essential to survival in our earliest evolution. If that is so, then the solution cannot be to rework our wiring. To rewire us is probably impossible, and certainly impossible within the time possibly available to us if we are to avoid sociological disaster in the next century or so. Nor is the solution to assert with whatever vigor that mankind is fundamentally benign; that "human rights" encompass universal values that will be acted upon as the world becomes smaller.

The solution must involve reprogramming ourselves. Reprogramming does not mean asserting that we are bound by any "law" that we refuse to obey when the circumstances arise that make obedience inconsistent with "wired" patterns of thought. Reprogramming means offering alternatives that make it in our interest to act more benignly when threatened. Dispute-resolution mechanisms must be put in place and made attractive to statesmen; solutions that do not transform a losing case into a total disaster, as the "legal" order frequently transforms a close case into an absolute "victory" for one party and a total loss to the other. An example might be the Malvinas/Falklands situation between Argentina and the United Kingdom in 1982, when the British offer to submit the Argentine case to a tribunal was necessarily viewed by the Argentines as disingenuous, because it would transform what might have been a substantial but not likely winning Argentine national issue from a colorable argument worth something politically, to nothing.[26]

---

[26] For background in the substance of the matter and the legal arguments, see Alberto R. Coll and Anthony C. Arend, *The Falklands War* (Boston: George Allen and Unwin, 1985), especially Alfred P. Rubin, "Historical and Legal Background of the Falkland/Malvinas Dispute" at 9–21.

"Monism" versus "dualism" again

"Incorporation"

It seems to be widely asserted today, perhaps even "conventional wisdom," that the substantive rules of the international legal order are "incorporated" into the law of the United States. That view seems clearly inconsistent with the municipal distribution of authority embodied in the United States Constitution by its framers. The view is not only inconsistent with the language of the Constitution taken in the jurisprudential context of its time, but was explicitly rejected by the Supreme Court under Chief Justice John Marshall, despite the vigorous argumentation of such "naturalist-incorporationist" giants as Joseph Story and Henry Wheaton. But the evidence analyzed above indicates at least four reasons for its persistence. Three of those reasons involved confusions of language and logic; the fourth probably underlies the entire debate.

The most superficial, but most often used, reason is the persistence of *jus gentium* language in admiralty and prize cases, like the 1900 prize case, the *Paquete Habana*,[27] taken by many far beyond their special context. As noted above, in admiralty and prize proceedings, *jus gentium* theory and language have persisted where not superseded by positive legislation. It is notable that nearly all the citations used to support "incorporation" theory are taken from admiralty or prize cases; supporters of "incorporation" then appear to assume that the language relating the American cases to the international legal order states traditional rules applicable outside of the admiralty and prize context. The assumption seems unjustifiable. It is relatively clear that when the decisions of foreign admiralty or prize tribunals are not considered persuasive by the judge in any particular forum, they are not followed and no problem of *stare decisis* appears to require an answer.[28]

The second reason is a bit deeper. The juristic confusions of the Age of Reason, particularly the period 1778–1810 or so, are reflected in some

---

[27] The case is cited and its key language quoted in chapter 3 note 48.

[28] See, for example, Joseph Story's dismissal in the *La Jeune Eugénie* case of Sir William Scott's very persuasive opinion in the *Le Louis*, discussed at some length at pp. 103, 110–114. There are many other such examples. For a very influential and oft-cited English admiralty judge, Stephen Lushington, ignoring the opinions of the United States Supreme Court in analogous cases to one before him, see the *Magellan Pirates*, 1 Spink Ecc. & Ad. 81 (1853), 3 *British International Law Cases* 780. The American cases involved were *US* v. *Smith*, 18 US (5 Wheaton) 20 (1820); *US* v. *Palmer*, 16 US (3 Wheaton) 610 (1818); and *US* v. *Klintock*, 18 US (5 Wheaton) 144 (1820). The situation is analyzed in Rubin, *Piracy* 233–236.

cases not involving admiralty or prize and in some diplomatic correspondence of that time. We have seen how the confusion was expressed in the debate between Gouverneur Morris and James Wilson during the drafting of our Constitution's provision empowering the Congress to "define and punish . . . offences against the law of nations."[29] We have seen also how it appeared in the reports of some early cases, although those cases were typically decided against the views of those arguing that universal law governed the outcome of cases heard by American judges or limited the powers given to the Congress by the new Constitution.[30] The overstatements of insupportable assertions of "conventional wisdom" of the period 1750 or so through 1834 left "precedents" for outmoded models of the legal order preserved in the language of some decisions and debates.

A third source of current confusion lies still deeper. *Jus gentium* theory has never been wholly abandoned by some jurists. Part of the bedrock of "naturalist" thinking has been the attempt to free it of the accusation of solipsism; the accusation by "positivist" scholars that many assertions of "law" by naturalist jurists assume that the jurist's personal value-based moral insights are universal. The argument that general principles of law to be found in many different legal orders represent empirical evidence that some moral values are "wired" into the human conscience and deserve to be categorized as rules of "law" applicable in all systems, including the international legal order, is implied in the Wen-Amon tale of about 1000 BC, is explicit in the Roman codes of Gaius and Justinian, and was "conventional wisdom" by the end of the eighteenth century in Europe. That this *jus gentium* argument was weak, indeed illogical and inconsistent with practicalities and empirical evidence, was repeatedly pointed out by such thinkers as Aristotle, Suarez and Pufendorf, but it continued to have a direct effect in the minds of many. That it had no bearing on the great moral-legal issue of the international traffic in humans, the slave trade, revolted self-confident, indeed brilliant, "naturalist" jurists like Joseph Story and Henry Wheaton. But the arguments of Sir William Scott and John Marshall proved unanswerable. The yearning continued. It continues today and surfaces in the notion that "inter-

---

[29] See pp. 73–74 above.

[30] Particularly *Henfield's Case*, 11 *Federal Cases* 1099 (1793), and the correspondence surrounding the case arising out of the voyage of *Romp* (see pp. 95–97 above) and other admiralty cases, like *The Charming Betsy*, 6 US 208, 2 Cranch 64 (1804), and the confusions in the mind of such eminent lawyer-statesmen as John Jay, e.g., his views regarding the superiority of international law to the Constitution, which were rejected the first time the issue was faced squarely by the Congress. See p. 77 above.

national law" is "incorporated" into the municipal law of the United States, bringing into that latter body of law rules based on the insights of scholars of comparative law and value-morality applied across cultural lines. That Joseph Story seems to have changed his mind and developed a very different approach, conflict of laws in its choice-of-law phase, that preserves the separate identity of different legal orders and enables judges in a common law system to adjudicate and enforce whatever "foreign" law they deem appropriate to a particular case, by the institutions of their own legal order, seems to be ignored. The argument that choice-of-law techniques allow United States courts to apply a foreign rule, say French law in some cases, without "incorporating" that foreign legal order or its rules into the American system, seems to be ignored.

Perhaps this last anti-"incorporation" argument is considered unpersuasive because American interpretations of French law are totally unpersuasive in France, as French interpretations of United States law are unpersuasive in the United States except perhaps in some cases of admiralty or prize. But if the international legal order is perceived as a "monist" system, with national tribunals serving a function in their municipal law systems and in the international legal order simultaneously (a *"dédoublement fonctionelle"*[31]), interpreting the law both for purposes of a municipal ruling and with persuasive precedential effect in the international legal order directly, the notion that the international legal order is "foreign" to the law of the United States is lost. It is only when the basic assumption of "monism" is questioned that the inconsistencies in this approach cease to require elaborate mental gymnastics and Occam's Razor makes the simpler "dualist" analysis persuasive. The tug of classical *jus gentium* thinking seems to be very strong indeed in the minds of many jurists, and the availability of a classically based alternative that is simpler does not appear persuasive to them.

A fourth root of "incorporation" theory is usually passed over in silence but may be the deepest of all. It is the struggle for authority. If the rules of "international law" are incorporated into a municipal legal order, then in a common law system lawyers and judges, plus foreigners, persons with authority under legal orders other than the one seeking to adjudicate or enforce the "law," become law-makers for the municipal legal order at the expense of the legislators and administrators of that order. But the lawyers are not selected for moral insight, and even the most learned

---

[31] The phrase entered the general vocabulary of international lawyers through the publication of Georges Scelle, *Précis de Droit des Gens, Deuxième Partie: Droit Constitutionnel International* (1934) 10–12.

judges do disagree with each other about important moral and legal questions. And foreigners are the products of foreign municipal legal orders with their own value systems and political pressures; it is hard to see them as importing moral objectivity into the international system.

In the British and American municipal legal orders, persons given the authority of law-makers by the constitutional processes of a democratic or popular-election system are likely to reflect public-relations campaigns, to be naïvely chosen or appointed for other reasons than their moral insight or legal acumen. The appeal of "incorporation theory" is to replace them with lawyers' and judges' evaluations of the persuasiveness of scholarly writings and judicial precedents. Joseph Story's handling of both *La Jeune Eugénie* and *US v. Smith*, the piracy case upholding the validity of the "Piracy Act" of 1819,[32] illustrates the technique and the rôle of the judiciary and the lawyers who argue before them. In evaluating this approach, it is well to bear in mind that scholars usually differ over any serious question; the Wen-Amon debate has been with them (us?) for more than 3,000 years. Except in rare cases, like Sir William Scott's opinion in *Le Louis* and John Marshall's in *Antelope*,[33] which carried along the very strong minds of those whose earlier opinions made it clear that they loathed the result in those cases, the selection of scholarly analyses as persuasive by a judge illustrates more the judge's prejudices than any consensus of scholars. And, as has been repeatedly seen, "conventional wisdom" is not a reliable source of insight.

The implications of a shift from amateur legislators selected by amoral, intellectually unreliable processes to professional jurist-legislators selected by other amoral educational and political processes are many; too many to be fully analyzed here. But the principal one in a representative form of government seems to be to remove authority from the elected and appointed representatives of "the people" or other existing constituency groups. Those municipally elected or selected legislators are replaced at least in part by the representatives of various governments and non-governmental organizations, lobbies, in international organizations and the judiciary of foreign legal orders, by lawyers whose training has been in rhetorical logic, argumentation, rather than in evaluating the relative weights of competing moral values, and by judges or, in a civil law system, administrators whose selection frequently rests on other factors than moral insight. The shift is profoundly anti-democratic; an illus-

---

[32] *La Jeune Eugénie*, 26 Fed. Cas. 832, No. 15,551 (D. Mass., 1822); *US v. Smith*, 18 US (5 Wheaton) 20 (1820). The pertinent part of the Act of 1819 is quoted at p. 91 above.

[33] *Le Louis*, 2 Dodson 210 (1817); *Antelope*, 23 US (10 Wheaton) 64, 113 (1825).

tration of the continued persuasiveness of Plato's *Republic* with its guardians to those who fancy that they would be in elite positions under such a government and, perhaps, those for whom the burdens of participating in a democracy seem too heavy. People who adopt such a model as their ideal might well be reminded of the aphorism that of all forms of government, democracy is the worst except for all the others.[34]

But many insightful and active statesmen and scholars will disagree. Fundamentally, the attempt to replace popular self-rule with benign aristocracy reflects a pattern of thought that cannot be refuted by logic; it rests on moral premises regarding the "good," the capacity of any human institutions to recognize and give authority to competent "good" people, and values about which reasonable people have disagreed since earliest records.

These four reasons for the continued appeal of "incorporation" as the current incarnation of *jus gentium* theory in the United States are not exclusive. There are surely other reasons; perhaps as many as there are adherents to the "incorporation" model of the current United States legal order. But these seem to be the major arguments that have so far been presented in favor of that model. On analysis they seem singularly unpersuasive.

On a somewhat more superficial level, in a somewhat disguised form not directly related to "incorporation" as such, there is a fifth argument supporting "incorporation" and *jus gentium* theory. This fifth argument is the one most often raised as this is written. It rests on an evaluation of the "trend" of international society; a perceived movement away from a competitive state-centered model and towards a more benign, cooperative, international institution-centered model; from a postulated "international law of competition" to a postulated "international law of cooperation."[35]

The argument seems unpersuasive for many reasons. For one, the moral or "soft law" or "imperfect obligation" to cooperate has been consciously part of the "conventional wisdom" of secular scholars of the law since at least the middle of the seventeenth century and the writings of Pufendorf. It is explicit in the frequent references the American founding fathers made to Burlamaqui and Vattel. But it is very hard to see any significant advance in moral enlightenment since that time.

---

[34] Usually attributed to Winston Churchill, but I cannot find it in the usual dictionaries of quotations.

[35] *Cf.* Wolfgang Friedmann, *The Changing Structure of International Law* (Columbia University Press, 1964) 70–71, 365–381.

For another, whatever the analyses of scholars, international organizations do not enact "law" for non-members or for members who have taken care that the terms of their membership do not include agreement to a law-making process binding on themselves without further consent. In a passage mocking popular theories of increasing legal interdependence through the radical growth of international organizations to help states coordinate their legal policies in matters of trade and other areas of useful cooperation without affecting their legal independence during the League of Nations period, Thomas Baty wrote:

It is universally agreed that, in spite of modern theories . . . International Law . . . nevertheless has something to do with States.[36]

Finally, whatever the assertions of scholars, statesmen, with real constituencies to protect at the risk of their own jobs or even their lives, live in a world in which benignity and cooperation are perceived as advantageous only if perceived as beneficial to their constituents and the cost is not too great. The assertion that "interdependence" has made the cost of competition too high to bear is far too broad to be convincing. There are large numbers of people and states in the world today that are willing to accept a cut in their standard of living, or endure an embargo, for the sake of ethnic purity, class dominance, political stability in their immediate region or other values that foreign scholars tend to under-value. "Realist" political theory, although seen as naïve and self-defeating to many international lawyers, cannot be opposed by bland assertions of the "legal" obligation to "cooperate" in contexts that put real constituencies at risk; such assertions seem naïve and self-defeating to many political scientists. To label such moral values as cooperation and humanitarianism "legal" obligations, to neglect the distinctions between "imperfect" and "perfect" obligations constantly reiterated during the Age of Reason when these parts of our current vocabulary were first formulated, seems to lead to a general denigration of the law, not an amelioration of the horrors at which the arguments are aimed. It is for that reason that it seems fair to ask whether "human rights" are "rights" in the legal order properly so called, with legal results flowing from their violation; or are they not better categorized as "rights" in a value-based moral order? We shall return to this shortly.

Many changes in policy as well as rhetoric would flow from rejecting

---

[36] Thomas Baty, *The Canons of International Law* (1930), quoted with obvious approval and amusement in Clive Parry, *The Sources and Evidences of International Law* (Manchester University Press, 1965) 8.

the "interdependence," "law of cooperation" model of the current legal order. Nor would it be necessary to accept an insular, "law of competition" model. The two extremes do not exclude each other in all cases; each applies to extreme circumstances. Nor is either the result of a realistic analysis of the actual trends of our time. For example, the Convention on the Prevention and Punishment of the Crime of Genocide[37] forbids various acts "committed with intent to destroy, in whole or in part, a national, ethnical, racial or religious group as such." But states refused to accept "universal" jurisdiction to adjudicate or enforce its substantive rules. The Convention as finally adopted is "dualist" in requiring only that states enact "the necessary legislation to give effect to" its provisions, and to establish the necessary criminal tribunals, or to submit by its own state act to the jurisdiction of an international tribunal with the appropriate jurisdiction to adjudicate or enforce, if ever one were to be established (presumably by yet other agreements of states):

Persons charged with genocide . . . shall be tried by a competent tribunal of the State in the territory of which the act was committed, or by such international penal tribunal as may have jurisdiction with respect to those Contracting Parties which shall have accepted its jurisdiction.[38]

Despite some very guarded language subject to much interpretation, it would be hard to maintain that Rwanda and the states or belligerent parties in what had been Yugoslavia, or, indeed, any other state party to the Convention has accepted the jurisdiction for its own people of any international tribunal. In light of Wheaton's and John Quincy Adams's objections to British proposals for international or mixed tribunals to try cases of accused slave-trading in the second quarter of the nineteenth century, objections that were based on interpretations of the United States Constitution whose pertinent provisions have not been changed or reinterpreted since then,[39] it is more than doubtful that the United States itself could accept for itself the very model it has been urging on the parties in contention in the former Yugoslavia. Moreover, as a matter of technical positive law, the complex legal train by which the United Nations Security Council construed itself into the authority to establish a criminal tribunal for the former Yugoslavia is not universally appreciated, whatever the moral revulsion provoked by the acts of the contestants in those benighted

---

[37] 9 December 1948, 78 UNTS 277. The Convention is very widely ratified as positive law and is generally regarded ("conventional wisdom"?) as codifying substantive rules of the international legal order, thus binding non-parties who participate in that order as well.

[38] Ibid., Article VI.   [39] See pp. 126–127, 130 above.

areas. It is not at all clear that the establishment of such a tribunal is in any legally significant way related to the maintenance of international peace and security. The attempt to argue that agreement on substance, that war crimes or genocide themselves constitute atrocities that should be punished, presupposes the existence of an enforcement mechanism based on international supervision which is simply not supported by the facts or the assumptions of a dualist, positivist legal order reflected in the actual text of the Conventions. The argument reflects instead the un-warranted assumptions of fact necessary to support a monist-naturalist legal model of the real world, or an attempt to alter that existing model to a monist-naturalist one, and the marshalling of rhetorical and political pressures on statesmen to adapt themselves to the change.

"Trends" of tribunals

Yet another argument is frequently raised by proponents of a resurgent *jus gentium*; a "natural law" to be enforced by "objective" lawyers applying what are posited to be universal moral standards as "legal" in real cases involving individuals. It is a reference to a supposed "trend" in dispute settlement; not "interdependence" in the sense discussed at pp. 155–156 above, but the use of arbitration with disinterested third-party foreign nationals to determine real disputes involving the interests of states, and the notion that those tribunals apply a "law" that directly binds states and individuals in an undifferentiated monist system.

There is no doubt that in the nineteenth century appeals to such arbitral tribunals increased, and in the twentieth have become common. Such tribunals have worked extraordinarily well to resolve real disputes. But it is frequently forgotten that their authority is based exclusively on positive submission and that it is the parties to the dispute, whether individuals or states, who determine the model to which the arbitrators are directed. The aim of such arbitrations is only secondarily "justice." It is primarily to end the dispute. Moreover, the generalities expressing an ontology coming out of these arbitrations, and, indeed, coming out of international adjudication since the creation by treaty of the Permanent Court of International Justice in 1920 and continuing under its successor International Court of Justice, have not indicated a consensus of the community of scholars as much as disagreement among the arbitrators and judges as to the model of the international legal order that best serves to resolve the dispute being addressed. For every "Chattin Claim," in which an international tribunal overruled a national tribunal on the basis of a supposed international standard of "justice" which the national tribunal did not meet,[40] there is either a dissent or a "Gelbtrunk Claim."[41]

Examples of these underlying truths abound. How more simply, in accord with Occam's Razor, is it possible to explain the refusal of Argentina to accept the arbitral award that was supposed to settle its quarrel with Chile over sovereignty in the Beagle Channel, at the entrance to the Straits of Magellan, and, with Chile's concurrence, the replacement of an arbitral tribunal's decision with a mediation guided by the Pope?[42] In fact, the advocates for a naturalist trend, in usual lawyerly fashion, cite only those submissions to arbitration and tribunals' decisions that support their argument, just as advocates for a positivist trend could cite other submissions and conclusions to support their positivist position.

An illustration of what happens when the parties disagree as to the fundamental model to be used in an arbitration is in the oft-cited *North American Dredging Company* arbitration of 1926.[43] The *compromis* submitting this dispute (among others) to the jurisdiction of the Claims Commission

---

[40] *B. E. Chattin Claim (United States of America)* v. *United Mexican States*, General Claims Commission 1927, 4 UNRIAA 282 at 295:

> An illegal arrest of Chattin is not proven. Irregularity of court proceedings is proven with reference to absence of proper investigations, insufficiency of confrontations, withholding from the accused the opportunity to know all of the charges brought against him, undue delay of the proceedings, making the hearings in open court a mere formality, and a continued absence of seriousness on the part of the Court. Insufficiency of the evidence against Chattin is not convincingly proven; intentional severity of the punishment is proven, without it being shown that the explanation is to be found in unfairmindedness of the Judge.

There was no showing that the Mexican tribunal had behaved more leniently or applied different procedures with regard to Mexican defendants. The arbitral award gave $5,000 damages to the United States. The Mexican arbitrator wrote an elaborate dissent (beginning at 302).

[41] *Claim of Rosa Gelbtrunk (United States v. Salvador)* (1902) in 1902 FRUS 876. Distinguishing between injury done by the state's action or culpable failure to act, the tribunal took the position that the injury done to the Gelbtrunks by insurgents was a risk they had assumed when investing in a country whose political situation was unstable. In the absence of discrimination by the state (which in fact offered the Gelbtrunks compensation at the same level compensation was offered to Salvadoran nationals after the rebellion was crushed), no damages were awarded.

[42] A concise summary of the complex situation involving Argentina's rejection of a 1977 arbitral award and leading up to the Pope's successful mediation may be found in 24 ILM 1–2 (1985). The documents pertinent to the final resolution of that contention are at 3–31. The 1977 award may be seen in 17 ILM 634 (1978); Argentina's rejection of the award and Chile's rejection of Argentina's position are in 17 ILM 738 and 750 (1978) respectively.

[43] *North American Dredging Company of Texas (USA)* v. *United Mexican States*, Mexico/USA Claims Commission decision of 31 March 1926, 4 UNRIAA 26.

waived the usual dualist-positivist rule requiring the exhaustion of domestic remedies before the dispute was considered truly "international." But the contract between the American private claimant and the Government of Mexico contained a "Calvo clause" placing the company on the same legal footing as a Mexican company doing business with its own government; forbidding the company to claim:

> any other rights or means to enforce the same than those granted by the laws of the Republic to Mexicans . . . and under no conditions shall the intervention of foreign diplomatic agents be permitted, in any matter related to this contract.

Mexico argued that the rule requiring exhaustion of domestic remedies was a substantive rule – that the waiver in the arbitral *compromis* affected mere procedure and did not affect the substance of the claim; that there was no claim under international law until the domestic remedies had been exhausted and the "denial of justice" established as between the alien and the country whose "justice" was being questioned. The United States argued that the rule itself was a mere procedural obstacle to the settlement of a dispute whose substance lay in the initial action of the government injuring the alien. Thus, in the United States view, the waiver in the arbitral *compromis* was sufficient to make the rule irrelevant to the actual case as presented. The Commission tried to take a naturalist-monist position. It held that in some cases an injured alien might have a valid claim against a foreign government without exhausting domestic remedies. But its only specific support for this proposition was a mention of the rejection of states being the sole parties before an international tribunal in an unratified 1907 Convention relating to the establishment of an International Prize Court.[44] Beyond that, there are generalities about:

> how largely the increase of civilization, intercourse, and interdependence as between nations has influenced and moderated the exaggerated conception of national sovereignty. As civilization has progressed individualism has increased; and so has the right of the individual citizen to decide upon the ties between himself and his native country.[45]

But prize proceedings have been conceived for several centuries as a special category in law, reflecting the "law of nations" conceptions of an earlier time, and an unratified convention is not much evidence of the evolution of anybody's conceptions except those of the negotiators. Negotiators are frequently carried away with enthusiasm for magic solutions to difficult problems. And generalities about trends perceived by

[44] Ibid., p. 28 (para. 6).   [45] Ibid., para. 7.

those with authority to make legal decisions are not persuasive to others who do not perceive the same trends, or, if perceiving the same trends, do not transfer the evolution of economic relations immediately to legal relations that have no direct connection to the economic. In this case, it is very difficult to see how even an increased interdependence in political and economic affairs can be read to diminish the authority of national law-makers to make law in their own territory or enter into whatever contracts they choose with whomever they choose, under whatever legal order the parties to the contract agree to be the law of the contract. The Commission clearly felt this difficulty, because it saw the same trends increasing the power of individuals to operate independently of their governments, thus making the Calvo clause valid. Under this approach, the naturalist-monist view was transformed from one upholding the direct application of some substantive rules of what could be argued to be "international law" to one upholding procedural rules that made irrelevant to the case the supposed substantive rules of the international legal order argued to apply to a mere commercial transaction. The result was to uphold the validity of the Calvo clause as between the alien claimant and the foreign government, but to deny it any effect as between the claimant and his own government, or to prevent the claimant's government presenting the positivist-dualist case it might have after the traditional requirement of a denial of justice had occurred through domestic procedures in Mexico. The American Commissioner, Edwin B. Parker, concurred in the result commenting that in his view the Calvo clause as construed by the Commission:

in effect does nothing more than bind the claimant by contract to observe the general principle of international law which the parties to their [compromis] have expressly recognized.[46]

In 1931 Fred K. Nielsen replaced Edwin B. Parker as the American Commissioner and took the opportunity of dissenting in another case to rip to shreds the decision of the Commission in the *North American Dredging Company* case. He particularly criticized the assertion that the decision was consistent with the *compromis*, arguing that the Commission had "ignored the effect" of its provision "stipulating that claims should not be rejected for failure to exhaust local remedies."[47] A claims commission

---

[46] Ibid., 34–35.
[47] *International Fisheries Co. Case* (1931), set out *in extenso* in William W. Bishop, Jr., *International Law Cases and Materials* (3rd edn.) (Boston: Little, Brown and Co., 1962) 817–821.

set up by the Government of the United States in 1942 to distribute among American claimants a lump-sum paid to the United States by Mexico to settle all the outstanding claims awarded a substantial settlement to the North American Dredging Company of Texas, expressly adopting Nielsen's view of the effect of the *compromis* as a positive document.[48]

In sum, it appears that despite the naturalist-monist view taken by the Claims Commission, its conclusion was consistent with the positivist-dualist orientation; and despite the American rejection of the Commission's view, its conclusion rested on a positive "waiver" of the rule of exhaustion of domestic remedies, so must also be considered an affirmation of the positivist-dualist model. As so frequently happens, then, a tribunal's language of trends and evolution is used to express a naturalist position that is not evident either by precedents, the perceptions of reality by others, or the conclusions actually reached by the tribunal itself. The criticisms of the tribunal, even when actually changing the result, can also be rationalized in naturalist-monist terms, but also seem to end with a result that could more easily have been reached through adoption of a positivist-dualist model.[49]

The Permanent Court of International Justice adopted the positivist-dualist model early on, and held on to that model to its end. In its second case, the *Mavrommatis Palestine Concessions Case (Greece v. Great Britain)*,[50] the court made it clear that it was Greece's complaint, not that of Mavrommatis, that was the nub of the dispute:

By taking up the case of one of its subjects and by resorting to diplomatic action or international judicial proceedings on his behalf, a state is in reality asserting its own rights – its right to ensure, in the person of its subjects, respect for the rules of international law.

---

[48] Ibid., 817, note 83.

[49] *Cf* A. A. Cançado Trindade, *The Application of the Rule of Exhaustion of Local Remedies in International Law* (Cambridge University Press, 1983) 48:

> A survey of specialized literature on the subject shows that authors have supported the application of the local remedies rule in the field of diplomatic protection; they have attacked the application of the rule in the field of diplomatic protection; they have defended the application of the rule in the field of human rights protection; they have contested the application of the rule in the field of humans [sic] rights protection . . .

Cançado Trindade's finely reasoned and exquisitely documented work concludes that the rule is solidly based, but, if human rights are to be advanced by legal means, the rule should be eroded by positive action, as through the European Human Rights arrangements: see ibid., 279–287.

[50] PCIJ, Ser. A, No. 2 (1924), 1 Manley O. Hudson, *World Court Reports* (1934) 293.

The question, therefore, whether the present dispute originates in an injury to a private interest, which in point of fact is the case in many international disputes, is irrelevant from this standpoint. Once a state has taken up a case on behalf of one of its subjects before an international tribunal, in the eyes of the latter the state is sole claimant.

Similar language appears in the last of the PCIJ's cases, the *Panevezys-Saldutiskis Railway Case (Estonia v. Lithuania)* in 1939:[51]

[I]n taking up the case of one of its nationals, by resorting to a diplomatic action or international judicial proceedings on his behalf, a State is in reality asserting its own right, the right to ensure in the person of its nationals respect for the rules of international law.

Now, in both of these cases, the language can be interpreted to affirm a "monist" position: that substantive rules of "international law" apply directly to transactions between a state and an individual. If that is so, the intervention of the state on behalf of its national must overcome only the procedural obstacle of exhaustion of local remedies. On the other hand, the language and the actual disposition of the cases is entirely consistent with a "dualist" view, that there was no violation of "international law" until justice had been denied; that the obstacle was not procedural, but substantive.[52] To the dualist scholar, the state owed to its fellow participants in the comity of nations not "justice" in the merits of the individual's complaint as measured by the opinion of a superior judge, but non-discrimination; merely treatment equivalent to that meted out to nationals of the states against which the complaint is lodged.[53]

Overview for the twenty-first century

Before looking more deeply into the issues of theory and structure that form the real subject of this study, it might be well to pause for a moment

---

[51] PCIJ, Ser. A/B, No. 76 (1939), 4 Manley O. Hudson, *World Court Reports* (1943) 341.

[52] See Alfred P. Rubin, "Review of Cançado Trindade, The Application of the Rule of Exhaustion of Local Remedies in International Law," 25(2) HILJ 517 (1984).

[53] See text at pp. 63–64 above. And see *United States (The Tattler Claim) v. Great Britain* (1926) reproduced in Herbert W. Briggs (ed.), *The Law of Nations* (2nd edn., New York: Appleton-Century-Crofts, Inc., 1952) 723. In that arbitration, a protested fine and renunciation of claims form, given by the vessel's American claimant to gain the release of a fishing vessel alleged to have been improperly seized by Canadian officials, was held to bar the claim on the ground that the United States "can rely on no legal ground other than those which would have been open to its national." The tribunal refused to place itself in a superior position judging the "justice" of the Canadian proceeding. But, as usual, with a little ingenuity the decision can be interpreted to support either a positivist-dualist rationale or a naturalist-monist rationale.

to address some other practical implications for current events of the evolution of concepts exposed above.

First, it is probably useful to restate a fundamental theme: the intellectual struggle to establish a model of reality on the basis of which some useful sense can be made of a messy world of facts has existed from time immemorial. We began with a papyrus of the end of the second millennium BC in which conflicting models were at issue. The practical result was a compromise in which neither disputant could convince the other to accept his model, but action was taken that could be rationalized as consistent with both models and the world got on. The priest of Wen-Amon was upset and felt hard used when he realized that his model, the one that required the Prince of Dor and Zakar-Baal to act as the priest believed they should, was not accepted by the Prince or by Zakar-Baal. But whether as a friendly concession, as a moral obligation or as a legal obligation under divine law, some other concept of natural law, or the Pharaoh's positive law, the Prince of Dor did undertake to do what he could in his territory: hunt for the thief of Wen-Amon's property, and hand him over to the priest for whatever treatment the priest's view of law would justify on board the Pharaoh's priest's vessel in Dor's waters. The clash between the Prince's territorial conception of prescriptive jurisdiction and the priest's universal conception based on an early notion that became *jus gentium* theory was resolved in practice in favor of the Prince's model. But that resolution was dictated by practicalities and the Prince's grace, not by the priest's concession or any consensus as to the "true" model of social organization. Indeed, it is the notion that a "consensus" would matter, that the issues could be seen as involving human opinion in any way, that lay at the root of the disagreement. Similarly, Zakar-Baal demanded payment in secular coin for the cedar of Lebanon, not merely the blessings of divine law; the compromise apparently (the Priest's tale is not wholly clear) involved the present blessings of Amon's divine law and at least a formal promise of secular payment in harder coin to follow delivery.

Skipping over the documented evolution of legal theory even more lightly than the text above (which at least attempts to hit some of the high spots), by the end of the eighteenth century, the heyday of the Age of Reason phase of the so-called Enlightenment, there seemed to be a "consensus" among scholars that morality and law were fundamentally the same; that value-based premises were self-evident and universally perceived by all civilized people; that rules of "law" were inherent in those moral premises and could be adduced by deductive logic; and that "objective" evidence for universal rules of "law" could be found in the coincident prescriptions of many different legal orders. Positive law was reduced to amoral matters such as customary law regarding wigs and clothing or, to remember the Roman law illustrations of Gaius, the technical forms of contracting. The positive law issue could be reduced to a question of whether the contracting form met local prescriptions, not whether consent freely and formally given was the basic requirement for a valid contract in the legal order of the forum.

Operating under this model, it could be asserted that "piracy," the taking of the property of another without following the forms of an accepted legal order, was "criminal" under the "law of nations." "Property" under this notion was regarded implicitly as a "natural law" concept. The fact that different legal orders defined "property" differently and differently provided for its non-contractual transfer (e.g., by descent or, to take a more telling example, by pillage or prize in war) were issues ignored. But the "crime" of "piracy" was thus reduced to acts done by persons who did not submit to a legal order "recognized" by whatever officials of whatever legal order had the question before it. Since territoriality had become a (if not the) dominant rule in Europe regarding the reach of prescriptive and enforcement jurisdiction, "piracy" was limited to acts beyond territorial claims to jurisdiction, the high seas, occurring between two vessels flying different flags, or involving at least one vessel not subject to an ascertainable "state's" order (symbolized by the legal right to fly a flag representing the legal order under which the ship's master had the authority to enforce discipline, possibly by flogging, and perhaps even in some circumstances to jettison cargo, the property of others).

Attempts in the United States to codify the rules relating to "piracy" ran afoul of the conflict of legal concepts implicit in the notion of "piracy" being within the jurisdiction to adjudicate of a particular legal order but being beyond its jurisdiction to prescribe, being prescribed already by a hypothesized "law of nations." That elected legislators of a legal order, as in the United States, would not have the authority to legislate, or would have the authority to legislate only for American nationals and not for foreigners whose acts violated the property rights of Americans on the high seas, those property rights having been granted by the law of the United States whether or not conforming to some abstract model of "property," was anomalous indeed. The result was incomprehensible legislation and the attempt to maintain "common law" crimes in at least this one area; "crimes" to be defined by judges on a case-by-case basis, and by reference not even to the legislation of other legal orders (which might reflect mere positive bargains by fallible humans within the foreign legislatures), but to the assertions of learned publicists and judges building abstract models of how the world should be organized.

But those charged with practical responsibilities in the world of political affairs were never wholly convinced. From Leoline Jenkins in the seventeenth century through the Law Officers of the Crown in the middle of the eighteenth, the emphasis was placed on who, what person or institution, had authority to determine the supposed "law," and what rules administered by that person or institution would enhance the amoral values (perhaps including some moral and political values) for whose protection and advancement that person or institution would be held politically responsible.

The clash between moral convictions and positive law reached its clearest expression in the early nineteenth-century moral struggle to abolish the abomination of human slavery. Blocked by the unwillingness of some societies to admit that chattel slavery itself was such an abomination,[54] the attempt by legal argumentation and moral suasion to abolish at least the international traffic in slaves succeeded only when bent to fit the model of a positive legal order. Treaties which restricted international policing to particular areas of the seas and to particular flag vessels were the only tool that worked to allocate the necessary authority to the British, the only country that seemed really to want to involve international law in the enforcement of the moral rules; a country whose official concerns quickly waned when the same legal authorities were sought to be asserted by smaller powers, like Haiti, with lesser navies and

---

[54] I do not wish to single out any particular society for moral condemnation here. The southern States of the United States were the notorious example; but, as Sir William Scott pointed out in the Le Louis, not only slavery, but even the traffic in slaves was tolerated in many other societies throughout known history. Indeed, it is unpopular to mention the fact, but it is nonetheless a fact that slavery existed in, and slaves were traded among, indigenous African communities in West Africa and elsewhere long before and during the time the Europeans entered the market. Nor is it clear that the practice was less horrific when religious-based tribalism rather than equivalent theories of "race" or pretensions to moral superiority were the excuses. The only real ameliorations of chattel "slavery" would have grown out of community moral pressures, religious convictions and the notion on the part of the slave-holder that a slave was property which, if it could be destroyed at the whim of the "owner," was still in the interest of that owner to preserve. Cf. T. E. Lawrence, Seven Pillars of Wisdom (1926, Penguin edn., 1962, 1982) 90: "[P]ublic opinion and self-interest deprecated any cruelty towards them [African slaves in what is now Saudi Arabia], and the tenet of the faith that to enlarge a slave is a good deed, meant in practice that nearly all gained freedom in the end . . . Those I saw had property, and declared themselves contented."

a municipal court system not subject to the controls of the British constitution. The United States's reasons for rejecting the British proposals were set out in strictly positivist terms by Henry Wheaton, an eloquent (perhaps the preeminent) spokesman for American "naturalism." It was the American federal government's lack of authority under the American Constitution that would prevent the United States joining even in the treaty regime the British hoped to erect; one involving an international court composed of judges from many countries to apply an asserted universal anti-slave trade "law."

The obvious parallel to the arguments of the late twentieth century is to the attempts now to create an international tribunal to adjudicate alleged violations of "international law" by individuals involved in "human rights" violations in the former Yugoslavia. The horrors of the civil (or international) wars in the former Yugoslavia,[55] ethnic violence in Rwanda and elsewhere in the world and, indeed, violations of the partially codified laws of war in all military engagements are hardly less than the horrors of the slave trade. The emotional revulsion of outside observers is probably quite comparable.

The inconsistencies created by attempting to categorize the world's operative dualist legal model as a monist one[56] are too obvious to belabor.

---

[55] Depending on whether one views the Bosnian Serbs as rebels within a single Bosnian state, or as agents of a separate Serbian state, the military activity in the territory of the former Yugoslavia can be categorized either as a war of non-international character or of international character under the terms of the four Conventions concluded in Geneva on 12 August 1949 which codified this distinction for purposes of current positive law. See Articles 2 and 3 of each. The four Conventions have been ratified by nearly all member states of the international community and are widely published: 75 UNTS 31–417 (reservations are on 419–468); 157 BFSP 234–423. I have used the version in Dietrich Schindler and Jiri Toman, *The Laws of Armed Conflicts* (3rd revised and completed edn.) (Geneva: Henry Dunant Institute, 1988) 373–562 (reservations are on 563–594). Two Protocols to the Geneva Conventions were adopted on 10 June 1977 (Schindler & Toman, *Armed Conflicts* 605–718), but have not yet been ratified by several major parties to the Conventions. Among the non-ratifying states as this is written, almost twenty years after 1977, are the United Kingdom, the United States and Russia.

[56] As noted in the text at p. 139 above, Hans Kelsen, the great organizer of modern "positivist" theory, rejected a dualist model in favor of a monist one. But his monist model exists on such a level of abstraction that in practical operation the positivist system he describes must be seen as dualist: see Kelsen, *Pure Theory* 328–344. Kelsen's model in its simplest interpretation certainly does not involve resurrecting the *jus gentium* or applying the rules of the international legal order directly to individuals. As with most, if not all, great works of scholarship, infinite variations can be attributed to Kelsen's basic model. In attempting to relate operative jurisprudential theories to reality today, it is no part of this study to defend or attack any particular interpretation of the details of Kelsen's "positivism."

They involve enforcing the substantive rules of what is asserted to be "international law" against individuals by tribunals other than those erected by one of the traditional legal orders, the states or belligerents involved in the struggle, thus implying a *jus gentium* model of the international legal order and ignoring the fact that absent the consent of the states necessarily concerned, the tribunal must lack the power to compel the production of exculpatory evidence that a defendant might seek from one of the warring factions. As shown above in connection with the British attempts to establish an international tribunal to consider violations of what was asserted to be a *jus gentium* forbidding participation in the international slave trade, there are likely to be problems of municipal constitutional law as well as of international legal theory in establishing a tribunal with the necessary powers.[57] From this point of view, it can be suggested that it is irrelevant to the human misery involved whether the struggle between some organized components of the former Yugoslavia following the disintegration of the unitary state in the early 1990s is categorized as non-international or international.[58] Nor is it legally important to outsiders how the participants in the struggle prefer to categorize the fighting between the Bosnian-Herzegovinian Muslim-dominated authorities and the Serbs basing themselves within the territory Bosnia claims as its own: it is discretionary in any state or organization, any revolutionary movement, indeed any legal order, to assert whatever legal model it considers appropriate; to label facts with whatever words it chooses. But its categorization is binding only on itself; indeed, that categorization is not "binding" even on itself if the labeling system prefers to face the sociological and moral consequences of inconsistency.

Similar problems arising out of confusion in the minds of monist-naturalist jurists attempting to adapt to a dualist-positivist world without

[57] They are belabored in Rubin, "Tribunal": an analysis of the Security Council resolution that established an international criminal tribunal for events in the former Yugoslavia (UNSC Res. 827 dated 25 May 1993, adopting the Secretary General's Report and annexed Statute, UN Doc. S/25704; reproduced in 32 ILM 1163*ff.*, 1203 (1993)).

[58] It might be borne in mind that the "war" which gave rise to the first great codification of the rules now nearly universally accepted by positive law was the American "civil war" of 1861–1865. During that "war" the Union never conceded that the legal status of "war" existed, and regarded the application of the Union's "Lieber Code" of the laws of war as a discretionary concession in the interests of humanitarianism and to ease the return to peace within the American "family." See *The Prize Cases*, 67 US (2 Black) 635 (1863); *Williams* v. *Bruffy*, 96 US 176, 183 (1878); Alfred P. Rubin, "The Status of Rebels under the Geneva Conventions of 1949," 21 ICLQ 472 (1972) (hereinafter cited as Rubin, "Rebels").

understanding its distribution of authority bedevil attempts to apply "international law" in its *jus gentium* guise to the genocidal struggle in Rwanda and Burundi. The monist-naturalist basic model in all its variations, including the much-cited Nuremberg "precedent," seems to rest on categorizing the actions or inactions of government officials or persons permitted to commit atrocities by those actions or inactions as crimes directly against a reservoir of "international criminal law." But the international criminal law remains an abstraction, an unadjudicable "common law crime," unless provision is made for clarifying prescription and for an institution capable of adjudication that takes account of either the traditional distributions of authority in the world, or, in the naturalist mode, of the "human rights" of the accused to call on evidence to defend themselves against false charges. And when the authorities that erect the prescribing or enforcement mechanism, be it a tribunal or something else, exempt their own leadership from its operation, it becomes very difficult to differentiate the model in their minds from the model in Metternich's mind immediately after the Napoleonic Wars; a model not of "community" sanction, but of great-power dictation to lesser powers coupled with great-power immunity from the operation of the system's own substantive rules.

If that is a model of "law," it should be discussed as such, with the lack of universal application of the supposed law at the center of debate. Is a "law" applied by some only to "others" really "law" in the sense asserted by adherents to a naturalist-communitarian model? Or is it a "progressive development" of the "law" which eventually gives to some person or organization the authority to decapitate a major state or its army in the interest of what its administrators define as a "community" demand for "justice"? If so, whose version of justice is to be the one enforced, and by whom? And who will command the military force that would obviously be necessary to exercise the jurisdiction to adjudicate or to enforce if "human rights" safeguards are to be observed, such as the "right" of an accused to require to be produced whatever evidence is relevant to his or her defense and to confront the witnesses against him or her?[59] And who, what individual or group, is presumed free enough of bias and pure enough in perception of "justice" to exercise the discretion all prosecuting authorities must have to determine if evidence is available to warrant the effort of a trial, to bargain with accomplices to gain their

---

[59] *Cf.* Christopher Blakesley, "Obstacles to the Creation of a Permanent War Crimes Tribunal," 18(2) FFWA 77–102 (1994).

testimony in return for lighter charges against themselves arising from the same incident?

It appears to me that an enormous amount of intellectual capacity and energy has been expended in trying to create a world organization based on a false model; a model in which the proposer assumes that he or she, or his or her like-thinking party, will dominate the system without submitting to the sort of selection processes that the world is in fact prepared at this time to accept.

The most frustrating result of this sort of analysis is the realization that it should be entirely unnecessary.

5   Implications for today

"Solutions" in a positivist legal order

"Legislating" a new constitution piecemeal

The simplest "solution" to the fact that ethical standards are not enforceable directly by the administrators of public international law, whether states in diplomatic correspondence or institutions or others, is to create a structure within the international legal order by the usual means available to "positivist" jurists. Of course, that requires states or belligerents or others sought to be bound by the new structure to consent to it. In some cases, that has been done very successfully. In Europe, major steps have been taken to modify the existing state structure by the creation of a single economic entity whose legislative and enforcement authority is, by agreement of the member states in the usual Westphalian pattern, given to new institutions organized specifically for the purpose of receiving and exercising the new authority.[1] In the "human rights" area, the Council of Europe's Human Rights Commission and Court serve as outstanding examples. General principles have been agreed among the state parties and an institutional structure has also been agreed with responsibility and authority to interpret those principles as they might apply to specific

---

[1] The history of the European Union is complex. See Eric Stein, Peter Hay and Michel Waelbroeck, *European Community Law and Institutions in Perspective* (Indianapolis: Bobbs-Merrill Co., Inc., 1963, 1976), especially the *Treaty of Rome*, 25 March 1957, in the Documentary Supplement to that volume at 40–83. See also the *Treaty on European Union* (Maastricht, 7 February 1993), ECSC–EEC–EAEC, Brussels, Luxembourg, 1992. For a learned positivist analysis of the entire arrangement as of 1973, see Giorgio Balladore Pallieri, "Le droit interne des organisations internationales," 127 RdC (1969-I) 1–38. For a learned naturalist analysis taking a very different view of the entire legal order, see R.-J. Dupuy, "Communauté internationale et disparités de développement," 165 RdC (1979-IV) 1 (1981).

cases; provision has been made allowing appropriate cases to be brought.[2] Similar institutions have been proposed in other contexts. The results vary with the willingness of the states involved to accept the sort of institutional structure that would actually implement agreed human rights principles.[3]

But even if there is no agreement on an institutional structure to which states are willing to submit questions involving their observance of human rights and other ethical standards, the positive legal order does not require people or states morally revolted by the actions of others to stand helpless. There are other ameliorations to such horrors in the existing international legal order which are being overlooked by those whose monist-moralist model has seemed to become an obsession. The simplest is merely for all morally concerned organizations to apply the positive law codified in the 1949 Geneva Conventions[4] to all struggles for authority that turn violent. Those four Conventions are very widely ratified and, despite many unclarities and inconsistencies in them, are usually regarded as definitive formulations of the substantive law binding as a matter of general practice accepted as law even if not expressly accepted by formal ratification. The Westphalian Constitution does pose major obstacles to this interpretation when arguments are sought to bind "guerrilla" or "terrorist" organizations to their terms.[5] But these issues are generally ignored by scholars and the laws of war have been widely treated as a matter merely of applying positive law; the relationship of the rules stated in the Conventions to general international law has only rarely been discussed.

The Conventions take a "dualist" view of the international legal order, obliging parties to the conflict to take action against individual violators of the substantive rules, but leaving open the possibility that

---

[2] The basic document is the European Convention for the Protection of Human Rights and Fundamental Freedoms (Rome, 4 November 1950), in HRD 191–204 (September 1983). For analysis, begin with Jochen Abr. Frowein and Wolfgang Peukert, *Europäische Menschenrechtskonvention, EMRK-Kommentar* (Kehl, Strassburg, Arlington: NP Engel Verlag, 1985).

[3] The basic document is the American Convention on Human Rights (San José, Costa Rica, 22 November 1969) in HRD 169–190. The Organization of American States maintains its own publications relating to the Inter-American Court of Human Rights and the Inter-American Commission on Human Rights. A useful "handbook" is OEA/Ser.L/ V/II.60, Doc. 28, in its revisions.

[4] Cited at chapter 4, note 55 above.

[5] Geoffrey Best, *War and Law Since 1945* (Oxford: Clarendon Press, 1994) *passim*. See also Alfred P. Rubin, "Is the Law of War Really Law? [review of Best, *Law and War Since 1945*]", 17(3) MJIL 643–666 (1996) (hereinafter cited as Rubin, *Best*).

an international tribunal might yet be established to exercise adjudicatory functions.[6] Whether the tribunal established by the Security Council to adjudicate alleged war crimes and human rights violations in former Yugoslavia represents a definitive shift to a "monist" legal order for purposes of enforcing "international criminal law" remains to be seen. It certainly represents an attempt in that direction, but the complications, reinterpretations of treaties and exceptions raise conceptual problems that are probably insuperable to those who are aware of Occam's Razor.

Under the "positive law of armed conflict," persons accused of "grave breaches" of any of the 1949 Conventions, including wanton murder, must be sought out, then tried or handed over for trial to another party concerned in the struggle that has established a *prima facie* case. If no party to the Convention or the conflict has establised a *prima facie* case, then the apparently absolute obligation to seek out those accused of committing a grave breach would lead to no clear result other than embarrassment. But if the problem were the reluctance of a party which has legal control of the evidence of the crime and of possible exculpations, then the positive legal order can easily give meaning to this provision. It would mean, in the case of former Yugoslavia, that if there were *prima facie* evidence against a person accused of killing or ordering a killing outside the privilege of soldiers to kill the resisting enemy, that person need not be tried by a third party which lacks the necessary jurisdiction to adjudicate or the access to exculpatory evidence necessary if the human rights of the accused are to be respected. The accused could be handed over to either his own command with a public commitment to apply the rules to which Yugoslavia was bound by treaty and its successor states by the normal law of state succession, if not by general international law developed by the practice of states accepted as law in diplomatic correspondence and other actions, and codified by the Conventions. If that "solution" is not trusted to do what the initial captor considers "justice," the accused could properly be handed over to the opposing side for trial and punishment under international safeguards set out in the Conventions, including the appointment of a "Protecting Power" and the presence of impartial observers at the trial.

Nor is it a valid criticism of this positivist approach that the fanaticism that accompanies armed struggle would make a trial by either of the

---

[6] For an analysis colored by the discussions taking place in the United States during the Viet Nam "war," see Rubin, "Rebels".

participants inherently unfair. Equivalent emotions and ambitions to alter the international legal order to the benefit of lawyers and the detriment of national leaders also cloud proposals by both positivist and naturalist scholars to establish an international criminal court. The reasons why British proposals along that line were rejected by the United States in the middle of the nineteenth century have been sufficiently discussed above. There does not appear to be any attempt to respond to those objections by advocates of an international criminal court today. Instead, discussions seem to proceed on the assumption that the officials of enlightened states would not commit such acts (which is patently unbelievable) or that the legal orders of those enlightened states would deal with those problems as they arise wholly within their own municipal orders; that the traditional distribution of authority will serve for us, but not for them, so we should impose our tribunals on them, but do not need to alter the system as it might apply to us. This approach obviously rejects the fundamental notion of sovereign equality of states. It is unlikely to be accepted for long by those societies whose people demand the same respect that our own friends demand. And it is no answer to them that they are wrong in their value systems or administration of "justice," and we are right.

Applying "ethical" remedies to ethical delicts

A variation on the positivist approach has been most usefully adopted in some states intent on internal reform and accepting the unwillingness, indeed the clear impropriety in a positivist legal order, of third states or an "objective" tribunal doing "justice." Indeed, there seems to be a growing movement on the part of a number of states to reject international supervision of their political order and punishment of those responsible for recent abominations. Their leaders also see the futility of "criminal" penalties under their own municipal orders when reconciliation, peace and an evolution towards democracy is their aim. Those societies have chosen to abandon the positive remedies of an inappropriate criminal law model, even if confined to their own municipal order. Instead, several have institutionalized a virtue-moral solution: "truth commissions." Under that pattern, confessions and exposure of atrocities are placed in the public record for history to know and, in return, criminal penalties are waived. If public opprobrium makes life difficult for those confessing to having committed atrocities to achieve what they had conceived to be the public good, the moral sanctions are working to punish present fanatics and deter future ones. Such punishment is not likely to be less severe than internment together with others who feel not that they have done wrong, but that they have lost a mere struggle for authority.

If there is no sense of public opprobrium that attaches to those who confess the truth, then it is likely either that the past has been "cleansed," that the public has matured as its political order has matured, or that the evils of the past still permeate the society and criminal sanctions would have been regarded as mere political suppression anyhow.[7]

In practice, "truth" commissions making amnesty conditional on confession seem to be more effective in the search for peace and reconciliation than would be positive law tribunals attempting to apply retributive justice, even if the state establishing the commissions has jurisdiction to prescribe, to enforce and to adjudicate as if applying its own criminal law. Examples (with variations) of such "ethics" tribunals exist as this is written. They result from political decisions made by South Africa in the aftermath of *apartheid*, several Latin American countries in the aftermath of military regimes and Eastern European countries in the aftermath of communist repression[8] to refuse to apply positive law sanctions, to "pardon" by positive law the violations of natural law by their various predecessor regimes, but to expose, thus leave to moral remedies, the facts that many would find shameful and the identities of those involved. In all those places there is opposition based on the sense that the books cannot be closed on a horrid chapter in national history unless retributive justice is done. Accepting that for many that will remain true, it is also true that for many others peace and reconciliation are regarded as the more compelling values, accepting the evils of the past as beyond effective remedy, but truth being essential to a better future. Reasonable people will surely continue to disagree as to the relative moral values of "justice" and "peace," but that is a problem to be worked out by each society for itself. The interposition of strangers with their own strong ethical commitments is unlikely to lead to either justice or peace in the

---

[7] Michael Scharf, "Swapping Amnesty for Peace: Was there a Duty to Prosecute International Crimes in Haiti?," 31(1) TILJ 1 (1996), argues that state practice does not support the existence of a legal "rule" requiring prosecution of crimes and suggests that the United Nations make such a rule by opposing unconditional amnesty as a matter of political and moral principle (at 40–41), although "truth" tribunals, making amnesty conditional on confession and cooperation in exposing the truth, would be permissible.

[8] See Tina Rosenberg, *The Haunted Land* (New York: Random House, 1995) for a semi-popular study of the controversies surrounding those tribunals in Eastern Europe.

contemplation of those most directly affected by the struggle and seeking a better future for themselves and their children.

An example of the conflict between "justice" and "reconciliation" occurred in the United States when Lieutenant William Calley was tried and convicted by a United States court martial for the breaches of military discipline which occurred when he committed undoubted atrocities at My Lai in Viet Nam. He was pardoned by President Nixon when it became clear that Calley in peacetime was no danger to anybody and that a significant part of the American populace felt that atrocities committed against an "enemy" in "war" (even though "war" had not been declared; but it was universally agreed that the international laws of war applied in that place at that time) did not justify significant punishment regardless of American commitments to various Conventions that seemed applicable. Many people were disturbed by the apparent lack of retributive justice. Many others were pleased by the formal confirmation of standards of military behavior; the reform of military procedures by the American institutions involved; moral sanctions, like discharge from the service regardless of the results of courts martial, applied to those involved above Calley in the military chain of responsibility; and being able to close an evil chapter in American military experience with a formal conviction regardless of what happened later.[9]

Another "solution" derived from the Calley precedent would be consciously to separate "legal" from "moral" condemnation, treat adjudication by a third party as simply not an option that the legal order permits, but deliberately to seek to apply moral sanctions to the villains, including the leaders of the force considered to deserve such sanctions and those who control the legal orders that have not discharged their moral, perhaps even positive legal, obligations to prevent or punish "grave breaches" of the 1949 Geneva Conventions and other "war crimes." Moral sanctions applied to states or belligerent parties to a conflict even if not "states," and to the individual villains, would include such things as refusing to establish diplomatic relations with the state or to "recognize" the capacities of the belligerent body to deal outside of the context of the belligerency. As to accused individuals, they need not be issued visas or invited to participate in conferences of interest to them or their constituents. Kurt Waldheim, at one time Secretary-General of the United Nations, later President of the state of Austria, faced such opprobrium as

---

[9] See Alfred P. Rubin, "Legal Aspects of the My Lai Incident," 49(3) OLR 260–272 (1970), reprinted in 3 R. A. Falk (ed.), *Vietnam and International Law* (Princeton, 1972) 346–358.

a result of the exposure of aspects of his past, which were probably not even criminal by any standard, but in the minds of many unethical. Since entry into a foreign country is not a legal right, there is no violation of the law in refusing to facilitate it. Such moral sanctions applied to states did have an effect in convincing the people of South Africa that a public policy of *apartheid* was not acceptable in a business partner. The pressures of moral sanctions are not quick and not sure, but they do express the revulsion that is felt by those applying them towards those accused of atrocities or lax enforcement of the law that condemns atrocities, and are as likely to have an effect as any other actions that do not reach the level of direct involvement in the foreign struggle.

Choice of penal law?

A third approach would be to develop Joseph Story's choice-of-law approach better to fit the current needs of the existing legal order. According to *dicta* of Chief Justice Marshall in the *Antelope*, "The courts of no country execute the penal laws of another."[10] Whatever the validity of this assertion as a rule of law, it is certainly a recognition of the complexities of the international legal order. A court, being the creation of a municipal legal order, is usually authorized to "execute" the penal laws only of the legislator who established the court. Why should the public purse of the establishing order pay for the enforcement of "laws" that its own public authority had only an attenuated voice or even no voice in making and that lie beyond the legal powers of its own ameliorating authorities, such as those empowered to grant amnesty? But are the criminal laws of the international legal order, if there are any, the penal laws of another "country"? Rather than attempt to analyze further the conceptions of Chief Justice Marshall and the apparently unanimous American Supreme Court in the *Antelope*, the working out of Joseph Story's conception of choice of law has pointed the way to a simple solution. Why should a legal order not make criminal *by its own law* the violation of some chosen foreign law, whether municipal or international (if there is any such thing as "international criminal law")?

---

[10] The *Antelope*, 23 US (10 Wheaton) 64, 113 (1825) at 123. See also Janis, "Recognition and Enforcement". By referring to the arguments of counsel in the *Antelope*, Janis concludes, as do I on the basis of this review of the evolution of jurisprudential postulates, that Chief Justice Marshall and the Supreme Court were taking a clear and general "positivist" and "dualist" line, not seeking to carve out a narrow exception to a "naturalist" or communitarian general rule of universal assistance in criminal matters relating to offenses which a foreign sovereign had the power to pardon.

Doctrinal complexities arise which seem insuperable when publicists or legislators attempt to ground state authorities' cooperation with the authorities of other states in criminal law enforcement on theories of natural law and perceptions of positive law that bear little relationship to the actual distribution of authority in the international legal order.[11] Rarely is it more desirable to remind scholars of the utility of Occam's Razor. But those complexities disappear when the requested state extends its own prescriptions on the basis of nationality or, in some cases, "effects" to cover the situation. In fact, at least one country, Germany, does effectively extend its jurisdiction to adjudicate in criminal matters to its own nationals violating foreign criminal law abroad when the same act would have been criminal under German law had it been committed within German territory. This extension of Germany's assertion of jurisdiction to adjudicate was apparently inspired to ameliorate the consequences of Germany's legal prohibition against extraditing its own nationals for acts done within the prescriptive jurisdiction of a foreign legal order and denominated crimes by both legal orders concerned in extradition proceedings,[12] but the open rationale goes much further. As to the exercise of German jurisdiction over German nationals committing crimes against foreign law only, the crime against the foreign law becomes a crime against German law and can be tried, and pardoned, by Germany as such.[13] International law already accepts the notion that a state's prescriptive jurisdiction in criminal matters can extend to the acts of its nationals wherever the acts are actually committed,[14] and the jurisdiction to enforce is satisfied by the physical presence of the defendant in the enforcing state's territory, and there seems little basis to dispute that any country has jurisdiction to adjudicate in criminal matters arising out of the acts of the forum state's nationals abroad. Indeed, if failure to exercise that jurisdiction would leave the requested state in breach of an extradition treaty, or in a position as potential asylum state for its own nationals who perform acts which are criminal by both its own municipal law and the municipal law of the place where

[11] See Istvan Szaszy, "Conflict-of-Laws Rules in International Criminal Law and Municipal Criminal Law in Western and Socialist Countries," in 2 M. Cherif Bassiouni and Ved Nanda (eds.), *A Treatise on International Criminal Law* (1973) 135, especially 159–168.

[12] See the German Constitution (*Verfassungsrecht*), Article 16(2): "*Kein Deutscher darf an das Ausland ausgeliefert werden* [No German may be extradited to another country]."

[13] For an outline of the German legal framework, see Kennedy, Stein and Rubin, *Hamadei* at 12–20 (by Professor Dr. Torsten Stein).

[14] See the *Lotus Case*, PCIJ, Ser. A, No. 10 (1927); 2 Manley O. Hudson, *World Court Reports* 20 (1935), and the discusion of John Bassett Moore's dissent at pp. 23–24 above.

those acts were actually performed or have effects, bringing them into the prescriptive jurisdiction of the requesting state, the failure to punish the national could well be interpreted to be a violation of at least the sociological "natural law" posited by Aristotle. The resulting strain in diplomatic relations, so easily avoidable by an exercise of jurisdiction to adjudicate, would seem unnecessary and a sound policy argument seems clear to encourage all states in the international order to follow Germany's lead in this regard.

But the German approach conceals an underlying monist-naturalist orientation that limits its utility. It cannot be applied too far under a dualist-positivist model. For example, there would be serious problems if a forum state's law were sought to be applied to the acts not of a national, but of a foreigner against other foreigners abroad. Even if the offense were classified "universal," there are very real problems in determining if all the "essential elements" of the offense are identical as between forum state law and the law of the place of the offense or the state of which the accused was a national. Worse, the jurisdiction to adjudicate would be lacking, and a "pardon" by the state primarily involved, perhaps as part of a "truth commission" action or some other form of reconciliation or plea bargain, would raise questions that seem to have no clear answers unless Germany and states adopting its approach were to pose themselves as adjudicators or policemen for the world. Such a radical change in the current legal order is unlikely to lead to stability and peace.

The same problems would arise if the offense were categorized not as a "universal" offense under international law, but solely as an offense against the foreign law of the place in which it occurred or of the state of nationality of the accused. It is very hard to see how German law can be justified in applying German versions of a foreign criminal prescription to the acts of a foreigner against other foreigners abroad. Not only are traditional lines of authority relating to jurisdiction to adjudicate ignored, but human rights implications seem obvious. Under whose public policy is a plea-bargain or pardon to be entertained? How can the accused subpoena his or her defense witnesses or physical evidence? Like it or not, territorial boundaries still determine the limits to the authority of a tribunal to issue binding orders and punish by contempt proceedings those who ignore or disobey them. At least some of these problems might be ameliorated if the rules were translated to positive law, perhaps treaties by which states undertook to cooperate with each other in criminal prosecutions that disregard jurisdiction to adjudicate. But there does not as yet seem to be a groundwork laid that would solve those problems.

To put it most kindly, the current German legislation is complex and not all observers would agree that the German perception of municipal jurisdiction to adjudicate is consistent with the simplest model of the international legal order or that Germany would feel comfortable itself if its model were applied by its neighbors; a practice under which those neighbors would provide their own municipal criminal penalties for persons accused of violating German criminal law within German prescriptive jurisdiction and not within what would be their own in the absence of a political decision not to extradite or deport the accused.

The arguments in favor of extending a state's jurisdiction to adjudicate to the acts of nationals, or even of foreigners, abroad seem even clearer in cases in which there already exist internationally agreed prescriptions, at least agreements in principle as to categories of action that all municipal legal orders should make criminal. Such agreements do exist when an accused has committed atrocities such as grave breaches of the 1949 Geneva Conventions, or acts, usually called "terrorism," which would be "grave breaches" except for a refusal by the political organs of the forum state, on policy grounds, to apply the legal labels that might imply recognition of a "belligerency."[15]

By this rationale, a person accused of violating a law of war which all parties to the 1949 Geneva Conventions have legally obliged themselves to make criminal in their own law,[16] when not "handed over" by reason of the lack of a *prima facie* case, a tribunal or fair trial safeguards that meet human rights standards or the standards of the Conventions, could be tried by any state that has the normal jurisdiction to adjudicate, perhaps based on the nationality of a victim. The state running the fair trial with

---

[15] International Law Association, Committee on Extradition in Relation to Terrorist Offences, *Final Report* (Warsaw, 1988). The full proceedings including the report and the debate that led to its adoption by the Association are reprinted in 11 TER 511–529 (1989). See also Alfred P. Rubin, "Terrorism and the Laws of War," 12 DJILP 219–225 (1983). The first proposal along this line appears to have been made by the Institut de Droit International in 1880.

[16] Each of the four Geneva Conventions of 12 August 1949 requires the state parties to try or "hand . . . over for trial to another High Contracting Party concerned," persons accused of a "grave breach" specified but not clearly defined in parallel articles of each of the four Conventions. The list of "grave breaches" is expanded but not clarified in two Protocols concluded in 1977. Several major nations, including the United States, have not ratified the Protocols. Nor is it universally agreed that ratifying the Protocols would lead to greater respect for international humanitarian law or the moral convictions on which it is based. See Rubin, *Best*. And see exchanges between Ambassador George H. Aldrich and Alfred P. Rubin in 85 AJIL 662–663 (1991); *Editorial Comment* by Professor Theodor Meron in 88 AJIL 678 (1994) and responding *Correspondence* by Alfred P. Rubin in 89 AJIL 363–364 (1995).

international observers according to the terms of the 1949 Conventions would not be enforcing substantive "international law" as an interloper, but its own municipal criminal prescription which, by treaty, should be more or less identical with the prescription of the defaulting state. In effect, it would be doing for a defaulting state what that defaulting state has a legal obligation to do. It would derive its jurisdiction to adjudicate from the legal detriment it suffers through the nationality of a victim or an effect in its territory, from the injury done to it by the default of another contributing to that injury by failing to perform *its own* duty of suppressing war crimes (or "grave breaches" of one of the 1949 Conventions). The rationale is "rectification."[17] In fact, the International Law Commission, a body of learned publicists formed to advise the United Nations General Assembly concerning areas in which the rules of international law could be usefully codified, as this is written seems to be moving in that direction.[18]

"International terrorism" has provoked substantial international concern and monist-naturalist actions that seem far less effective than a dualist-positivist approach would be. At this writing, in actual practice two states, the United States and Germany, have gone so far as to ignore the normal requirement for *jus standi*, the legal interest necessary to

[17] See Jeffrey Sheehan, "The Entebbe Raid: The Principle of Self-Help in International Law as Justification for State Use of Armed Force," 1(2) FFWA 135 (1977) at 144–146. This conception has not yet been evidenced in diplomatic correspondence or state practice; nor has it been rejected. It has been ignored. It is suggested here, that the precedent and its "rectification" rationale should become increasingly persuasive to those wishing to find a basis consistent with the current international legal order for some foreign military action to ameliorate some of the horrors perpetrated in former Yugoslavia, Rwanda and other places too depressing to list. One precedent that might be revived involves British action in 1879 to suppress "piracy" against British commerce that by an earlier (1847) British interpretation of the rules of the legal order should have been suppressed only by Turkey. *Cf.* 1 Arnold Duncan McNair, *International Law Opinions* (Cambridge University Press, 1956) 270 and 2 ibid. 274–276.

[18] On the origin of the International Law Commission and its relationship to the United Nations General Assembly, see Goodrich, Hambro and Simons, *The Charter of the United Nations* (3rd and revised edn., 1969) 137. The ILC draft of 16 July 1993 is reproduced in 33 ILM 253 (1994). See James Crawford, "The ILC Adopts a Statute for an International Criminal Court", 89 AJIL 404 (1995) especially 408–409 and points 3 and 5 at 410:

(3) a court of defined jurisdiction over grave crimes of an international character under existing international law and treaties . . .

(5) . . . As the preamble states, the Court 'is intended . . . to be complementary to national criminal justice systems in cases where [their] trial procedures may not be available or may be ineffective.'

The ILC approach looks very like "rectification," although not using the term. Their analysis *de lege ferenda* seems to reach the same conclusion that Sheehan reached analyzing the *lex lata* and state practice.

establish jurisdiction to adjudicate. They seem to consider "terrorism," as defined by themselves and as performed by persons whom no state appears willing to protect or to discharge against them the obligations incumbent upon parties to the 1949 Geneva Conventions, to be a matter for universal jurisdiction not only to prescribe, but also to adjudicate.[19] Parenthetically, it might be observed that the rationale used to support assertions of universal jurisdiction to adjudicate in those cases seem much broader than would seem warranted by the facts or a model of the legal order that conforms to the traditions of the Westphalian "constitution"; would seem thus to violate Occam's Razor.

There seem to be no cases applying national versions of the hypothesized international criminal law to the acts of a foreigner against strictly foreign interests abroad other than two "terrorism" cases in which the accused were in the position of Klintock in the leading American case asserting jurisdiction over the acts of the foreigner against foreign interests abroad, professing allegiance to no legal order (i.e., belligerent or government) recognized by the state seeking to expand its adjudicatory authority.[20] The two cases arising recently involved Arab "terrorists" of either no reliably asserted nationality or no state willing to press diplomatic correspondence to protect them. The two cases are the conviction of Mohammed Hamadei by a German tribunal and the conviction by a United States tribunal of Fawaz Yunis.[21]

To say that this abstention from engaging in diplomatic correspondence was evidence of a conviction that the law would not support the argument that the prosecuting state lacked *jus standi* is far more than the political realities would seem to bear. The European and American outcry at Iran's *fatwa* condemning Salman Rushdie for violating Iran's version of divine law while the secular law of the current international legal order would categorize Rushdie as a foreigner outside of Iran and doing no sufficiently direct injury within Iran seems strong evidence the other way. And yet, the push to extend at least adjudicatory and enforcement jurisdiction seems well underway as this is written. Article 6 of the German Penal Code asserts the applicability of German criminal law to a list of actions "affecting internationally protected interests [*Auslandstaten gegen internationale geschützte Rechtsgüter*]" such as genocide, crimes involving nuclear energy or explosives, attacks on air and sea traffic, slave trade, narcotics

[19] See Kennedy, Stein and Rubin, *Hamadei*, especially 27–35.
[20] See *US* v. *Klintock*, 18 US (5 Wheaton) 144 (1820).
[21] See Kennedy, Stein and Rubin, *Hamadei*.

dealing, diffusion of pornography, counterfeiting and a few other things; and Article 7 expanding the applicability of German penal law to acts of foreigners outside of Germany where the territorial law forbidding those acts is not enforced and the victim is a German national, or where the foreign jurisdiction should be applied but extradition is not feasible ("*die Auslieferung nicht ausführbar ist*").[22]

Signalling a possible future direction in which the urge to punish foreigners committing atrocities against other foreigners seems to have been subordinated to the more traditional use of municipal criminal law to protect the public order of the particular state enacting and enforcing that law, Belgium has a much more limited statute. First, it nods in the direction of international cooperation to help suppress the commission of war crimes; "grave breaches" of the 1949 Geneva Conventions and their 1977 Protocols. Its Law of 16 June 1993 asserts for Belgian tribunals whatever jurisdiction is necessary to implement the penal provisions of the 1949 Geneva Conventions and their 1977 Protocols. In light of a number of serious problems in interpreting those provisions,[23] it is very difficult to say just what the effect of this law might be in practice; no cases are known to have been brought under them. But much clearer is the Belgian Law of 13 April 1995. Article 8 provides for criminal jurisdiction over a foreigner found in Belgium (thus within Belgian jurisdiction to enforce) who has committed any of the listed offenses outside of Belgium. But all of the offenses listed involve pornography, sexual or similar moral delicts involving minors under 16 years of age.[24] Since the accused must have been found in Belgium, it appears that extradition to Belgium is not envisaged, although, again, a definitive interpretation of the statute must await actual practice under it. It can certainly be argued that the Belgian approach assumes a distinction among jurisdiction to prescribe, jurisdiction to adjudicate, and jurisdiction to enforce. It remains to be seen whether those traditional distinctions will be maintained in light of the general wording of the statutes, their intended effect, and the increased flow of people across European borders.

[22] I am indebted to Florian Thoma for the texts of the original German and a useful English translation.

[23] For a critique of those provisions, and of the 1977 Protocols in general, see Rubin, *Best*.

[24] I am indebted to Professor Pierre d'Argent of the Centre Charles de Visscher pour le droit international, Université catholique de Louvain, for the French texts of these statutes.

Non-legal ameliorations of inevitable inaction

A fourth course of action consistent with the current international system is in fact inaction. Do nothing. This is the course most likely in fact to be taken once the problems of national tribunals exercising a purported universal jurisdiction to adjudicate have become clearer, and the enthusiasm for international criminal tribunals has died down, as seems likely if they fail to reduce the horrors occurring in former Yugoslavia, Rwanda and elsewhere and today's tribunals' advocates begin to speak more of "useful precedents" than of immediate effects. This has in fact been the fate of the "Nuremberg precedent." Volumes have been filled with analyses of the illogic of trying some of the accused for "conspiring to wage aggressive war" when representatives of their partners in the conspiracy were sitting at the prosecution table and on the bench.[25] The first attempt to apply the precedent to another defeated enemy, Japan, provoked a persuasive formal dissent from one of the judges, a partial dissent from another and a rather confusing concurrence from a third. The Nuremberg and Tokyo "precedents" have then not been repeated in a legal proceeding for fifty years. It surely cannot be argued that during that period there were no "aggressions" or unprosecuted "war crimes" or "crimes against humanity" as those phrases were defined for purposes of the Nuremberg and Tokyo tribunals.

In my opinion, the use of the forms of law to achieve a necessary political aim regardless of legal principle and consistency has demeaned the law more than it has strengthened it. But in some cases, as at Nuremberg, it has also achieved its political and some moral purposes, so perhaps was the best course available to the victors. In my opinion, the problem is not with using the forms of law to expose the horrors of an unspeakable episode in human history, but with attempting to use those forms to justify redistributing authority in the international legal order without considering the full range of consequences: Precisely *who* should have the authority to order *whom* to justify his or her acts before *whom*, and *who* selects the judges, the "guardians"? Meanwhile, for the international community to do nothing about such moral horrors as the likely genocide in Rwanda and the probable violations of the laws of war in former Yugoslavia seems to be a true reflection of the international legal order in its usual practice. That practice is probably dictated by the unwritten constitutional law of a society of separate legal orders, states,

---

[25] See pp. xiii–xiv above.

and no universal authority; a "horizontal" legal order.[26] The practice is to confine the horrors to the territory controlled by rogues and encourage the escape of potential victims. Those who cannot escape, like Jews and Gypsies in territory under Nazi control or Cambodians in territory controlled by Pol Pot's villains, are likely to be killed or worse. But those who escape that territory face only the more civilized horrors of starting life afresh, if they can. And there is no legal obligation on a potential asylum state actually to offer asylum.

This is the approach in fact normally taken by municipal law when confronted with analogous horrors. One obvious example is child abuse. The child escaping his or her abusive family is welcomed (or not) by a neighbor, and the abusive parent cannot invade the neighbor's house without other consequences that in fact involve community reactions. Meantime, the community response to the abusive situation itself is notoriously dubious. Few trust social case-workers to make the decisions that could finally break up even a dysfunctional family, and other community organs normally will not step in until it is too late to help. The evils of being too late are normally regarded as less than the evils of acting too quickly in light of the other interests involved in a family situation. So the abuse is confined to that family, and the moral indignation of the neighbors is the only effective social response the system cannot stop. So in international affairs, the genocide is confined by the system to the territory which the villains control, and the neighbors look on aghast but legally powerless to help. Those that feel that moral sanctions are appropriate can apply them.

There is nothing wrong with that system except in the minds of those who feel secure enough in their own moral insight and perception of facts to try to govern the lives (and deaths) of others. From a strictly personal point of view, I would not trust anybody from outside the circle of those immediately involved who asserted such certainty to make those decisions for me or my family or my country. To those who would argue that the evils of genocide can be apparent, and the moral obligation to stop it so compelling that the use of third-party force is legally as well as morally justifiable in response, the legal system poses two answers. First, the notion that moral conviction by an outsider justifies the use of force by that outsider is an open invitation to chaos: rule by the strongest outsider with the most persuasive demagogues, and scrapping the fundamental

---

[26] See Gidon Gottlieb, "The Nature of International Law: Toward a Second Concept of Law," in 4 Cyril Black and Richard A. Falk (eds.), *The Future of the International Legal Order* (1972) 331*ff*.

rule of sovereign equality of states. In some cases the human benefits might be worth the cost to the system, but the possibility that the moralist is fallible in his or her appreciation of the facts or the moral issues, and the cost to the system should be measured before anybody should be persuaded to act on the basis of strong moral pressures. Second, as pointed out above, the alternative response of the legal order is not negligible. Admitting into one's own protective system those fleeing the horrors of a neighboring country, as was *not* generally done in the case of German persecution of Jews in the middle of the twentieth century, is a legal response both cheaper in lives and property than war, and more effective than war if humanitarian concerns are really the dominant issues in the minds of those counseling action.

Summary and conclusions

From earliest times in which political and philosophical notions were recorded there have been conceptions of morality, law in its various guises, jurisdiction and the rôle of force. The intellectual and practical political problems of twisting these strands into a single thread that can both reflect reality and provide a useful lever for affecting it in desired ways have divided people of obvious intelligence, moral insight and conviction. And it is frequently forgotten that if there were any easy way to determine the law or virtue-morality it would have been found by thinkers as profound as Plato and Aristotle. I know of no evidence that the current generation is much more insightful than its ancestors in such matters. And if "enforcement" were easy, then each of us would rule the world or the world would necessarily be a world of each against all. Fortunately, both notions, that the world is ultimately based on force and that concepts of justice are common to all mankind who can "reason," are false. Models built upon those notions and turned to action have always failed to achieve either justice or stability. The simplistic notions on the one side that "force is the bottom line" and adherence to moral standards weakens a state in an amoral world, and on the other that "law" and value-based morality are identically based on reason available to all and binding on all alike in all capacities, have proved throughout history to lead to simplistic actions, "unintended consequences," and futility. It is time to remind ourselves of the relationships between morality, law and the international political order.

First, I can dispose quickly of the most simplistic notions. Plato, in the *Gorgias*, has Polus assert that the ruler of the state is "a man who can do what he pleases in the state, killing and banishing and having his own way in everything." Socrates responds mockingly:

Suppose I were to meet you in the marketplace in the middle of the morning with a dagger up my sleeve . . . Such is my power that if I decide that any of the people you see around you should die on the spot, die he shall.[27]

The notion that a madman in the agora is the ruler of a polity is absurd. Power is not the bottom line, authority is; no army is necessary to support the authority of the king who is obeyed because the law that makes him king is respected. The President of the United States is President because he achieved that position by law; he is commander-in-chief of the United States armed forces[28] because he is President; not President because he is commander-in-chief. As a corollary, the state that ignores moral obligations does not establish a viable order. It loses allies and soon finds itself enmeshed in the very complications that its "model" of the international legal and political orders had defined out of consideration.

Applied to international society the result is the same. He who takes force for the bottom line finds life in international society to be solitary, expensive, and probably nasty and brutish although perhaps not short.[29] The historical precedents seem to confirm this. In Livy's account of the rise of the Roman Republic and then Empire, treaties and a reliable alliance structure form the basis of Rome's international position, not the Roman legions alone. Force is part of the system, but not the bottom line. Force might at times even have been part of the legislative process, but it was that process and respect for its results that held the Empire together under the Republic, and the administrative system based on law defining the authority of those within the system held it together for centuries when those with the command of armies used force to grab what they thought were the strings of authority at the center.

---

[27] Plato, *Gorgias* (Walter Hamilton, translator) (Penguin Classics, 1960, 1971 revision, 1985) 54.

[28] Actually, the United States Constitution, Article II, section 2, clause 1, makes him "commander-in-chief of the army and navy of the United States; and of the militia of the several States, when called into the actual service of the United States." For present purposes, there is no need to explain the Constitutional bases for his authority over the United States Air Force, the Marine Corps and Coast Guard.

[29] Thomas Hobbes, *Leviathan* (1651) (Michael Oakeshott, ed., Collier Books edn., 1962) 100:
Whatsoever therefore is consequent to a time of war, where every man is enemy to every man; the same is consequent to the time, wherein men live without other security, than what their own strength, and their own invention shall furnish them withal. In such condition, there is no place for industry . . . and the life of man, solitary, poor, nasty, brutish, and short.

As to the moralists, the notion that the legal is the same as the reasonable assumes that reasonable people agree on all essential questions of morality and order. But very few products of human law-making effort are adopted through a legislative procedure by unanimous vote or equal enthusiasm in any consensus. And the experience of the ages is that group decisions are at least as likely to be immoral as individual decisions. Indeed, Cicero himself argued that the true law, the *"vera lex,"* might well require an honorable person to violate the positive law passed by the Roman Senate.[30] So the result of the notion that morality and law are identical leads to each individual being his own law-maker, and little likelihood of a cohesive community.

Classical and medieval theorists found the tools with which to analyze these questions of human governance. They divided the rules asserted to be "law" into categories depending on the sources of the rules and their enforcement mechanisms. Human law, usually called "positive law," was that law which resulted from legislative processes in which human discretion was the decisive factor, whether the discretion of a single ruler or a council or the customs of society as a whole. It was enforced by human agency. Divine law was the law of God, discoverable through holy myth, holy writ and revelation delivered through agencies accepted as possessing the necessary authority to determine or interpret divine law by those expert in the system. Natural law was originally the law derived from the needs of man, such as the need to procreate, protect the family, thus form societies in which defense and a degree of prosperity would be possible. As the conception developed, an increasingly important aspect of it focused on virtue-morality, which was abstracted from what was attributed to the human "reason." But that reason was regarded as the natural embodiment of mankind's uniqueness in nature and assumed that all reasonable people would come to the same conclusions regarding issues of virtue. Cicero's ringing phrases regarding "right reason in harmony with nature" struck a deep chord. Finally, eternal law was the law implicit in God's will, on which all other systems rested, and was discoverable, if at all, by analysis of the other systems of law as a consistent whole.

To St. Thomas Aquinas, it was only the unknowable eternal law, otherwise the knowable intersect of all these systems, that could without doubt be regarded as "law" in its fullest sense. And to be such, law had to be promulgated by an agency with the authority to promulgate it. This

---

[30] See pp. 8–9 above.

meant for the natural law in its "virtue-moral" phase that each person is the keeper of his own conscience, because natural law is promulgated by reason implanted in each mind by God or nature, and no group decision can replace an individual's responsibility to God or his natural heritage to use his reason as God or nature gave it to be used. On the other hand, while denying that human or positive law is "law" in its entirety or deserves the general label "law," St. Thomas did not deny the existence of a positive law system which has in each positive legal order its own legislative processes and its own enforcement mechanisms. He who violates the positive law because he finds it inconsistent with conscience, nonetheless violates the positive law and is quite likely to suffer the consequences of that violation in this world, even if praised in the next.

Within the political order of Europe, struggles for authority occurred with frequency and violence between the institution of the Church, the claimants to secular authority by descent from the Roman Empire, and various identifiable legal orders descended from Germanic tribal, Mediterranean and other political groupings. Each had its own view of law, and under the view taken by each, it had some claim to dominance over the others. In the main, as long as the Germanic tribes based their legal orders on oaths of fealty either to replace sacerdotal kingship or to supplement it, and oaths were conceived as made to God rather than to the beneficiaries of the promises made under oath, the organized and universal (in Europe) Church was in a position to dominate the system. But with the increasing secularization of society, and with the loss of general confidence in the Church as an institution capable of maintaining order in an increasingly mobile and economically competitive society; with the Protestant movement undercutting both the secular and religious authority of the Church as perceived by those whom it sought to rule; a reorganization of thought was necessary. The events and underlying conceptions were too complex to summarize with coherence here, but the new order is exposed fully developed with the Peace of Westphalia in 1648, when the continental European powers agreed that the Protestant Dutch Republic was in fact and in law independent of the Catholic Spanish Empire despite the undoubted "right" of Spanish inheritance under the organized Catholic Church's version of divine law and under the Germanic and Spanish Visigothic laws of inheritance, not to belabor the customary inheritance law of the Holy Roman Empire, the positive law of the Empire and all the other systems that had been thought applicable. It was not force as such that won the independence of the Netherlands; the Dutch armies lost just about every battle. It was the impossibility of maintaining Spanish authority among a people who felt themselves different. It had nothing to do with right reason or, except in a rather stretched or circular sense, the will of God or the working of nature. It was an independence achieved through the discretionary acts of people determined to exercise their discretion as a people regardless of the theories espoused by others. If their exercise of discretion was conceived by some to be compelled by a divine plan or by the workings of a "natural law" of history or human motivation, so be it; but such rationales seem merely polemical when applied prospectively, and mere rationalizations when applied retrospectively.[31]

The difficulties that jurists had grappling with the new realities of authority distribution produced works of extraordinary depth and subtlety. But a truly exhaustive review of the slow evolution of thought by which jurists adjusted their mental images, their "models," of international society to fit the realities of their times, and the legal implications of those realities, is far beyond my capacity to produce, and, I suspect, beyond the patience of anybody to read. For those familiar with the evolution of political thinking, it bears some resemblance to the adjustments in thought that the English revolution of an overlapping later generation, 1642–1688, required of those trying to analyze the distributions of legal authority under the unwritten English constitution.

In both cases, old words and old patterns of thought persisted among traditional lawyers. Meanwhile, statesmen, grappling with realities that had been affected by force, even in part effected by force, were developing new models to rationalize their actions and support their claims to authority. The picture clarifies by the end of the eighteenth century in both municipal constitutional law in Europe and in the *jus inter gentes* with one notable difference: in the municipal systems the judiciary survived and with it the "rule of reason" implicit in the English and other common law systems, where judges take part in an attenuated way in the legislative process; in the international legal order, compulsory third-party dispute settlement was rejected in principle, and statesmen were far less persuaded by the arguments of "reasonable" advocates than by

---

[31] These views were "conventional wisdom" in the Age of Reason: see, e.g., Alexander Pope, *An Essay on Man*, Epistle I (1732), line 294: "One truth is clear, Whatever is, is right." Voltaire mocked this notion in Candide (1759), pointing out that if God had His unknowable reasons for various natural disasters, like the earthquake that devastated Lisbon in 1755, then this must be the best of all possible worlds. If that is so, he asked, "What then are the others?" To those inclined to seek a rationality in nature graspable by humans, or a world in which mankind is the center of creation, it is a terrifying question.

what they felt to be the need to maintain national independence, thus national discretion even to the point of going to war, in matters of interest to their constituents.

From this point of view, the great age when theory was developed to rationalize political realities and stabilize them with a sense of constitutional order was the generation of Bentham. In legal theory it was the age between Blackstone and Austin. In politics, it was the time of the American Revolution and Constitution-making, the French Revolution, the Napoleonic Wars and the grand settlement of Vienna.

By the end of the eighteenth century, "natural law" thought had reduced itself to two major models. One, that "law" was moral principle determined by deductive logic from basic moral premises derived from the perceived values of the overall system. The great publicists of the time called its rights "imperfect" until translated into positive law by one or another mechanism acceptable to whoever was making the decisions. Taken to its logical end, it yields primacy to the positivist statesmen who determine as a matter of discretion whether that transition had occurred; it leaves them free to pursue "moral" policy based on perceptions of "imperfect rights," like the right to trade, which is "perfected" only by agreement with a willing trading partner. It also leaves them free to abstain from the pursuit of any particular "moral" policy, or even to pursue an immoral policy. It is unavoidably dualist.

The violations of "morality," even if called violations of "law" by naturalist jurists, seemed to have had no impact on the international relations that were the arena within which the statesmen were operating. The pressures necessary to influence policy were constituency pressures, and, for them to work, the constituencies to whom the statesmen looked for support had to be prepared to impose their moral choices on those who acted for them. That happened only rarely, most notably in the British anti-slave-trade agitation of the immediate post-Napoleonic time. It failed to affect the fundamentally amoral, positivist conceptions of the system held by statesmen whose internal constituents were more concerned with national independence than with British views of "moral law." It survives today most notably in the language and logic of those who would have their states and others take direct action to vindicate "human rights" somewhere other than within their own country, or within their own country when the political processes of municipal legislation or enforcement seem unpersuaded of the value of the action proposed. The British anti-slave trade and anti-slavery movements form what seems a precise parallel, and the reasons for the failure of this naturalist logic to work the legal changes in the system conceived by legislators and statesmen as positivist, remain; also the reasons for those movements' ultimate success in influencing the necessary constituency groups to support the actions necessary within the legislative process of the positive law to translate their moral values into legal rules. The legal arguments of the American (indeed, international) anti-nuclear movement and the international environmental movement seem less obvious modern reflections of the same basic assumptions of legal thought, but just below the surface the parallel seems clear.

The other mainstream attempted to bring the virtue-based moral law into the positivist system by reverting to the *jus gentium*'s "objective" evidence of "natural law." By that conception the rules of substantive law common in many parallel systems were argued to be parochial reflections of some underlying general principles of law binding on all directly, even if imperfectly perceived in some specific municipal legal orders. This orientation was felt intuitively by many, but failed repeatedly to pass close examination by those whose intuitions placed national discretion and the integrity of the positivist law-making process over the coinciding moral perceptions of those not responsible for the national security and wealth of particular statesmen's constituencies. *Jus gentium* theory was intellectually insupportable after the elaborate argumentation by the early positivist, Francisco Suarez, writing around the turn of the seventeenth century. It survived as a repeated and powerful theme in legal thought for 200 years more, reaching the status of conventional wisdom. It was repeatedly asserted as if beyond question during that time although, as far as research can show, never actually used as the basis for any legal decisions in international correspondence.

Jus gentium theory was explicitly rejected by the logic of those who developed conflict-of-laws theory. Nonetheless, it remains as an undercurrent and surfaces from time to time in naturalist writings urging the international implementation by international institutions of a presumed universal law merchant, maritime law, or other subset of legal regulation where uniformity of rule is an ease to commerce, or security of title to moving assets, like ships, a necessity. It also supports the notion of indefeasible property rights based on law beyond the municipal property law of any country, thus has acquired a strong constituency among the advocates of capital-exporting states' investors in areas in which spasms of shortsightedness might encourage expropriations for either short-term or ideological political or economic purposes by the governments of states whose constituents' interest in the sanctity of property is small.

Professor Ian Brownlie of Oxford University has said in an unrecorded presentation at a conference of the International Law Association that there is no Rubicon between morality and law in the international landscape. To naturalist jurists, the statement is a platitude because there is no theoretical distinction in their fundamental model of the legal order between virtue-based morality and law: the "moral law" is as much part of "law" as the "positive law." Positivist jurists can agree with the formulation even if they disagree on the fundamental legal model with mainstream naturalists: Indeed, there is no Rubicon between law and morality in the real world of affairs, because the legislative process accepted by mainstream positivists today includes the evidences of consent given by diplomatic correspondence and analogy; the law to them is not confined to matters of express treaty interpretation.[32]

But there is a fundamental distinction between the two main camps. Based upon the analysis above, it seems to me that between morality and law there is a fairly well-defined swampy area that should be shown on the map as dangerous to enter without some notion of the paths by which moral conceptions are translated into legal rules. The paths are not well marked.

The major signpost is the summary of the sources of law adopted in 1920 to guide the Permanent Court of International Justice.[33]

The strength of the underlying positivist system is evidenced by the history of the International Court of Justice's gradual drift into naturalism. In a series of cases seeking to find a legal basis for terminating South Africa's treaty-based rights to administer South West Africa (Namibia), the court repeatedly upheld the South African rights as a matter of fairly straightforward treaty interpretation; after all, South Africa would certainly not have joined the United Nations had there been any hint in the Charter that it contained any express threat to South Africa's "rights" as the treaty-based "Mandatory Power" in Namibia. But as soon as the court indicated that it might take a more "human right to self-determination" or similar view opposed to the continued Mandate, arguments based on the "Non-Self-Governing Territories" provisions of the United Nations

---

[32] The seminal work on this remains Leo Gross, "States as Organs of International Law and the Problem of Autointerpretation," in 1 Leo Gross, *Essays on International Law and Organization* (1984) 367. The term "autointerpretation" was invented by Professor Gross in this essay, and has been much misinterpreted by others ever since it first was published in 1953.

[33] See pp. 139–140.

Charter[34] were dropped by advocates for "natural law," and the positivist underpinnings to the entire system eventually forced an end to the series of cases, by the narrowest of technical margins in the judges' votes, on the ground that no state had the legal interest, the *jus standi* necessary to support a legal claim against South Africa based merely on its continued authority in Namibia.[35]

At that point, the positivist system was deployed, and non-binding resolutions of the United Nations General Assembly were ostensibly made binding by a "decision" of the Security Council. Under Article 25 of the United Nations Charter, at least some "decisions" of the Security Council are binding as law for all members of the United Nations, including South Africa. But whether a "decision" terminating a League of Nations Mandate treaty would be binding is a matter of some legal doubt. Indeed, many legal doubts surrounded this resolution. Not only were there doubts as to whether the authority of the Security Council under the Charter extended to a "decision" not involving "international peace and security" in the sense of various related parts of the Charter, but also doubts stemming from the deliberately evasive language of the key resolution itself as to whether a "decision" in the sense of Article 25 had actually been made to require the legal result sought. Ultimately, the court held in an Advisory Opinion that various General Assembly and Security Council resolutions had legislated an end to the Mandate.[36]

In my opinion, the court's argument is logically weak in purporting to find positivist support for a position taken for what seem to be unstated moral reasons. The result was South Africa's continued presence in Namibia and the United Nations General Assembly erecting a symbolic but powerless Council for South West Africa to administer Namibia until independence. The Council's regulations seem to have had no significant legal effect in the real world. Meantime, moral and political action quite different from the sort of legal action that would be available if the positive law were involved, but effective within the moral and political

---

[34] Articles 73 and 74 of the Charter bind South Africa, as a member of the United Nations which has "responsibilities for the administration of territories whose peoples have not yet attained a full measure of self- government," to ensure the political, economic, social and education advancement, and just treatment of the people there, and "to develop self-government."

[35] *Southwest Africa Case (Ethiopia and Liberia v. South Africa)*, Second Phase, ICJ Reports (1966), 3, majority opinion at 25–51.

[36] *Advisory Opinion on the Legal Consequences for States of the Continued Presence of South Africa in Namibia (South West Africa) Notwithstanding Security Council Resolution 276 (1970), ICJ Reports (1971)*, especially dissenting opinions of Judges Fitzmaurice and Gros.

systems which produced them, continued. Under that moral and political pressure, Namibia finally achieved independence. What was demonstrated has not been the weakness of the law, but the inability of naturalist jurists to trigger the positive enforcement mechanisms of the law when the positivist underpinnings of the system are ignored. Of course, it is possible to argue that the opinion of the court gave additional weight to the moral sanctions already contemplated or being imposed on South Africa and thus hastened the end of *apartheid*. I cannot speculate about that, but would caution that the price paid in the coin of the court's integrity has been very high indeed. If speculation were to be allowed, I would speculate that the end of *apartheid* was already in train, and I am not convinced that the benefit to enlightened humanity of the additional pennyworth of naturalist "legal" pressure, achieved by a strained inter-pretation of the United Nations Charter's authority-distributing provi-sions forming a precedent for even more dubious assertions of authority by the Security Council[37] was worth that cost.

Going further, the court in 1974 disposed of Australian and New Zealand complaints against France's atmospheric nuclear testing in the Pacific by discovering a new rule under which "unilateral declarations" given with what the court construed to be an intention to be bound, were to be accorded the effect of a universal treaty. A series of French statements indicating some limits to the current phase of testing was then construed to be a binding undertaking as if contained in a treaty and the case was dismissed for mootness. No such rule existed in positive law; even if it had it is very hard to see how the French unilateral statements could be construed to have been given with an intention to be bound.[38] The result was France's withdrawal from the jurisdiction of the court. The decision has proved futile to achieve the policy result sought by the court. When France resumed nuclear testing in the Pacific in 1995 her withdrawal from the jurisdiction of the court placed the testing beyond

---

[37] For example, the attempt to apply "peace and security" authority to condemn Libya for its refusal to extradite its own public officials two years after the incidents giving rise to the claim and with no future incidents threatened, to countries with which Libya has no positive extradition obligations and in circumstances which, if reversed, would surely not be construed by those countries to oblige them to extradite any of their officials to Libya. See Rubin, *LLL*.

[38] See Alfred P. Rubin, "The International Legal Effects of Unilateral Declarations," 71 AJIL 1 (1977). I predicted the weakening of the Court as a direct result of that decision and hinted as broadly as the editorial policy of the journal would permit that the United States would be well advised to reconsider its general submission to the court's jurisdiction.

the reach of the easiest and most highly visible and persuasive legal forum before which the arguments might have been posed with significant political effect. The tests were underground and thus would not have been forbidden even had the earlier case been decided as Australia and New Zealand had requested. The French withdrawal from the jurisdiction of the Court foreclosed the option of appeal to the court, which might have held that evolving notions of environmental protection by law had by now made even underground tests illegal in the global commons. As it is, even without judicial action, political and moral pressures were marshalled and it can be speculated that the cost to France in that coin has been far higher than an adverse decision of the court in 1974 would have been. The loss has been not to international law as a moral, sociological and otherwise persuasive force in world politics, but to the tribunal; the perversion of the substantive positive law by its highest tribunal has led to a loss of authority by that tribunal and a general mistrust of the positive law and its enforcement mechanisms.

It would be excessive in this place to run down the evolution of the court from a highly persuasive, highly influential organ of the positivist international legal order to its present position.[39] Many of the cases in its active calendar now deal with maritime boundary delimitations. Those posing issues of fundamental importance, such as cases involving the legality of possessing nuclear weapons or the authority of the Security Council of the United Nations to declare the existence of a "threat to the peace" when no facts exist to support such a categorization, cannot be resolved without causing serious statesmen to question the place of the court in the international legal order.

Nonetheless, the system survives the court, indeed, it is the court's misunderstanding of the system and attempt to exercise a legislative authority even greater than that of common law judges and without the restraints the common law system puts on its judges[40] that is probably at

[39] A rather more tempered statement tending in the same direction was the result of the detailed analysis undertaken by the American Society of International Law in the 1970s and published as Leo Gross (ed.), *The Future of the International Court of Justice* (1976), concluding essay by Leo Gross in Volume II, 727.

[40] For an example, in one case recently the United States federal Court of Appeals for the 2nd Circuit in New York actually held torture in Paraguay involving only Paraguayans to be a "tort in violation of the law of nations," and took jurisdiction, applying its naturalist conception of the substance of public international law to a private tort action (actually, a wrongful death action to which none of the cited principles could logically have been held to apply). Many cases in other federal courts of the United States followed. To date few have succeeded. The leading case is *Filartiga* v. *Peña-Irala* 630 F. 2d 867 (2nd Cir, 1980). In addition to the works cited there, see the summary of

the root of the problem; a misunderstanding of the constitutional distribution of authority in the international legal order and its positivist base.

What is to be done? That depends on what result is sought. If the advancement of particular values, like human rights, then a recognition that those "values" may be implicit in the legal order but are not enforced by its positive institutions could result in a better direction of effort than the current hectoring approach. If the enforcement by the means made available by positive law is sought with regard to the substantive rules of positive law, like the rules that forbid a state to take foreign diplomats prisoners, then the procedures for rule-enforcement must be followed, as they were not by the United States following the successful submission to the International Court of Justice of the case of Iran's imprisoning American diplomats, among others, for over a year in 1979–1981.[41] If cooperation among affected countries in support of mutually agreed policies, like the suppression of "terrorism," then the tools the law makes available must be used instead of being disregarded in favor of bombast and futile military demonstrations that alienate the very constituencies abroad whose cooperation is so badly needed.[42] Indeed, the more the current scene is contemplated, the more clear it becomes that the greatest inhibitions on the use of law to support the order, stability and rationality on which we all depend for economic development and military and political security are the misapprehensions on both sides of the scales: The argument on one side that the law is futile because it rests on idealism in a harsh world, and on the other that the law is futile because it does not embody our highest humanitarian ideals.

The other great misapprehension is that the law can be refined in substance to please a consensus, more or less (even if not to satisfy

the current situation in Buergenthal and Maier, *Public International Law in A Nutshell* (2nd edn., 1989) 212–214. The reasons Buergenthal and Maier abstract from the cases rejecting jurisdiction in Filartiga-like situations reflect considerations of judicial administration only. In light of the jurisprudential considerations analyzed in this work *passim*, those reasons seem very superficial, although the conclusions of Buergenthal and Maier appear consistent with precedent and theory and in practice make it unnecessary for judges or other scholars to reexamine their operative models of the legal order.

[41] *United States Diplomatic and Consular Staff in Tehran, Judgment, ICJ Reports (1980)*, 3.

[42] See, for some suggestions as to how this could be done, the series of columns printed in the *Boston Herald* (BH) and the *Christian Science Monitor* (CSM) concerning the Beirut TWA hijacking (BH, 10 December 1985, 20), Libya (BH, 1 April 1986, 21; CSM, 13 May 1986, 15), Nicaragua (BH, 8 July 1986, 21; CSM, 15 July 1986, 13; CSM, 18 August 1986, 14). This merely scratches the surface.

everybody; a patent impossibility in any legal order in which individual views are respected), but that enforcement of the law creates problems that require community attention. It is frequently forgotten that if there is any "general principle of law recognized by civilized nations," any remnant of the old *jus gentium*, it lies not in the substantive law, but in the distribution of authority. In no known legal order is *jus standi* universal. In none can a stranger to a dispute who is not acknowledged by the parties to be a representative of the community whose legal order is supposedly violated require the parties to the dispute to submit to judicial or other "legal" settlement procedures. *Jus standi* in this sense lies at the root of the recent American rediscovery of implicit legal limits on the "jurisdiction to adjudicate." This fundamental rule of restraint is referred to by international legal scholars familiar with it as *"res inter alios acta* [thing done among others]," implying a lack of the minimal legal interest in the third party necessary in any particular legal order to trigger the enforcement mechanisms of the law. The rule is implicit in the system itself, as in all known legal orders, and places out of reach except in cases of post-war victors' tribunals the sort of supervision that many had hoped the international community would find to force an end to the worst miseries of humans engaged in organized political and economic competition.

In what might be the most significant failing of positivist international jurists to date, the reach of jurisdiction to adjudicate, including an analysis of the legal interest necessary to bring into play the adjudicatory agents of Westphalian society, has not been fully analyzed by any scholar to my knowledge. Not even police agents of a society organized with a rigid criminal law enforcement system claim authority to act in the private law realm, and attempts to categorize some violations of the rules of international law as "criminal" rather than the basis for international claims,[43] have notoriously failed.

The reason for the failure is not that "states" cannot be jailed. Corporations cannot be jailed either, but many municipal law systems attach results in their criminal law systems to the acts of corporations. Nor is it simply the difficulty of piercing the corporate veil to "get at" the true actors. The laws of war do that routinely, although problems do remain with regard to the plea of "superior orders" in cases in which those orders are not on their face atrocious, as would be direct orders to commit

---

[43] See International Law Commission, "Draft on State Responsibility," Article 19, in 18(6) ILM 1568 at 1573 (1979).

torture or rape.[44] It is the lack of authority in any truly international body to define and to enforce anything analogous to "criminal law" in the international legal order.

When the laws of war are violated, enforcement becomes the responsibility of states and belligerent parties, which fail in their international obligations under conventional or general international law if they do not enforce the rules within their jurisdiction to adjudicate. That failure is not regarded as "criminal" activity by the failing legal orders, but as a basis for legal argument and claims, torts, in the usual way.

When there is no injured party with standing to present such a claim, recourse is restricted to the moral and political counter-measures available in those orders. They are not ineffective, but are "legal" only under a naturalist model, and cannot be enforced by courts or other positive legal institutions without degrading their authority in the positive law. When other rules of the international legal order are violated, there is no reason why similar responsibilities cannot be attributed to states. But states will not accept that responsibility in any known area outside of the laws of war. Given the basic positivist system, without acceptance by states, the "solution" of requiring by international law that states exercise their jurisdiction to adjudicate in ways the community finds satisfying must fail until the great powers themselves are willing to submit voluntarily to the sort of community supervision that many advocate for others.[45] Until the United States is willing to let General Schwarzkopf and former American President Bush be brought before an international tribunal to defend their ordering the bombing of what turned out to be a civilian bomb-shelter in Baghdad in 1992, attempts to assert that Saddam Hussein, the ruler of Iraq who ordered the invasion of Kuwait in 1991, should be brought before such an international tribunal must ring hollow. It is not that President Bush or General Schwarzkopf have necessarily committed war crimes or crimes against humanity. But how can an honest analyst distinguish between Iraq's failure to bring Saddam

---

[44] See L. C. Green, *Superior Orders in National and International Law* (Leiden: Sijthoff, 1976).

[45] In addition to making this argument with regard to the Security Council's attributing to Libya in connection with the Lockerbie incident an "extradition" obligation the members would be very unlikely to accept for themselves and seeming to have nothing to do with current threats to international peace and security as mentioned in note 37 above, I have also criticized in some detail its erecting a tribunal for the former Yugoslavia in apparent disregard of the sovereign equality of states and its corollary of reciprocity, and the limitations implicit in the authority granted it by Articles 24 and 25 of the UN Charter. See Rubin, *LLL* and Rubin, "Tribunal." There are many other examples that could be discussed.

Hussain to Iraqi courts for trial for his acts, and the United States' failure to bring its leaders before a national court? And how can an honest analyst argue that "international law" should be applied to punish Saddam Hussain's actions as "illegal" in a criminal sense but should not be applied to the acts of other persons wielding public authority within or beyond national legal orders? Should there be an international tribunal to hear a case, valid or not, against former President Bush for the American invasion of Panama? Or former President Reagan with regard to Grenada? Of course, we "Westerners" would not trust such a tribunal: Who would be the judges? How could it be reconciled with our forms of democracy under which we select our leaders, and they act for all of us whether we agree with them or not? But why do we insist that people from other parts of the world should subordinate their national leaders' policies to our supervision, even though we call it "law"? It would be surprising if this obvious failure to apply principles of "sovereign equality" when piercing a corporate veil were not one of the factors leading many of the less powerful people in this world to consider the entire system hypocritical. The result has not been political stability, but apparently has been a contribution to widespread instability.

The Statute of the International Court of Justice is now a positive law document, binding on its parties, which include all members of the United Nations whatever their attitudes towards the court. So, even though the Statute of the court does not require states to submit to the court's jurisdiction to adjudicate; even if it is agreed that the positive law does not permit the court to decide cases according to ethical or virtue-moral principle (i.e., *ex aequo et bono*) unless the parties to a particular case agree to that; and even if it is agreed that prior cases and the writings of the most eminent publicists can be only a "subsidiary" source of law;[46] there remains the descendant of the *jus gentium*, Article 38.1.c, making "general principles of law recognized by civilized states" a formal source of the rules of law.

But there was a gap in the positivist jurisprudential writings when

---

[46] Precisely what "subsidiary" means in this context is notoriously elusive. Certainly within the world of jurists, court decisions that are well reasoned have considerably more weight than publicists' writings; and publicists' opinions regarding the basic theoretical models of the legal order and their implications are usually far more influential than their parochial opinions as to specific points on which diplomatic correspondence exists. See Sir Gerald Fitzmaurice, "Some Problems Regarding the Formal Sources of International Law," in *Symbolae Verzijl* (The Hague: Nijhoff, 1958) 153, and the same author's "Judicial Innovation – Its Uses and Its Perils . . .," in *Cambridge Essays in International Law* (Dobbs Ferry, NY: Oceana Publishers, 1965) 24.

conflict-of-laws theory, which superseded the concept of *jus gentium* in the *private* international law field, was reintroduced into the formal sources of *public* international law. That reintroduction appears to have occurred with very little positivist discussion, just as today talk of the universal "law merchant" seems to be creeping back into the writings about private international law with very little positivist analysis. In the case of public international law, the gap was partially filled by a brilliant virtue-morality "naturalist"-oriented book, the first of many such by Judge Sir Hersch Lauterpacht, in 1927.[47] In that book, aside from a very sophisticated analysis of the concept of "general principles," Lauterpacht actually isolates many municipal law concepts, like the invalidity of contracts procured by force, and shows how the "principles" that underlie them are far higher on any plane of generalities than most publicists and courts suppose. His basic conclusion, although perhaps he would disagree with my simplistic summary, is that principles common to many or all municipal law systems are not directly transferrable to public inter-national law, but can usefully serve as analogies whose validity requires an examination of the differences as well as the similarities between any (or all) municipal law systems and public international law.

The principal point is that most "civilized" legal orders are almost automatically assumed to be based on a "vertical" command structure. That image is not only seriously misleading with regard to the inter-national legal order,[48] but is not true even of such familiar complex constitutional systems as that of the United States. John Austin him-self, the founder of modern "positivism," had grave difficulties fitting federal and other dispersed-power orders like that of the United States into his system.[49] He regarded public international law as a system of "positive morality," and not "law" at all within his framework of defini-tions because lacking a political superior able to give commands and lacking a "sanction," i.e., a direct enforcement mechanism similar to police. The naïve positivism of Austin remains a constant undercurrent of naïve "realism" in American jurisprudential writing today when ques-tions of international law are raised.[50] Of course, I in no way want to

---

[47] Sir Hersch Lauterpacht, *Private Law Sources and Analogies of International Law* (Longman, Green & Co., London 1927, reprinted Archon Books, 1970).

[48] See Gidon Gottlieb cited at note 26 above.

[49] John Austin, *The Province of Jurisprudence Determined* (1832, Weidenfeld & Nicolson reprint, 1954). Lectures I, VI at 15–18, 233, 245–251.

[50] See, e.g., Robert Bork, "The Limits of 'International Law,'" 18 NI 3 (Winter 1989/90), and my response and Bork's "surrebuttal" in 19 NI 122 (Spring 1990).

imply that naïveté is restricted to "naturalist" jurists in current American writing.

This analogistic approach avoids many of the confusions of the direct *jus gentium* approach, and can be highly enlightening. For example, it is immediately apparent that the usual unstated analogy between municipal criminal law and the public international law system is wholly misplaced. Public international law is not a defective municipal criminal law system. Most large cities in the world, and many small towns, have criminal law systems that are almost wholly ineffective to control anti-social behavior even in defined communities whose prescriptions, adjudicative processes and other enforcement and sanctioning systems are wholly within the legal control of a positive municipal order. Public international law has highly effective subsystems analogizeable (with differences) to municipal contract law (treaties), tort law (claims), property law (law of the sea, natural resources, pollution), corporation law (international organizations), and, most importantly, constitutional law. In the last of these, constitutional law, the analogy is often overlooked; the United States did not need police to force a president to resign under threat of impeachment in 1974, nor is impeachment or military or police action the spur to a restructuring of the American Government's administrative and some substantive policies today. So it is more than odd to find objections to the fundamental definitions of an international legal order to rest on the lack of military enforcement of its rules.

But the clearest example of the utility of analogy to clarify the relationship between law and morality comes with regard to the history of *apartheid* in South Africa, a moral evil, few would deny, but the subject of much futile rhetoric and frustration on the part of those who believe that unless the "law" forces their version of morality on others, the law is useless.

The analogy between war crimes and municipal family law was briefly noted above. The obvious analogy to *apartheid* in the municipal law familiar to most scholars who abhor *apartheid* is to family law and child abuse; also a moral horror. But how do municipal systems handle it? In the municipal system we see so clearly the value of trying to maintain a family, the incompetency of "objective" or "outside" state administrators to evaluate the facts and weigh the many interests involved, the frustration of municipal legislatures in trying to find general rules that can be applied in practice without creating the likelihood of abuses at least as great as some of those they are supposed to cure. We know the problem and we lament the inadequacy of both the social and the legal order in dealing with it, but we do not blame the law; we blame ourselves and wish we were more clever, or more stable as people, or had a more benign and caring society with a tribal or extended family structure able to take over the raising of children at least at certain ages and in some cases. We accept all this and call the police or other social services only as a last resort, knowing that it is likely to be useless. On the other hand, when the opportunity comes to protect a battered spouse or child within our own jurisdiction, or house, we accept that opportunity with moral gratitude and hope that the law will protect us from the counteraction of our aggrieved neighbor, who regards a rigid and vertical family structure and a degree of violence to maintain it as "natural," and his neighbors as "officious intermeddlers." In the most extreme cases, we watch with horror as an abused child murders his or her oppressor and, if the police come, we hope that the procedures implicit in the municipal system, like jury trials in common law countries, will result in acquittals even if the strict operation of law would not.

So would we have looked with relief at a successful revolution in South Africa, and welcomed the successor government as long as it did not in its turn become as oppressive as the system against which it grew. In fact, the evolution of the pattern of governance in South Africa followed a much more enlightened line. Instead of bloody revolution, the dominant elite saw its own interests best served by abandoning *apartheid* and establishing by South African municipal law a truly multi-racial government. Those who still fancy *apartheid* to be an expression of some phase of "natural" or "divine" law evidenced by some apparent physical distinctions resting on rather superficial genetic inheritances involving skin pigmentation and the shapes of noses or lips, still consider themselves justified in their models of law in resorting to force to maintain an impossible system. Their "logic," if it can be called that, on a more abstract level involving religious, historical and cultural definitions instead of arbitrary apparent physical characteristics, is similar to that visible in Rwanda, the former Yugoslavia and Nazi Germany, among too many others.

There are differences between the American family law system and the international legal order that would have to be analyzed also. For example, in our municipal legal order once the child kills a parent or other abuser, the criminal law steps in; the matter ceases to be one of family law alone. In the international legal order, there is no aspect closely analogous to municipal criminal law, although perhaps the collective security arrangements of the United Nations and the general law of collective self-defense fill that gap. But, as noted above, the municipal criminal law is at its weakest in such situations anyhow. In the United States the result in a sufficiently wrenching case is likely to be an acquittal because few juries would convict the victim of abuse for killing the abuser even if the law of self-defense did not technically apply (as, for example, if retreat were still considered by a jury to be possible). The fact that some juries might convict is a sign of capriciousness in our criminal law administration, not that our municipal law is stronger or more "law-like" than public international law. The solution preferred by naturalist jurists like Wooddeson at the end of the eighteenth century, conviction followed by a discretionary pardon, seems to be included in the international legal order's division of authority in such a way as to avoid the first conviction, thus to make the "pardon" unnecessary; the moral values are already built into the law by replacement of a formal court system with a less formal political enforcement system that takes morality, with many other things, into account. In any case, since Metternich failed to establish "legitimacy" of constitutional succession as a lasting principle of the legal order of Europe, there would be no violation of the international legal order in nationals of a single country deposing and replacing its constitutional order, even by force. Indeed, I suppose all states in the international community have constitutional orders built upon the use of force somewhere in their histories, and probably a lot of bloodshed as well, legally approved after it was successful.

The interesting questions involve assistance to rebels, like assistance to the abused children in our analogy, and the use of community pressures analogous to those a neighborhood or Church congregation would want to use to alleviate a family abuse problem within their ken. If the victim were not in your Church congregation or immediate circle of friends and relatives and the abuser were the local supermarket manager, would you take your custom to a more expensive and inconvenient supermarket?

Would a critical number of those opposed in principle to South Africa's *apartheid* policies have supported an economic embargo against South Africa that could be expected to decrease its standard of living beyond the petty decrease that might accompany some merely symbolic gesture? Indeed, there is much to explore in the analogy, and much light to be shed on major policy decisions once it is clear that, when the focus is on a true analogy, the simplistic assertions that some supposed universal "rules" of "law" are more accurately categorized as rules of "virtue-morality" and are by themselves not enough to guide action. From this point of view, the law is a help to moral analysis, and morality can be seen as underlying some important parts of the legal analysis. But the two are not the same.

A final analogy might help to tie a number of strands together. It appears to me each society and, indeed, each individual and each group within a given society, defines "law" to suit his (her, its, their) ontology; the perception of "reality" on the basis of which things are organized. Law, thus, is an aspect of social perception, reflecting morality, political values and traditions that vary with time and in place. The positive law represents an attempt to impart an element of clarity, certainty, predictability, into the legal order. Natural law in its various phases exists independently of the positive law, and its impact on the positive law varies with the degree to which different social/political/legal orders confer authority to "legislate" on different persons or groups within the system.

Historically, it would be surprising if perceptions of "law" did not vary according to perceptions of reality and order. In a sense, it would be possible to draw a parallel between the evolution of European consciousness of the legal order and the evolution in Europe of greater movements. Baroque music features independent instruments playing independent melodies in counterpoint, coming together at key places, each fitting the coming-together into its own melody. In a baroque fugue, a single simple melody is repeated in different keys, at different tempi and with different melodic embellishment. The analogy to a state asserting a rule of law and hearing its own assertion played back to it in unforeseen circumstances and with unforeseen variations seems compelling. Classical music insists on clear rules being followed by all at the same time; variations on the rules are deliberate and done for specific effects, which can be glorious. They can also be dull. Romanticism plays games with the supposed rules. It emphasizes the emotions of individual instruments within the whole and the dynamics of the orchestra as a whole.

Baroque music provides the most compelling analogy to the international legal order. If the society of nations is conceived as an exercise in counterpoint and fugue, with comity requiring a certain coming together at key points, the effect is comprehensible, even if at times the disharmonies of some melodic lines are disturbing to all. The urge to classicism seems to involve a coming together at points which some players refuse, and disputes as to the relationship of the parts and even the clef leave us dissatisfied and yearning for a unifying force: a "world government." Romanticism leads us to believe that each of us is that leader, and carried to its extreme leads to Armageddon. I find classicism inconsistent with the variety of melodies that I hear in the world, and romanticism loud and insistent, but requiring a submission that seems inconsistent with natural law in all its forms.

Conflict of laws theory in its jurisdictional and choice-of-law phases, a consciousness of the limits on jurisdiction to adjudicate inherent in conflict of laws theory in its jurisdictional phase and a perception that international law is a "foreign" legal order to which a municipal legal order's choice-of-law reference should in some cases be made, provide unifying conceptions. And I see the arguments for it and against it in patterns of dispute evident through at least 3,000 documented years, with the underlying counterpoint always visible.[51]

Four approaches are suggested consistent with the "baroque" dualist-positivist model of the current international legal order: (1) continued institution-building through treaty by which each member of the community yields a degree of its discretion to an international organization in which it participates, in return for the benefits of community decision-making; (2) of particular use in the human rights area, disaggregating the notion of a "legal" order to make "non-legal" remedies more obviously a useful reaction to tensions in the system with which no positivist system can cope without paying a price probably too high for realistic discussion; (3) accepting that "international law" is a "foreign" legal order to any municipal system, applying choice-of-law techniques within the existing positivist legal order; using an existing "jurisdiction to adjudicate" in criminal matters to bring before a traditional municipal or belligerent's tribunal applying its own legal order's "law" to cases involving the activities of foreigners impacting primarily on other foreigners abroad; and (4) accepting as inevitable in a positivist legal order that there are

---

[51] Like everything else in this study, these observations are not entirely original. See *The Originality of Machiavelli*, in Sir Isaiah Berlin, *Against the Current* (1979, Penguin edition, 1982) 25 at 67:

> Or it [a doctrine of unity in international society] has been represented by an analogy drawn from music, as an orchestra in which each instrument or group of instruments, has its own tune to play in the infinitely rich polyphonic score. When, after the seventeenth century, harmonic metaphors replaced polyphonic images, the instruments were no longer conceived as playing specific melodies, but as producing sounds which, although they might not be wholly intelligible to any given group of players (and might even sound discordant or superfluous if taken in isolation), yet contributed to the total pattern perceptible only from a loftier standpoint.

Berlin goes on to aver that this penchant towards classicism was fatally wounded by Machiavelli's published insights: "The purpose of this study is to suggest that it was Machiavelli who lit the fatal fuse" (at 68). I regret that I did not read Berlin's perceptive essay until after this study was nearly completed.

some problems that cannot be solved by the application of "law," and that some "reprogramming" and education divorced from "rule-making" and "enforcement" in their usual senses might be the only effective responses.

From this point of view, there is a simple answer to the question posed: Do rules that bind the conscience bind the state? Rules that bind the conscience bind the conscience; rules that bind the state bind the state. To make the one set of rules applicable in the other sphere, a bridge is necessary. The bridge exists, but is not often used. It is not used because it is narrow and difficult, as all legislation is except that passed in a fit of hysteria that were better not passed. The difficulties that surround legislation in the international legal order stem not from a lack of conscience but from the deeper values of the international legal order that will survive our ignorance and our adversarial approaches to policy and legal problems. If there is a bottom line in the moral sphere as applied to the positive law, it is the value of respect for the municipal legislative systems of others, and respect for the opinions of others, even when we believe them to be morally wrong, as fellow participants in the comity of nations.

Bibliography

Adams, George Burton, *Constitutional History of England* (revised edn., by Robert L. Schuyler, ed.) (New York, 1921, 1934, 1949)

Aldrich, George H., "Correspondence," 85 AJIL 662–663 (1991)

José E. Alvarez, "Review of Danilenko, Law-Making in the International Community," 15(3) MJIL 474 (1994)

American Heritage Dictionary (1969)

Anonymous, *Extracts from the Several Treaties Subsisting Between Great-Britain and Other Kingdoms and States . . .* (London, 1741)

Aquinas, St. Thomas, *Summa Theologiae.*

Aristotle, *Organon*
   Rhetoric
   Politics, in *The Politics of Aristotle* (Ernest Barker, ed. and translator) (Oxford, 1946, 1975)
   Nichomachean Ethics (extracted in *The Politics of Aristotle* (Ernest Barker, ed. and translator) (Oxford, 1946, 1975), Appendix II
   Nichomachean Ethics (H. Rackham, translator) (Loeb Classical Library, Harvard University Press, 1939)

Austin, John, *The Province of Jurisprudence Determined* (1832, 1954)

Balladore Pallieri, Giorgio, *Le droit interne des organisations internationales*, 127 RdC (1969 I)

Barak, Aharon, *Judicial Discretion* (New Haven, CT: Yale University Press, 1989)

Bartlett's Familiar Quotations (14th edn., 1968)

Bassiouni, M. Cherif and Nanda, Ved (eds.), *A Treatise on International Criminal Law* (Chicago, 1973)

Baty, Thomas, *The Canons of International Law* (1930)

Bemis, Samuel F., *Jay's Treaty* (1923, 1962) (Yale University Press)

Bentham, Jeremy, *An Introduction to the Principles of Morals and Legislation* (1789) (Wilfrid Harrison, ed.) (Oxford, 1948)

Berlin, Sir Isaiah, *Against the Current* (1982)

Berman, Harold, *Law and Revolution* (Harvard University Press, 1983)

Best, Geoffrey, *War and Law Since 1945* (Oxford, 1994)

Bishop, William W., Jr., *International Law Cases and Materials* (3rd edn., Boston, 1962)

Blackstone, Sir William, *Commentaries on the Laws of England* (1765, 1897)

Blakesley, Christopher, "Obstacles to the Creation of a Permanent War Crimes Tribunal," 18(2) FFWA 77 (1994)

Bok, Sisela, *Lying; Moral Choice in Public and Private Life* (Pantheon Books, 1978)

Boole, George, *An Investigation of the Laws of Thought* ... (1854, Dover edn., 1958)

Bork, Robert, "The Limits of 'International Law,' " 18 NI 3 (Winter 1989/90) "Correspondence," 19 NI 122 (1990)

Bosch, William J., *Judgment on Nuremberg* (Chapel Hill, NC; University of North Carolina Press, 1970)

Bowring, John (ed.), *The Works of Jeremy Bentham* (1838–1842, 1962)

Bradford, William, *Of Plymouth Plantation* (S. E. Morison, ed.) (New York: Alfred E. Knopf, 1975)

Briggs, Herbert W., *The Law of Nations* (2nd edn., New York, 1952)

Buergenthal, Thomas and Maier, Harold, *Public International Law in a Nutshell* (2nd edn., 1989)

Burlamaqui, Jean Jacques, *The Principles of Natural and Politic Law* (1751, 1807, 1972) (Nugent, translator)

Burley, Ann-Marie, "The Alien Tort Statute and the Judiciary Act of 1789: A Badge of Honor," 83 *American Journal of International Law* 461 (1989)

Bynkershoek, Cornelisz van, *Questionum Juris Publici* (1737) (Tenney Frank, translator) (Carnegie Endowment Classics of International Law, 1930)

Cançado Trindade, A. A., *The Application of the Rules of Exhaustion of Local Remedies in International Law* (Cambridge University Press, 1983)

Cardozo, Benjamin, *The Nature of the Judicial Process* (New Haven, CT: Yale University Press, 1921)

Carr, Craig L. (ed.), The Political Writings of Samuel Pufendorf (Michael J. Seidler, translator, Oxford University Press, 1994)

Casto, William R., "The Federal Courts' Protective Jurisdiction over Torts Committed in Violation of the Law of Nations," 18 CLR 467 (1986)

Cavers, David F., "A Critique of the Choice-of-Law Problem," 47 HLR 173 (1933)

Cicero, Marcus Tullius, *De Legibus* (C. W. Keyes, translator) (Loeb Classical Library, 1928, 1977)

   De Re Publica (C. W. Keyes, translator) (Loeb Classical Library, 1928, 1977)

Coke, Sir Edward, *Fourth Institute of the Laws of England* (1644)

Coll, Alberto and Arend, Anthony C., *The Falklands War* (Boston: George Allen & Unwin, 1985)

Corbin, Arthur L., "Legal Analysis and Terminology," in *Readings in Jurisprudence* (Jerome Hall, ed., 1938); extracted from 29 YLJ 163 (1919)

Coupland, Reginald, *The British Anti-Slavery Movement* (London, 1933)

Crawford, James, "The ILC Adopts a Statute for an International Criminal Court," 89 AJIL 404 (1995)

D'Amato, Anthony A., *The Concept of Custom in International Law* (Cornell University Press, 1971)

Dickinson, Edwin, "Changing Concepts and the Doctrine of Incorporation," 26
    AJIL 259 (1932)
Dictionary of American Biography
Documents of the Christian Church (Henry Bettenson, ed.) (Oxford, 1943, 1956)
Dodgson, Charles L. (Lewis Carroll), *Through the Looking Glass and what Alice Found
    There* (1861)
    The Annotated Alice (Martin Gardner, ed., New York, 1960)
Dupuy, R.-J., "Communauté internationale et disparités de développement,"
    165 RdC (1979–IV) 1 (1981)
Eco, Umberto, *The Name of the Rose* (1980, English translation, 1983)
    Semiotics and the Philosophy of Language (1984)
    "Language, Power, Force," in Eco, *Travels in Hyperreality* (1986)
Ehler, S. Z. and Morrall, J. B., *Church and State Through the Centuries* (London,
    1954)
Falk, Richard A., (ed.), *Vietnam and International Law* (Princeton University Press,
    1972)
The Federalist Papers (Clinton Rossiter, ed.) (Mentor Books, 1961)
Ferrand, Max, *The Records of the Federal Convention of 1787* (revised edn., Yale
    University Press, 1966)
Fitzmaurice, Sir Gerald, "Judicial Innovation – Its Uses and Its Perils," in
    Cambridge Essays in International Law (New York, 1965)
    "Some Problems Regarding the Formal Sources of International Law," in
    Symbolae Verzijl (The Hague, 1958)
Forsyth, Murray, "The Tradition of International Law," in Terry Nardin and
    David R. Mapel (eds.), *Traditions of International Ethics* (Cambridge University
    Press, 1992)
Franck, Thomas M., and Glennon, Michael, *Cases and Materials on the Foreign
    Relations Law of the United States* (1987)
Friedmann, Wolfgang, *The Changing Structure of International Law* (Columbia
    University Press, 1964)
Frowein, Jochen Abr. and Peukert, Wolfgang, *Europäische Menschenrechts-
    konvention, EMRK-Kommentar* (Kehl, Strassburg, Arlington: NP Engel Verlag,
    1985)
Gaius, *The Institutes*, Part I (*c.* 165 AD) (F. de Zulueta, translator) (Oxford, 1946)
Gentili, Alberico, *Hispanicis Advocationis* (1613, 1661) (F. F. Abbott, translator)
    (Carnegie Endowment Classics of International Law, 1921)
Goodrich, Leland, Hambro, Edvard and Simons, Anne, *The Charter of the United
    Nations* (3rd and revised edn. 1969)
Gottlieb, Gidon, "The Nature of International Law: Toward a Second Concept of
    Law," 4 Cyril Black and Richard A. Falk (eds.), *The Future of the International
    Legal Order* (Princeton University Press, 1972) 331
Green, Leslie C., *International Law Through the Cases* (2nd edn., London, 1959)
    Superior Orders in National and International Law (Leiden, 1976)
Green, Thomas Hill, *Prologomena to Ethics* (A. C. Bradley, ed., 1883) (Thomas Y.
    Crowell, 1969)

Gross, Leo, "The Peace of Westphalia, 1648–1948," in 42 AJIL 20 (1948)
"States as Organs of International Law and the Problem of
Autointerpretation," in G. A. Lipsky (ed.), *Law and Politics in the World
Community* (Berkeley, 1953), and in Gross, *Essays on International Law and
Organization* (Transnational Publishers, 1984, 1993)
Gross, Leo (ed.), *The Future of the International Court of Justice* (1976)
Grotius, Hugo, *De Iure Belli ac Pacis* (1625, 1646) (F. W. Kelsey, translator)
(Carnegie Endowment Classics of International Law, 1925)
Hart, H. L. A., *The Concept of Law* (Oxford, 1961)
Herodotus, *The Histories* (Aubrey de Sélincourt, translator 1954, Penguin,
1986)
Hobbes, Thomas, *Leviathan* (1651, Collier Books edn., 1962)
Hohfeld, Wesley, *Fundamental Legal Conceptions* (Yale University Press, 1923)
Holmes, Oliver Wendell, Jr., *The Common Law* (1881) (Howe, ed., Boston 1963)
Holt, J. C., *Magna Carta* (Cambridge University Press, 1969)
Howell's State Trials
Hudson, Manley O., *World Court Reports* (1934, 1943)
Huff, Toby E., *The Rise of Early Modern Science* (Cambridge University Press,
1993)
Indian States Committee Report, Cmd. 3302, *Parliamentary Papers 1928–1929*
International Law Association, Committee on Extradition in Relation to
Terrorist Offences, *Final Report* (Warsaw, 1988) in 11 TER 511 (1989)
International Law Commission, *Draft on State Responsibility* (1979)
Janis, Mark, "The Ambiguity of Equity in International Law," 9(1) BJIL 7 (1983)
"Recognition and Enforcement of Foreign Law: The Antelope's Penal Law
Exception," 20(1) IL 303 (1986)
Jessup, Philip C., *A Modern Law of Nations* (New York, 1946)
Transnational Law (Yale University Press, 1956)
Justinian, *Institutes* (T. C. Sandars, translator and notes) (7th edn., 1922, 1970)
Kelsen, Hans, *The Pure Theory of Law* (1934, revised edn., 1960) (Max Knight,
translator 1967)
"Recognition in International Law," 35 AJIL 604 (1941)
Kennedy, David M., Stein, Torsten and Rubin, Alfred P., "The Extradition of
Mohammed Hamadei, 31(1) HILJ 5 (1990)
Latham, R. T. E., *The Law and the Commonwealth* (Oxford, 1937, Greenwood Press,
1970)
Lauterpacht, Hersch, *Private Law Sources and Analogies of International Law*
(London, 1927, 1970)
Lawrence, T. E., *The Seven Pillars of Wisdom* (1926, Penguin edn., 1982)
Lewis, Walker, "John Quincy Adams and the Baltimore 'Pirates' " 67 ABAJ 1011
(1981)
Lindsay, T. M., "Occam, William of," in 19 *Encyclopaedia Britannica* (11th edn.,
1911) 965
Luard, Evan, *Types of International Society* (New York, 1976)

Maier, Harold, "Extraterritorial Jurisdiction at the Crossroads: An Intersection Between Public and Private International Law," 76 AJIL 280 (1982)

Malloy, W. (ed.), *Treaties, Conventions, International Acts, Protocols and Agreements between the United States and Other Powers, 1776–1909* (1910)

Marsden, R. G. (ed.), *Documents Relating to Law and Custom of the Sea* (Naval Records Society, Volume L) (1916)

McNair, Arnold Duncan, *International Law Opinions* (Cambridge University Press, 1956)

Meron, Theodor, "Editorial Comment," 88 AJIL 678 (1994)

Moore, George Edward, *Principia Ethica* (1903) (reprinted, Cambridge University Press, 1968)

Moore, John Bassett, *Digest of International Law* (Washington, 1906)

Morison, Samuel Eliot, *John Paul Jones* (New York, 1959)

Nussbaum, Arthur, *A Concise History of the Law of Nations* (revised edn., 1954)

O'Brian, Patrick, *Master and Commander* (1970, Norton Paperback, 1990)

Ogilvie, R. M., *A Commentary on Livy Books 1–5* (Oxford, 1965)

Onuma, Yasuaki, "Conclusion: Law Dancing to the Accompaniment of Love," in *A Normative Approach to War* (Yasuaki Onuma, ed.) (Oxford, 1993)

The Oxford Dictionary of Quotations (2nd edn., Oxford, 1955)

The Oxford English Dictionary (1971)

Parry, Clive, *The Sources and Evidences of International Law* (Manchester University Press, 1965)

Petrie, Donald A., "The Piracy Trial of Luke Ryan," 5 *The American Neptune* 185 (1995)

Pfeffer, Leo, *This Honorable Court* (Boston, 1965, 1967)

Plato [all mentions not specifically cited to a different translation are from Benjamin Jowett (translator), *The Dialogues of Plato* (1892, 1920, 1937) (Macmillan, Oxford, Random House)]

    Cratylus

    Crito (Hugh Tredennick translator, Penguin, 1954, 1959, 1984)

    Gorgias (Walter Hamilton, translator, Penguin, 1960, 1985)

    Laws

    Phaedrus (Walter Hamilton translator, Penguin, 1973, 1985)

    Protagoras

    Republic (Desmond Lee translator, Penguin, 1955, 1974, 1983)

Pope, Alexander, *An Essay on Man*, Epistle I (1732)

Pritchard, James K., *The Ancient Near East* (5th edn., Princeton University Press, 1971)

Pufendorf, Samuel von, *Elementorum Jurisprudentiae Universalis* (1660, 1672) (W. A. Oldfather, translator) (Carnegie Endowment Classics of International Law, 1931)

    De Jure Naturae et Gentium (1672–3, 1688) (C. H. and W. A. Oldfather, translators) (Carnegie Endowment Classics in International Law, 1934)

    De Officio Hominis et Civis Prout Ipsi Praescribunter Lege Naturali (Frank Gardner

Moore, translator) (Carnegie Endowment Classics in International Law, 1927)

Quine, W. V., *Methods of Logic* (Harvard University Press, 1950, 4th edn., 1982)
  Philosophy of Logic (Harvard University Press, 1970, 2nd edn. 1986)

Reichenbach, Hans, *Elements of Symbolic Logic* (1947, Free Press Paperback, 1966)

Restatement (3rd) of the Foreign Relations Law of the United States (adopted by the American Law Institute, 14 May 1986) (Philadelphia, 1987)

Robertson, David W., *Admiralty and Federalism* (New York, 1970)

Rosenberg, Tina, *The Haunted Land* (New York: Random House, 1995)

Rubin, Alfred P., *The Law of Piracy* (Newport, RI: Naval War College Press, 1988)
  International Personality of the Malay Peninsula (University of Malaya Press, 1974)

  Piracy, Paramountcy and Protectorates (University of Malaya Press, 1974)
  "Are Human Rights Legal?", 20 IYBHR 1990 45 (1991)
  "The Concept of Neutrality in International Law," in 16 DJILP 353 (1988)
  "Correspondence" (reply to Aldrich) 85 AJIL 662–663 (1991)
  "Correspondence" (reply to Meron) 89 AJIL 363–364 (1995)
  "Enforcing the Rules of International Law," 34 HILJ 149 (1993)
  "Evolution and Self-Defense at Sea," in 7 TSA 101 (1977)
  "Historical and Legal Background of the Falklands/Malvinas Dispute," in Coll and Arend, *The Falklands War* (Boston, 1985)
  "An International Criminal Tribunal for Former Yugoslavia?," 6(1) PILR 7 (1994)
  "International Law in the Age of Columbus," 39 NILR 5 (1992)
  "The International Legal Effects of Unilateral Declarations," 71 AJIL 1 (1977)
  "Is the Law of War Really Law? [*Review of Best*, War and Law Since 1945]," in 17 MJIL 643 (1996)
  "Legal Aspects of the My Lai Incident," 49 OLR 260 (1970), reprinted in 3 Richard A. Falk (ed.), *Vietnam and International Law* (Princeton University Press, 1972) 346
  "Libya, Lockerbie and the Law," 4 D&S 1 (1993)
  "Private and Public History; Private and Public Law," 28 PROC 1988 30 (1990)
  "Review of Beitz, Political Theory and International Relations," in 47(2) CLR403 (1980)
  "Review of Cançado Trindade, The Application of the Rule of Exhaustion of Local Remedies in International Law," 25 HILJ 517 (1984)
  "Revising the Law of Piracy," 21(1) CWILJ 129 (1990–91)
  "The Status of Rebels under the Geneva Conventions of 1949," 21 ICLQ 472 (1972)
  "Terrorism and the Laws of War," 12 DJILP 219 (1983)
  "US Tort Suits by Aliens Based on International Law," 18(2) FFWA 65 (1994)

Scelle, Georges, *Précis de Droit des Gens, Deuxième Partie* (1934)

Scharf, Michael, "Swapping Amnesty for Peace: Was There a Duty to Prosecute International Crimes in Haiti?," 31 TILJ 1 (1996)

Schindler. Dietrich and Toman, Jiri, *The Laws of Armed Conflicts* (3rd revised and completed edn.), (Geneva: Henry Dunant Institute, 1988)

Sheehan, Jeffrey, "The Entebbe Raid: The Principle of Self-Help in International Law as Justification for State Use of Armed Force," 1 FFWA 135 (1977)

Stein, Eric, Hay, Peter and Waelbroeck, Michel, *European Community Law and Institutions in Perspective* (Indianapolis: Bobbs-Merrill Co., Inc., 1963, 1976)

Story, Joseph, *Commentaries on the Conflict of Laws* (Boston, 1834, 1972)

Suarez, Francisco, *De Legibus, ac Deo Legislatore* (1612) (G. L. Williams, Ammi Brown and John Waldron, translators) (Carnegie Endowment Classics of International Law, 1944)

Szaszy, Istvan, "Conflict-of-Law Rules in International Criminal Law and Municipal Criminal Law in Western and Socialist Countries," in 2 M. Cherif Bassiouni and Ved Nanda (eds.), *A Treatise on International Criminal Law* (1973)

Textor, Johann Wolfgang, *Synopsis Juris Gentium* (1680) (Carnegie Endowment Classics of International Law, 1916)

Thucydides, *History of the Peloponnesian War* (Rex Warner, translator 1954, 1972, Penguin, 1985)

Trimble, Phillip, "A Revisionist View of Customary International Law," 33 UCLALR 665 (1986)

Tuchman, Barbara W., *The First Salute* (Ballentine Books, 1988)

Twain, Mark, (Samuel Clemens), "Was it Heaven? Or Hell?" (1902), in *The Complete Short Stories of Mark Twain* (Charles Neider, ed., Bantam, 1958) 474–491

United States House of Representatives, 69th Congress, 1st Session, Doc. 398, *Documents Illustrative of the Formation of the Union of the American States* (Washington, 1927)

Vattel, Emmerich de, *Le Droit des Gens* (1758) (Charles G. Fenwick, translator) (Carnegie Endowment Classics of International Law, 1916)

Vitoria, Francisco de, *De Indis* (1532) (E. Nys, ed., J. P. Bate, translator) (Carnegie Endowment Classics of International Law, 1917)

Voltaire, *Candide* (1759)

Waltari, Mika, *The Egyptian* (1949)

Wheaton, Henry, *Elements of International Law* (1836) (Charles Henry Dana, ed., 1866) (Carnegie Endowment Classics of International Law, 1936)

 Enquiry into the Validity of the British Claim to a Right of Visitation and Search of American Vessels Suspected to be Engaged in the African Slave Trade (Philadelphia, 1842) (cited as Wheaton, *Enquiry*)

Wittgenstein, Ludwig, *Tractatus Logico-Philosophicus* (London and New York: Routledge & Kegan Paul, 1922, corrected bilingual edition, 1933)

 Philosophical Investigations (G. E. M. Anscombe, translator) (New York: Macmillan Publishing Co., Inc., 1953, revised 3rd edn. 1968)

Wolff, Christian, *Jus Gentium Methodo Scientifica Pertractatum* (1749, 1764) (Joseph H. Drake, translator) (Carnegie Endowment Classics of International Law, 1934)

Wooddeson, Richard, *A Systematical View of the Laws of England* (1792–1794)

Wynne, Sir William, *The Life of Sir Leoline Jenkins* (1724)

Zouche, Richard, *Iuris et Iudicii Fecialis, Sive Iuris Inter Gentes, et Quaestionum de Eodem Explicatio* (Oxford, 1650) (J.L. Brierly, translator) (Carnegie Endowment Classics of International Law, 1911)

Index

Adams, John Quincy (Secretary of State
  1817–1824; President 1824–1828)–
  furious at *Romp* verdict (1817), 97
  rejects international policing (1818), 126
  rejects international tribunal (1823), 126,
    156
admiralty tribunals–
  established in England in fourteenth
    century, 33
  apply "universal" substantive law, 33, 90
  and Richard Zouche, 52
  and Sir Leoline Jenkins, 55
  and Cornelisz van Bynkershoek, 59–60
  apply *jus gentium*, not *jus inter gentes*, 61,
    63–65, 66, 90, 104
  define "piracy" as political offense
    (1693), 62–63
  in Blackstone, 64
  in American Articles of Confederation
    (1777), 71–72
  in American Constitution (1787), 72
  jurisdiction over "piracy" in England, 84
  jurisdiction over "piracy" in America, 86
  retain *jus gentium* language, 97, 150
  Story as judge (*La Jeune Eugénie*), 102–104,
    110
  British precedent persuasive in America,
    106
  British restrict authority (*Le Louis*),
    110–115
  British deny Haitian authority, 129–130
Aldrich, George H., 179 note 16
"alien tort claims," *see* Judicature Act of
  1789
Alvarez, José E., 145 note 23
ambassadors–
  responsibility of sending state, 66–67
  responsibility of receiving state, 67–68
  subject to receiving state law, 53–54,
    67–68
Aquinas, St. Thomas–
  definition of "law," 16–17, 187–188

definition questioned, 17–18
"*lex*" and "*jus*," 29–31, 49
notion of "just war," 30–31
apparently influenced Sir William Scott,
  112
Arend, Anthony C., 149 note 26
Aristotle–
  and "logic," 5 note 8
  and "natural" law, 7, 16, 57, 62, 185
  and "positive" law, 7–8, 62, 83
  and "sociological" law, 7–8, 57, 132, 178
  and "justice," 7–8, 12, 83, 185
  Rhetoric, 5 note 8, 22
  influence on Pufendorf, 41
  influence on Suarez, 49–50
  rejects universality of *jus gentium*, 7, 12,
    16, 83, 112, 151
  influence on Philip Jessup, 144
Austin, John–
  founder of modern "positivism,"
    138–139
  difficulties describing constitutional law
    and international law, 200
Austria, Austro-Hungarian Empire–
  at London Conference (1817), 115
  at Aix-la-Chappelle (1818), 118
  at Verona (1822)–
    agrees to Convention subject to French
      consent, 120
    Mediterranean power, but not in
      tropics, 120–121
    Metternich not a moralist, 121
  and Hans Kelsen, 139
  and Kurt Waldheim, 175–176

Balladore Pallieri, Giorgio, 170 note 1
Barak, Aharon, 20 note 35
Bassiouni, M. Cherif, 177 note 11
Belgium–
  legislation extending jurisdiction to
    adjudicate criminal activities by
    foreigners, 182